ILLINOIS IN 1818

ILLINOIS IN 1818

by Solon J. Buck

with an introduction by Allan Nevins

Second edition, revised, and reprinted
on the occasion of the Sesquicentennial of the state of Illinois

UNIVERSITY OF ILLINOIS PRESS Urbana, Chicago, and London, 1967

✠ *An Illinois Sesquicentennial Publication*

At the beginning of its existence the Illinois Sesquicentennial Commission decided that the observance demanded a program of historical publications. That program was formulated with the advice of a committee of Illinois historians. The committee agreed that *Illinois in 1818*, by Solon J. Buck, published in connection with the Illinois Centennial, deserved to be made available again. The person to write the introduction which the new edition called for was obvious: the distinguished historian Allan Nevins, a native of Illinois and a graduate of its state university.

RALPH G. NEWMAN
Chairman, Illinois Sesquicentennial Commission

✠ *The Illinois Sesquicentennial Commission*

Ralph G. Newman, *Chairman*
Hon. Hudson R. Sours, *1st Vice Chairman*
Hon. J. W. "Bill" Scott, *2nd Vice Chairman*
Gene H. Graves, *Secretary*
James W. Cook
Hon. Lawrence DiPrima
Hon. G. William Horsley
Patrick H. Hoy
Goffrey Hughes
Hon. George P. Johns
Hon. Richard R. Larson
Lenox R. Lohr
Virginia L. Marmaduke
Hon. Robert W. McCarthy
Hon. Elmo "Mac" McClain
Hon. Tom Merritt
Hon. Clarence E. Neff
Hon. Richard H. Newhouse
Hon. Paul Powell
Hon. Paul J. Randolph
Hon. William J. Schoeninger
Walter Schwimmer
John H. Sengstacke
Glenn H. Seymour
Hon. Paul Simon
Burnham P. Spann

✠ *Introduction*

Some Midwesterners whose memories reach back to the opening of World War I will recall that a thrill ran through the embattled state of Illinois at the intelligence that a centennial commission had been created to make sure that the centenary of statehood was properly commemorated in 1918. The chief figures in that commission were well known from Chicago to Cairo, for few were the high schools and normal schools which Professor Evarts B. Greene, tall, spare, austerely shy and yet somehow inspiring, had not visited, and few also were the communities which did not have some personal acquaintance with Clarence Walworth Alvord, professor of history at the University of Illinois since 1901, and widely known for his researches in the records of the old French settlements in Cahokia and Kaskaskia. Alvord was increasingly known also for his labors in promoting the new Mississippi Valley Historical Association and the *Mississippi Valley Historical Review* that it fostered and protected.

Less well known, but much respected, was Solon J. Buck, who had taken degrees at the University of Wisconsin and at Harvard, and had then become a research associate in history at the University of Illinois in 1910. Everyone who watched the activities of Dr. Buck as a research worker, archivist, and librarian soon perceived that, while he was less a scholar than Greene and less proficient a writer than Alvord, he had remarkable gifts of his own as an organizer of historical activities and an executive of historical groups. He was particularly interested in western travel and in agricultural history. As an editor of historical documents he was meticulously careful and precise.

The Centennial Commission soon brought forth its first fruits. It was required by the Illinois legislature to compile and issue a commemorative history of the state and it laid plans for five volumes to cover the record of Illinois from the advent of the first Europeans to a recent date. This record was to be carefully documented, and full enough to justify the statement of some historians that Illinois might well be called the keystone state of the Mississippi Valley. A large public greeted the initial volume of 326 pages in 1917 with enthusiasm. This volume by Solon J. Buck was entitled *Illinois in 1818*. Its treatment of the politics of territorial Illinois and of the movement which resulted in the writing of the first constitution, and of the holding of the first state elections, was especially praised. The comprehensive bibliography was greeted as a document of primary usefulness to all students of western history.

Dr. Buck penned a sterling volume. The Illinois of 1818 was sufficiently picturesque and promising to deserve a rich and appealingly human depiction.

The infant state that year had some 40,000 people. In its western reaches, a belt of settlement occupied the rich "bottom" lands along the Mississippi, where Illinois history had begun. The term "bottom" land can be traced far back; it is used, for example, in Mrs. Gaskell's classic life of Charlotte Brontë, as a phrase familiar in Yorkshire. Everyone who has dwelt along the Mississippi, the Ohio, the Illinois, or their tributaries, is familiar with the ring marks left on great trees—oaks, ashes, beeches, and elms —as the waters in flood during winter and spring receded with the summer. These waters washed a fertile alluvial soil over the valley country or "bottom" lands.

The year 1818 was part of the flat-boat age for all western river country. A half-century later, E. L. Godkin was to speak of the United States as culturally in "the chromo age." The culture of the Illinois country in 1818 might be said to be in "the camp-meeting age." A reader of that illuminating social document, *The Autobiography of Peter Cartwright*, an itinerant Methodist preacher of wide experience, will understand what that age was. As population increased and as horse thieves and murderers were driven out, Peter Cartwright declared, ministers of different denominations—Presbyterian, Baptist, and Methodist—competed vigorously for popular support. He described one great camp meeting in or near the year 1800-1801 to which multitudes flocked on foot, horseback, and in carriages or wagons. "It was not unusual to see three, four, or even seven ministers exhorting the listening thousands from different stands at the same time, with such effect that more than one thousand persons might break into shouting simultaneously." If the concourse seemed indifferent, such a "bearer of the word" as Lorenzo Dow would call upon Almighty God to "Rip them up!"

The camp meetings with their evangelistic piety, their emphasis on conservative tenets in religion and conservative attitudes in ethics and morals, their cultivation of fervent styles of oratory and a loose emotionalism in manners, exhibited some of the virtues and more of the vices of pioneer life as many Midwesterners knew it. Later Cartwright was at pains to defend the camp meetings against Calvinistic strictures, not very convincingly. Mark Twain, who knew them well, took a severe view in *Huckleberry Finn,* and was still more severe in some of his random observations in later life, such as his directions to the illustrator of *Huckleberry Finn.* Readers of Edward Eggleston's novel of Illinois in Lincoln's time, *The Graysons,* will recall that the murder on which the plot turns took place amid the excitement of a camp meeting.

This was the West in which the fastidious N. P. Willis, as Mrs. Christiana Holmes Tillson relates in *A Woman's Story of Pioneer Illinois* (Lakeside Classics, 1919), was shocked at the rudeness of Quincy as displayed at the Quincy House. It was the West in which the principal hotel of Shawneetown, managed by a "poor white" from the South, who seemed a whiskey keg in the morning, had floors without carpets and unplastered walls. It was the West of profanity and drunkenness, of savage fights in which men tried to gouge out each other's eyes. It was the West of rough corduroy roads, of rougher speech, of people burdened, as Mrs. Tillson puts it, with "poverty, ignorance, and filthiness"—in short, the West that Frances Trollope has so vividly described. But people of cultivation and character, like John Tillson, a native of Plymouth County in Massachusetts, and his energetic wife Christiana, could establish attractive homes, and place before their neighbors a high set of standards. The literature of pioneer times makes it plain that from the very beginning a latent antagonism existed between Yankee migrants to Illinois and Southern-born migrants.

The most remarkable fact about the Illinois of 1818 or 1820 was the rich diversity of its population. Already it was plain that New England, New York, and the easternmost Canadian provinces would soon pour a steady stream of emigrants along the Great Lakes to the valley of the Illinois River. The French had already made a large contribution to the nascent state. The Germans of Pennsylvania and the Scotch-Irish or Ulster Scots of the same state, and the Shenandoah Valley in Virginia, stood ready to make full use of the Ohio River highway. Few states have had so remarkable a community in their early history as the English settlement at Albion, which owed its special character and its very real distinction to Morris Birkbeck, a man of varied gifts and many accomplishments, and his equally remarkable companion, George Flower. Flower's classification of the pioneers of the early West deserves to be better known than it is. The work of Birkbeck and Richard Flower in establishing a library at Albion, and in organizing a society for the promotion of agriculture, was especially promising. Buck's *Illinois in 1818* and the companion volumes by Alvord and Cole make it plain that the new state, so largely Northern in its spirit of enterprise and idealism, and in certain reform tendencies, and so clearly indebted to the South for its graces of temper and politeness, contained the seeds of future greatness as a society.

For all its distressing faults and shortcomings, the pioneer society of Illinois contained in embryo the institutions of the future. From this society were to be born, in due course, the great universities, the splendid libraries, the museums devoted to art and to a rich diversity of fields—history, biology, industry, and technology—which were later to rise from the prairies and the lake shores.

It is a remarkable "profile of emergent Illinois" that Solon J. Buck has drawn for us in this book, not so much an "introductory volume" for its history, as he modestly called it, but as a foundation volume. He brings out the fact that the special glory of Illinois lay in its rich diversity of folk who flocked to settle the new state. They included the family of the Rev. Jesse Townsend, who at an early date moved to Edwardsville to establish a school, and whose daughter-in-law, Mrs. Edwin Townsend, formerly a Miss Durfee, came from Palmyra, New York. A considerable part of the population, including the Tillsons, was of New England origin.

Another considerable part traced its forebears to Kentucky and Tennessee, or more remotely to Virginia and the Carolinas. The parents of the senior Adlai E. Stevenson (Vice-President of the United States in Cleveland's second term), for example, had lived in Christian County, Kentucky, whence Adlai E. Stevenson, Sr., removed to Bloomington, Illinois, before he was twenty. Carter Henry Harrison's parents lived near Lexington, Kentucky, at the time of his birth in 1825, and he had time to graduate from Yale at the age of twenty before he removed to Chicago, where he rapidly grew rich in business. Mrs. Carter Henry Harrison came from Louisiana, where she was born on a plantation that had been purchased by her Kentucky-born grandfather, Charlton Beattie. The most poignant legend in his family dealt with the obliteration of Lost Island, a fashionable resort for Southerners of ease, off the coast of Louisiana. It was overwhelmed by a sudden tidal wave, whipped on by a hurricane, and the story has been told with immortal vividness and eloquence in Lafcadio Hearn's *Chita: A Tale of Lost Island*. Mrs. Harrison's mother gave Hearn much of the information he used. But on her father's side she also traced a relationship with an old New Jersey family of high repute, that of John Ogden, the first "acting governor"— so she describes him—of New Jersey. So mixed were the strands of pioneer society in Illinois. That the Northern elements gave the state much of its restless enterprise, and that the Southern elements contributed unforgettably to its grace and polish, there can be no doubt.

No man of cool judgment and measured language would call this volume a historical masterpiece. It is journeyman's work, but journeyman labor at a high level of craftsmanship. It is honest in every phrase and sentence. It reflects careful thought and thorough inquiry. It never sinks below the level of complete competence, and this is perhaps more highly important than the fact that it never rises to a real flash point. It does not possess the cool elegance of style and thought that James Lane Allen gave to his graceful volume on *The Bluegrass Country*. Nor does it possess the richness, the fire, and the verve that William Allen White put into some historical passages that he wrote about Kansas. Thoroughly good as it is as a profile of Illinois in 1818, it might have been bettered if the author had included a discussion of the main points of Frederick Jackson Turner's classic essay on the frontier; while a few touches of the imagination, displayed by Willa Cather in her descriptions of early Nebraska, would have given it additional grace.

The settlement of the raw new country was a rough, dirty, dangerous undertaking that required courage and endless hard work. But, as Solon J. Buck shows, it bred character. And the Americans who flocked to settle there had three great advantages. First, they entered a rich, empty, challenging new land where they had to fight savages and wild beasts, but could do so with hope of success. Second, they created a new people to do the work of conquering this land, an amalgamation of numerous national stocks: English, Scots, Irish, Dutch, Germans, Huguenot French, Swedes, Jews from eastern Europe. This new society had traits all its own, and prized social equality and tolerance. Third, the settlers insisted on a common language and institutions—English —and so kept their unity. They remained one nation. America, as Crevecoeur wrote, became a new nation, quite unlike any in the Old World.

ALLAN NEVINS

About the Author

Before the publication of *Illinois in 1818* Solon J. Buck had left the University of Illinois to become superintendent of the Minnesota Historical Society. In 1931 he was appointed professor of history at the University of Pittsburgh and director of the Western Pennsylvania Historical Survey. Four years later he joined the staff of the newly established National Archives, and in 1941 was appointed Archivist of the United States. Moving to the Library of Congress in 1948 he served first as chief of the Manuscript Division and then as assistant librarian until his retirement in 1954. He died in 1962 at the age of seventy-eight.

Before *Illinois in 1818* Buck had published two scholarly books, *The Granger Movement* and a fine Illinois bibliography, *Travel and Description 1765-1865*. These were followed by *The Agrarian Crusade* (1919), and, with Mrs. Buck, *The Planting of Civilization in Western Pennsylvania* (1939).

Buck was honored with the presidency of the Mississippi Valley Historical Association and the Society of American Archivists, of which he was a founder.

✠ Contents

The state of Illinois is about to celebrate the centennial of its admission to the Union. If the observance of this anniversary is to be of any permanent value to the commonwealth, it should furnish the occasion for a survey of progress during the century that has passed in order that future development may be built upon a solid foundation. The full significance of 100 years of statehood cannot be understood without a knowledge of the Illinois of 1818, when the state had its beginnings. This work is an attempt to portray the social, economic, and political life of Illinois at the close of the territorial period, and, in addition, to tell the story of the transition from colonial dependence to the full dignity of a state in the Union. It opens with a description of certain elements, then dominant in the whole northern part of the state, which have long since disappeared from its boundaries—the Indians and the fur trade. The next chapter contains a discussion of the system by which the United States disposed of the soil to settlers and a survey of the extent to which such disposition had been effected by the close of 1818. An examination of the distribution of population, with an attempt to locate the extreme frontier of settlement in the year of admission, leads to a study of the settlers themselves—who and what manner of people they were and whence they came. The two succeeding chapters deal with economic, social, and intellectual conditions, which are depicted principally by means of extracts from contemporary newspapers and books of travel.

The first half of the book is primarily descriptive; the latter half, narrative. Chapter 7, which furnishes the transition, consists of a rapid sketch of political developments during the territorial period designed to bring out the political situation in 1818. The movement for admission is then narrated from its inception under the influence of Daniel Pope Cook to the passage of the enabling act by Congress. Chapter 9, dealing with the campaign for the election of members of the convention, contains extensive quotations from newspaper communications, and finds its principal significance in the slavery issue. The work of the convention in framing a constitution for the embryo state is then discussed on the basis of a careful study of its journal recently rescued from oblivion. The last chapter tells of the establishment of the state government—the first election and the first session of the legislature—and finally of the passage by Congress of the act which made Illinois one of the United States of America.

When the work on this volume was begun, I was connected with the University of Illinois. My departure from the state and the assumption of obligations to the University of Minnesota and the Minnesota Historical Society delayed and made difficult the completion of the work; and that it has been accomplished at all is due largely to the assistance which I have received from others. I am especially indebted to Dr. Wayne E. Stevens and Mr. Ralph Linton, who furnished most of the material for the first chapter; to Dr. Frances Relf, who served as my assistant in the assembling of material and the drafting of the other chapters; and, above all, to Dr. Otto L. Schmidt, the chairman of the Illinois Centennial Commission, whose personal support alone made much of the essential material available and enabled the work to go on during the interval between the two commissions. After the manuscript left my hands it received extensive revision at the hands of the editor, Professor Clarence W. Alvord, and his staff. Because of the illness of Professor Alvord, the work of seeing the book through the press has been supervised by Professor Evarts B. Greene, with the assistance of Dr. Theodore C. Pease. The selection of the illustrations and the compilation of the bibliography and index have been handled by the editorial staff.

Solon J. Buck
St. Paul, Minnesota
February, 1917

ILLINOIS IN 1818

Chapter 1

The Indians and the Fur Trade

One hundred years ago, the Illinois country formed the far western edge of the wave of American civilization which was slowly advancing across the continent from the Atlantic seaboard. Less than a third of the area included within the boundaries of the state of Illinois, when admitted to the Union in 1818, was occupied by permanent settlements of white men. North of an east and west line drawn through the mouth of the Illinois River, the vast treeless prairies, interspersed with wooded valleys along the streams, were still the domain of the Indian and the fur trader. The irresistible westward movement of the American people, seeking new homes in the wilderness, had carried them across the Alleghenies, down the Ohio valley, and into the region of mingled forest and prairies in southern Illinois. Already extensive cessions of land in the northern part of the state had been secured from the Indians; and, although they continued to live and hunt in the ceded as well as the unceded districts, their elimination as a factor in Illinois history was soon to be completed. Nevertheless, no account of Illinois in 1818 would be complete without some consideration of these remnants of the aboriginal inhabitants and their relations with the white men.

When the French explorers first came to the Mississippi valley, they found a confederacy of five tribes inhabiting the country which was named, after them, the Illinois. During the eighteenth century, these tribes were almost annihilated by the surrounding peoples. By 1818, the Cahokia, Michigamea, and Tamaroa had disappeared as distinct tribes; the Kaskaskia, much weakened, lingered on in a reservation of 350 acres left them by the whites near the town of Kaskaskia; while the remnants of the Peoria still lived near the former habitat of the confederacy on the Illinois River.

Next to the Kaskaskia, the nearest neighbors of the white settlers in the south were the Kickapoo, who were scattered along the valley of the Sangamon from the headwaters of the Kaskaskia River to the Illinois. They also appear to have had one or two villages west of the Illinois. Farther north were the Sauk and Fox, who, although not completely amalgamated, mingled with each other a great deal and sometimes lived in the same villages. In spite of the nominal cession of all their lands in Illinois, the principal villages of these tribes were still located near the mouth of the Rock River with other villages extending along both banks of the Mississippi and into the interior. Generally speaking these tribes may be said to have occupied the western part of the triangle between the Mississippi and the Illinois and between the Mississippi and the Rock rivers. The greater part of the domain of the Winnebago was in what is now Wisconsin, but a small wedge-shaped portion of it extended into Illinois between the Rock River and the eastern watershed of the Mississippi. Some of the villages of this tribe were located on the Rock. The whole northeastern part of Illinois was occupied by the Potawatomi with the associated bands of Ottawa and Chippewa. They had villages on the Rock, the Fox, the Kankakee, the Illinois, and also in the interior between these streams and in the neighborhood of Chicago.[1]

The best available evidence as to the population of the Indian tribes living in Illinois in 1818 is an estimate made by the Secretary of War in 1815, but unfortunately the figures refer to the tribes as a whole and not merely to the groups living in Illinois. According to this estimate the Potawatomi were the most numerous, having 4,800 souls. The Sauk numbered 3,200 and the Fox 1,200, making a total of 4,400 for the two tribes. The Winnebago were credited with 2,400 souls but only a few of these lived south of the boundary line. Nearly all of the 1,600 Kickapoo, on the other hand, were within the limits of Illinois. The Kaskaskia tribe had been reduced to 60 souls and the Peoria were not in-

---

[1] For condensed information about the different tribes, consult Hodge, *Handbook of American Indians*. See also *American State Papers, Indian Affairs*, vol. 2; *Wisconsin Historical Collections*, vols. 11 and 20; Morse, *Report on Indian Affairs*; Blair, *Indian Tribes of the Upper Mississippi Valley*; Schoolcraft, *Narrative of an Expedition*; Brown, *Western Gazetteer*; Michelson in *American Anthropologist*.

cluded in the count at all. In each instance it was estimated that about one-fourth of the members of the tribe were warriors.

All these tribes belonged to the Algonkin linguistic group with the exception of the Winnebago, who were of Dakota stock. The material culture, social organization, and religious beliefs of the different tribes were fairly uniform. They were people neither of the forest nor the plain, but lived along the water courses and in the groves much as did the first white settlers. Their time was divided about equally between hunting and agricultural life. "They leave their villages," says Marston,

as soon as their corn, beans, etc., is ripe and taken care of, and their traders arrive and give out their credits and go to their wintering grounds; it being previously determined on in council what particular ground each party shall hunt on. The old men, women, and children embark in canoes, and the young men go by land with their horses; on their arrival they immediately commence their winter's hunt, which lasts about three months. . . . They return to their villages in the month of April and after putting their lodges in order, commence preparing the ground to receive the seed.[2]

The principal crop was Indian corn, of which they often had extensive fields. Speaking of the Sauk and Fox near Rock Island, Major Marston says: "The number of acres cultivated by that part of the two nations who reside at their villages in this vicinity is supposed to be upwards of three hundred. They usually raise from seven to eight thousand bushels of corn, besides beans, pumpkins, melons, etc. . . . The labor of agriculture is confined principally to the women, and this is done altogether with the

---

[2] Blair, *Indian Tribes*, 2:148-151. The most detailed accounts of Illinois Indians in the early nineteenth century are to be found in two memoirs dealing with the Sauk and Fox, published in this volume. The first is in the form of a "Letter to Reverend Dr. Jedidiah Morse, by Major Morrell Marston, U.S.A., commanding at Fort Armstrong, Ill., November, 1820," and was first published in Morse, *Report on Indian Affairs*. The second is "An account of the Manners and Customs of the Sauk and Fox Nations of Indians Tradition," by Thomas Forsyth, Indian agent, January 15, 1827. Much of the material in the following paragraphs is drawn from these memoirs and from Appendix B of the same volume, containing "Notes on Indian social Organization, mental and moral Traits, religious Beliefs, etc." The volume contains also a very comprehensive annotated bibliography. See also Hodge, *Handbook of American Indians*.

hoe."[3] While corn formed the staple of the Indians' diet, they made some use of wild vegetables and roots. They ate meat of many varieties, preference being given to venison and bear's meat. They cared little for fish but ate it when other food was scarce. "They most generally boil everything into soup," says Forsyth in his memoir. "I never knew them to eat raw meat, and meat seems to disgust them when it is not done thoroughly. . . . The old women set the kettle a boiling in the night, and about day break all eat whatever they have got, they eat in the course of the day as often as they are hungry, the kettle is on the fire constantly suspended from the roof of the lodge, every one has his wooden dish or bowl and wooden spoon or as they call it Me-quen which they carry along with them when they are invited to feast."[4]

The ordinary garments of the Indian men were a shirt reaching almost to the knees, a breechclout, and leggings which came up to the thigh and were fastened to the belt on either side. In earliest times all their clothing was made of leather, but by 1818 this material had been generally replaced by trade cloth. The shirt and leggings were often dyed a deep blue or black, while the breechclout was usually of red cloth; all were more or less elaborately decorated with bead and quill work. The women wore a two-piece garment, short leggings reaching to the knees, and moccasins; they also employed the customary Indian ornamentation of quills and beads. Both sexes wore the robe, and later the trade blanket. The men painted their faces in various ways, while the women painted very little or not at all. Except when on the warpath the men of most of the tribes let their hair grow long, wearing the scalp lock braided and a band of otter skin or a woven sash bound around the brows. The women ordinarily wore their hair in a single braid down the back.

The principal manufacturing operations of these tribes were tanning, weaving, and the making of pottery; although the last named industry had practically been given up by 1818. The

[3] Blair, *Indian Tribes*, 2:151.
[4] Blair, *Indian Tribes*, 2:229.

central Algonkin were not familiar with the use of the loom, but they twisted a twine from the inner bark of the linden, and with this wove excellent bags of various sorts, which they used for a great variety of purposes. These were decorated by weaving in geometric designs and conventional representations of animals. They also made reed mats sewed with twine, which were used as covering for the floors, and as roofing for the winter houses. The pottery was of a rather inferior sort, burned in an open fire, or simply sun-dried, and decorated with a few incised lines. With the coming of the whites, this native ware was rapidly replaced by the trade kettle.

All the tribes living in Illinois used two types of houses, one for summer, the other for winter. The summer houses, as described by Forsyth, were

built in the form of an oblong, a bench on each of the long sides about three feet high and four feet wide, parallel to each other, a door at each end, and a passage thro the center of about six feet wide, some of those huts are fifty or sixty feet long and capable of lodging fifty or sixty persons. Their winter lodges are made by driving long poles in the ground in two rows nearly at equal distances from each other, bending the tops so as to overlap each other, then covering them with mats made of what they call puc-wy a kind of rushes or flags, a Bearskin generally serves for a door, which is suspended at the top and hangs down, when finished it is not unlike an oven with the fire in the center and the smoke omits thro the top.[5]

The basis of the social organization and government of these Indians was the clan, all the tribes being divided into a large number of gentes or groups based on descent in the male line and strictly exogamous. Each clan took its name from some special animal or thing to which the members thought themselves related. Thus the gentes of the Kickapoo were Water, Bear, Elk, Bald Eagle, Tree, Berry, Fox, Buffalo, Man, Turkey, and Thunder. The heads of these clans acted as civil chiefs, although the braves or principal men had considerable influence in matters of war and peace. The authority of the chiefs was hereditary, descending to the oldest male of the family, but it

---

[5] Blair, *Indian Tribes*, 2:227.

was not by any means absolute. So loose was the organization of a tribe that the office of chief entailed more trouble than advantage and was sometimes refused. Indeed the power of an individual chief depended primarily on his personal influence rather than on the prestige of his office. The function of the council appears to have been not so much judicial as administrative—the determination of matters of tribal policy—and in its deliberations substantial unanimity was necessary for a decision. "There is no such thing," says Forsyth, "as a summary mode of coercing the payment of debts, all contracts are made on honor, for redress of civil injuries an appeal is made to the old people of both parties and their determination is generally acceded to." [6] Atonement for murder was made in the manner customary among primitive people, usually by payments or presents to the relatives of the dead. Even war was a matter of individual initiative rather than of tribal concern. Any individual might become a war chief for the time being, if he had sufficient influence to induce a party of warriors to follow him.

Most of the tribes were also divided, without regard to clans, into two great phratries, the Blacks and the Whites. This division was applied to both sexes, and the phratry was fixed at the time of birth. Usually the first child of a Black was a White, the second a Black, and so on, but there was no fixed rule. The explanation given by the Indians for this division was that it tended to promote emulation within the tribe. The two colors always played against each other in athletic games and in gambling. They seem to have had some ceremonial significance also, for at clan feasts the Whites took the south and the Blacks the north side of the lodge; and certain offices were definitely assigned to each.

The religion of the Algonkin Indians was essentially a nature worship, pure and simple. An object around which associations had clustered would become the recipient of adoration, and either the object itself or an interpreted manifestation of the object would be looked upon as a manitou capable of bringing pleasure

[6] Blair, *Indian Tribes*, 2:186.

or inflicting pain. In everyday life the elaborate ritual of the Indians' religion centered about the medicine bundle—a collection of charms, amulets, or fetishes sometimes thought to have a consciousness of its own and to enjoy offerings. Some of these bundles were used in clan ceremonies connected with the naming of children, others were thought to give magical protection and help in battle, while still others were supposed to aid their owners in various affairs of life, such as hunting, love, friendship, sickness, athletic sports, gambling, and witchcraft. Frequently the same bundle would be used for several purposes, but there was always an elaborate ritual in connection with it.

In addition to the cult of the medicine bundles, the Indians of Illinois, in common with other central Algonkin, had the society of the Midewin, or grand medicine lodge. This was a secret organization, varying in its minor details with the different tribes, but having certain fundamental features common to all. Admission was on the recommendation of some member, or in the place of some member who had died. Membership was open to both men and women, and in some tribes even children were taken to succeed deceased members. The applicant had to pay a certain fixed sum for admission, and at the same time buy from some member a certain number of formulae and charms. Among several of the tribes the society was divided into four degrees, admission to each one of which had to be bought. The initiation seems to have been little more than a notification to the public that the initiate was qualified to practice magic, the scope of his power becoming greater with each succeeding degree. The badge of the order was a medicine pouch, usually made of the skin of an otter tanned whole, and always containing the megus—a small white shell which was supposed to be the carrier of the magic power. Usually there were also other magicians and witches, not members of the medicine lodge, whose powers were supposed to result from some special dispensation of the manitous.

It is evident that the Indians had nothing that could be called a formal civil government. Most affairs were left to individual initiative; the love of freedom was one of the Indians' chief characteristics; and they suffered their personal liberty to be only slightly limited even by the authority of the chiefs and sachems. This lack of political organization among the Indians inevitably caused many complications in dealing with the whites, complications which were increased by the fact that the whites with whom the Indians first came in contact were generally the most lawless and unruly representatives of their race.

The fur traders, who were always the first to penetrate the Indian forests, were usually hardy adventurers whose one concern was to secure as large a profit as they could from their traffic with the savages. The Illinois country had long been a fertile field for these rovers, and the problem of their control had been one of the most serious which had been handed down first by the French to the British, and then by the British to the Americans. The advent of the pioneer farmer, however, was an even more prolific source of friction than the irregularities of the fur traders, for the Indians regarded with the most jealous disfavor the permanent clearance and settlement of the hunting grounds over which their ancestors had roamed in perfect freedom. The whites, on the other hand, regarded the land as theirs by a sort of racial right and considered that they were justified in using every means to wrest it from the aborigines.

In 1818, the Indians in Illinois retained but little of the independence and self-sufficiency of their forefathers. Their agriculture was of a rude and primitive sort, and they had come to rely upon the white trader for a large number of articles which, once unknown, had become necessities of life; and these they secured in exchange for the returns of their hunts. Their resources not having kept pace with their growing wants, their condition was a rather wretched one; and they were regarded by the government as wards to be cared for as well as possible enemies to be feared. Governor Cass of Michigan Territory, speaking of the Indians in 1816, said: "Since the establishment of the National Government provisions have always been gratuitously distributed to them, and more recently goods to a considerable [amount] have been given. Without these annual gratuities, it is difficult to conceive how they could support and clothe themselves. And even with all this assistance their condition is wretched, their wants increasing their feelings disponding and their prospects dreary." [7]

While the Indians of Illinois and the adjoining frontier were comparatively peaceful and quiet in 1818, there was always a danger that they might take up the hatchet and wage war against the whites, and this ever-present danger was never lost sight of by the United States government. A complicating factor in the situation was the influence which the British still exerted over the tribes of Illinois and the Great Lakes region as late as 1818. The great majority of these tribes had sided with the British in the War of 1812; and, after peace was concluded between Great Britain and the United States, it was necessary to conclude treaties with the Indians likewise. Thomas Forsyth was sent as agent to invite various tribes, including the Chippewa, Menominee, Kickapoo, Potawatomi, and Sauk and Fox, to send deputations to meet with Governor Clark of Missouri Territory, Governor Ninian Edwards of Illinois Territory, and Auguste Chouteau, who had been appointed commissioners by the President to conclude treaties of peace and amity.[8] In the course of time, formal peace was established between the United States and the various tribes which had taken up the hatchet on the British side in the war, but the problem of British influence still remained. The proposal of the United States government after the close of the war to establish military posts at Chicago, Green Bay, and Prairie du Chien aroused considerable opposition among the Indians; in this they had a certain degree of moral support from the British, who naturally were not anxious to see the military forces of their late enemy occupy the frontier region resorted to by the British traders.[9]

[7] Indian Office Papers, Michigan Letter Book, 1 (1814-17):362.

[8] Draper Manuscripts, 2M. 24, 26, 27, 28, and 29.

[9] *Wisconsin Historical Collections*, 19:430. A smouldering hostility toward the Americans persisted among certain Indian tribes for some little time after the war. When the Illinois fur brigade arrived in the vicinity of Peoria Lake in 1818, the trader in charge of the expedition informed the Indians that Gurdon Hubbard, a young American apprentice just arrived in the Indian country, was his adopted son from Montreal. One young brave insisted that Hubbard was an American and showed him a number of scalps, which he claimed were those of his countrymen. Hubbard, *Autobiography*, 48.

During the period following the war, the British endeavored to preserve the good will of the Indians of the northwest by a lavish distribution of presents at Drummond's Island, not far from Mackinac, and at Malden, at the mouth of the Detroit River. In the summer of 1817, Major Puthuff, agent at Mackinac, reported that a considerable band of Sauk and Fox from the lower Mississippi, of Winnebago from the Wisconsin River and Prairie du Chien, as well as some Potawatomi and other tribes from the Illinois, had visited Mackinac and Drummond's Island that season. At the latter post, the British had distributed presents, and it was reported that large quantities of arms and ammunition had been given out. Two years later, Governor Cass said in a letter to Calhoun, then Secretary of War: "The British Indian headquarters are at Malden at the mouth of this River, and to that place the Indians east of Lake Michigan, many west of that Lake, and those upon the Wabash & Miami Rivers and their tributary streams make an annual journey to receive the presents, which are distributed to them and to confer as they express it, with their British father." [10] Needless to say, the practice was most objectionable to the United States, and in 1819, Calhoun gave Governor Cass instructions to prevent any Indians living within the United States from passing into Canada, save as individuals. Still, as late as 1820, certain of the Sauk and Fox living in the vicinity of Fort Armstrong on Rock Island had British medals in their possession and were displaying British flags considerably larger than the American army standards.

The presence of British traders among the Indians of the northwest was also a source of considerable uneasiness to the Americans. In 1818, many of the private traders in Illinois, as well as throughout the entire Great Lakes region, were British in their political allegiance and in their sympathies; many of them had taken an active part against the Americans in the War of 1812. The correspondence of the time is filled with complaints concerning the evil influence of these British traders.

[10] Indian Office Papers, Michigan Letter Book, 3 (1818-22) :80.

Jacob Varnum, who had charge of the government trading factory at Chicago in 1818, said: "The indiscriminate admission of British subjects to trade with the Indians, is a matter of pretty general complaint, throughout this section of the country. There are five establishments now within the limits of this agency, headed by British subjects." [11] Governor Cass likewise had little love for these traders. "They systematically seize every opportunity of poisoning the minds of the Indians," he wrote. "There is no doubt but they report every occurence of any importance to their Indian Department, and the Indians are taught to consider our Government as their enemies and the British as their friends." [12] It is very probable that American army officers and Indian agents somewhat overestimated the danger to be anticipated from the influence of British agents and traders with the savages. At the same time, in the light of experience, and in view of the actual situation of affairs on the frontier, the government of the United States was certainly justified in exercising the greatest diligence in its efforts to check all intercourse between the Indians and the British.

The United States government had, then, three ends in view in its administration of Indian affairs upon the northwestern frontier during this period: to preserve peace between the red man and the white settler; to destroy British influence and to render the Indians dependent upon the United States; and, last, to improve the condition of the savages or, if possible, to civilize them. There was a rather widely spread feeling that the whites owed a certain moral obligation to the Indians on account of the occupation of so goodly a portion of their best hunting grounds. The government sought to carry out its policy by means of three separate and distinct agencies; the military posts upon the frontier, the Indian Department, and the system of government fur-trading factories.

[11] Morse, *Report on Indian Affairs*, 46. In *Niles' Weekly Register*, 8:263, is printed a list of names of traders who sided with the British in the War of 1812. The correspondence in which the list occurs is dated April 29, 1815. There are included the names of three traders who formerly resided at Peoria: "Mitchell" La Croix, Louis Buisson, and Louis Bennett.

[12] Indian Office Papers, Michigan Letter Book, 1 (1814-17):365.

The principal military establishments upon the northwestern frontier in 1818 were at Detroit, Mackinac, Fort Wayne, Green Bay, Prairie du Chien, and Chicago. Fort Dearborn, it will be remembered, was destroyed during the War of 1812, but it was re-established in 1816. There were three other posts in Illinois in 1818, besides the one at Chicago: Fort Armstrong, on Rock Island; Fort Edwards, opposite the mouth of the Des Moines River; and Fort Clark, on the Illinois River near the outlet of Peoria Lake. The last-named post was abandoned, however, in the same year. These posts were located at strategic points upon the water communications of the northwest and were designed to overawe the Indian tribes in their vicinity and to act as a check upon foreign interference. In addition, they gave aid and protection to the Indian Department and to the government trading factories.

The Indian Department, under the supervision and direction of the United States Department of War, had its agencies at Mackinac, Green Bay, Prairie du Chien, Chicago, Vincennes, Fort Wayne, and Piqua. There was a special agent for the Illinois Territory, with headquarters at Peoria, besides scattered sub-agents. Before Illinois was admitted into the Union, Governor Edwards was *ex officio* superintendent of Indian affairs in the greater part of the territory and as such directed the administration of affairs at the different agencies within his jurisdiction. Thus the agent for Illinois Territory, as well as the one stationed at Prairie du Chien, was prior to 1818 responsible to Governor Edwards. The agents at Green Bay and Chicago, however, although within Illinois Territory, were under the direction of Governor Cass of Michigan Territory. The reason for this arrangement was that Chicago and Green Bay were more easily accessible from Detroit by way of the lakes than from Kaskaskia. After Illinois became a state, the agency at Prairie du Chien and that for Illinois Territory became independent establishments, responsible directly to the War Department; Chicago and Green Bay remained under the supervision of Governor Cass.[13] In 1818 Charles Jouett was in charge

[13] Indian Office Papers, Letter Book, D (1817-20):326 *et seq.*

of Indian affairs at Chicago, while Richard Graham acted as "agent for Illinois Territory"; the two sub-agents within the limits of Illinois were Pierre Menard and Maurice Blondeau.

The Indian agents and sub-agents were entrusted with the duty of supervising the political relations between the various tribes and the United States. They discharged treaty obligations on behalf of the United States government, and acted as the medium of communication with the Indians. They granted licenses for the Indian trade and generally supervised its conduct. One of the most important of the duties regularly performed was the payment of the annuities due the Indians. These were usually paid in goods and were delivered in accordance with treaty stipulations, most often as the price agreed upon for the cession of lands by the Indians. The amounts paid over in this way, however, were very modest. The annuity due the Kaskaskia in 1818 was $1,000, while an equal amount was paid the Ottawa, Chippewa, and Potawatomi residing upon the Illinois River. The Kickapoo received only $900.

Another important service rendered by the Indian agents was the distribution of presents, which was of the utmost importance as a means of securing the attachment of the savages. The lavish distribution of presents by the British agents at Malden and at Drummond's Island dictated a similar policy on the part of the United States, for the Indians usually bestowed their favor upon the party which bid highest for it. The annuities were divided among the different villages of the various tribes in proportion to their numbers, while the presents were usually bestowed upon the principal chiefs and other influential individuals. Those familiar with the state of affairs upon the frontier were almost unanimous in advocating a liberal distribution of presents as the most effective and the cheapest means of controlling the savages. Governor Edwards in 1816 recommended that presents be distributed to the Indians of the Illinois River and vicinity with a free hand, for a few years at least; "nothing less," he said, "can wean them from British influence to which they more than any other Indians in those territories have long been devoted." [14]

[14] Letter of Ninian Edwards, September 24, 1816, in Chicago Historical Society Manuscripts.

The giving of presents may also be regarded as the price of peace along the frontiers, and of freedom from petty annoyance, such as cattle and horsethieving. A threat to withhold presents was a much more effective argument with the Indians than any appeal to their higher sensibilities. It was also considered necessary to distribute presents in order to give dignity and prestige to the agent himself. Invoices sent out by Thomas L. McKenney, superintendent of Indian trade, in 1818, indicate that merchandise to the value of $2,000 was destined for Kaskaskia for distribution among the Indians, while equal amounts were sent to Peoria and Prairie du Chien.

Besides the presents which were distributed among the Indians each year, it was also customary to feed those who visited the various posts from time to time for business or other purposes. It took nearly as much food to supply the visiting savages as the regular garrisons. Governor Cass described the situation in the following words:

A long established custom, a thousand wants real or imaginary, and the restlessness and impatience of their mode of life send them in upon us. They come with trifling articles to barter, they come to get their arms repaired, to get their farming utensils, to enquire about their annuities, to complain of injuries from some of our Citizens and messages of every kind from their chiefs. It would [be] equally troublesome for me to enumerate and for you to read the various causes which influence them to make these visits. They generally bring with them their women & Children, and they are so importunate in their applications, and their necessities so obvious, that an Agent must frequently yield to them.[15]

The agents of the Indian Department also performed a number of small services, often trifling in themselves, but important for the maintenance of friendly relations. They received all visiting Indians, endeavored to secure such information from them as might be of value to the United States, attempted to prevent the introduction of liquor into the Indian country, and in fact did anything which might operate to secure the good will or promote the welfare of the Indians. Blacksmiths were sometimes maintained at the agencies to repair the tools and

[15] Indian Office Papers, Michigan Letter Book, 3 (1818-22):105.

weapons which the savages brought in from their villages and hunting grounds. In 1820, Pierre Menard, sub-agent at Kaskaskia, expended $13 "for ferriage of the Delaware chief and his party over the Mississippi"; $19.50 "for supper and breakfast furnished thirteen Indians, corn and hay for their horses"; and $23 "for four hundred pounds of beef, and making a coffin for a Delaware Indian who was accidentally killed." [16] In the performance of their various duties the agents usually had the assistance of interpreters, whose knowledge of the languages and intimate associations with the Indians enabled them to secure information of value to the department.

One of the most important functions of the Indian agents was the supervision of the fur trade and the enforcement of such regulations as the President or Congress might prescribe from time to time. In 1816, Congress passed an act excluding foreigners from engaging in the fur trade unless granted special permission by authority of the President. The power of determining who were to receive licenses was delegated by the President to the Indian agents, inasmuch as they were in a better position to decide what foreigners might with propriety be allowed to trade within the limits of the United States. Since the American capital employed in the industry was not sufficient to supply the needs of the Indians, it was not thought wise at this time to exclude foreigners entirely, but the agents were allowed to grant passes only "under such regulations as shall subject them [the traders] to a strict observance of the laws of the United States upon this subject; secure their exertions in maintaining peace between the Indian tribes, and this government, and between themselves; and present additional inducements to respect the laws against smuggling." [17] More stringent regulations were prescribed in 1818, when the President gave orders that no foreigners were to be licensed to trade with the Indians, nor were American traders to be allowed to take with them foreign *engagés*. But as it was almost impossible for American

[16] *American State Papers, Indian Affairs*, 2:302.
[17] *Wisconsin Historical Collections*, 19:406.

traders to dispense with the services of the French-Canadian *voyageurs* and interpreters, there was later a slight relaxation from this strict ruling, and permission was given to employ foreign *engagés* under certain conditions, one of which was that none should be employed who were obnoxious to American citizens by reason of their conduct during the War of 1812. The various agents did not hesitate to refuse licenses to foreigners on occasion. In 1816, Charles Jouett, agent at Chicago, announced that he had refused to one Beauveaux a license to trade because of "his having held up to odium those Indians who are remarkable for their attachment to the American Government." [18] In the following year, Governor Ninian Edwards, believing that the hostility of the Winnebago and other Indians living along the Mississippi was due to the influence of British traders, declared his intention of refusing all British traders permission to enter Illinois Territory. The regulations looking to the exclusion of foreigners, however, do not appear to have been very effective. Licenses were taken out in the names of American citizens, but often as soon as the outfit in question entered the Indian country, a foreign trader who was nominally an *engagé* in the expedition took charge and directed the commerce with the Indians.

As a means of destroying the influence of the private traders, particularly the British, and of attaching the Indians to the American government, the United States placed great confidence in a system of government trading factories which had its origin as far back as 1795. These factories were not intended to be money-making enterprises but were designed rather to supplement the Indian Department in the administration of the frontier. Certain provisions of an act of 1811, which was still in force in 1818, will serve to illustrate the general nature of the plan. The president was given authority to establish factories at such places on the frontier as he might deem most convenient and to appoint a superintendent of Indian trade who should manage the business on behalf of the government. The agents

[18] Indian Office Papers, Michigan Letter Book, 1 (1814-17):395.

appointed to take charge of the various factories were to be responsible to the superintendent and render their accounts to him. The prices of the goods employed in the trade were to be regulated in such a manner that the original capital stock furnished by the United States should not be diminished, no effort being made to secure a profit in the conduct of the business. The furs, skins, and other articles obtained from the Indians in the course of trade were to be sold at public auction under the direction of the President at such places as should be deemed most advantageous.[19]

In 1818, the United States maintained four factories in the northwest, at Chicago, Green Bay, Prairie du Chien, and Fort Edwards. Before the War of 1812, there had been government trading houses at Mackinac, Chicago, Fort Madison, and Sandusky; but during the course of hostilities all were lost to the British, together with their buildings, supplies, and furs. In 1816, shortly after the close of the war, factories were established at Green Bay and at Prairie du Chien, both of which places were within Illinois Territory, and at Chicago. This last was placed under the supervision of Jacob B. Varnum. Matthew Irwin and John W. Johnson were appointed factors at Green Bay and Prairie du Chien, respectively. A trading house was built at Fort Edwards in 1818, as a branch of the establishment at Prairie du Chien, with Robert Belt as the assistant in charge; but the next year this was made an independent establishment. It was designed to supply the tribes between Prairie du Chien and St. Louis, and to drive out the unprincipled private traders operating in that quarter, who, the superintendent of trade declared, had during the past two years supplied the Sauk and Fox Indians with no less than 50 barrels of whiskey.

The goods used at the government factories were all purchased under the direction of the superintendent of Indian trade, Thomas L. McKenney, who had his headquarters at Georgetown, District of Columbia. The articles designed for Fort Edwards and Prairie du Chien were generally sent to Pittsburgh to be

[19] *Statutes at Large*, 2:652.

shipped down the Ohio to St. Louis. There they were received by James Kennerley, who acted as forwarding agent and sent them up the Mississippi to their respective destinations. The peltry received from the Indians at Fort Edwards in 1818 included deer, bear, beaver, otter, raccoon, and muskrat. A portion of the goods was also traded for lead, obtained by the Indians from the mines below Prairie du Chien, and for beeswax, tallow, and Indian mats. These furs and other goods were sent to Kennerley at St. Louis and forwarded by him up the Ohio to Pittsburgh. The trade at Chicago and Green Bay was conducted in a manner very similar to that at Fort Edwards and Prairie du Chien, with the exception that the goods were forwarded to the factories and the returns shipped back by way of the Great Lakes. Not all the goods received at the trading houses in the northwest were exchanged directly with the Indians by the factors. At times some of them were made up into outfits and sold to private traders, who carried them out into the interior. Sometimes the factors at the government houses sold the peltry which they received to private traders, but in December, 1818, strict orders were issued by the superintendent that it was all to be forwarded to the Indian trade house at Georgetown. The furs from the posts in the northwest were generally disposed of at Georgetown by means of annual public sales.[20]

Insofar as the object of the government in establishing the factory system was to destroy the influence of the private trader and attach the Indians to the United States, the plan must be pronounced a failure. The power of the private trader increased rather than diminished, while the tribes of the northwest still regarded the United States with suspicion and distrust. The system was likewise a failure from a business point of view. Taking into consideration the cost of maintaining the factory at Chicago, the trade there was conducted at a loss estimated, by March 31, 1818, at nearly $2,000. In December of that year the factor reported that he had hardly done sufficient business that season to clear the wages of his interpreter.[21] Two years later the super-

[20] *American State Papers, Indian Affairs*, 2:335.

[21] Morse, *Report on Indian Affairs*, 46.

intendent of trade, in a letter to the Secretary of War, wrote, "I conceive it proper to make known to you for the information of the President that the u. s. factory at Chicago has ceased, almost to do business." [22] The trade at Fort Edwards in 1818 was somewhat more prosperous than that at Chicago, but even there the returns in furs and skins obtained by the government factor were probably insignificant in comparison with those secured by the private traders who operated in the region.

Many reasons for the failure of the government factories in their competition with private traders were advanced by persons supposedly familiar with the situation. The factories were so few in number and so widely scattered that it was often necessary for the Indians who wished to deal with the government agents to make long journeys with their furs. The private trader, on the other hand, went out into the wilderness, carrying his goods to the Indians at their hunting grounds or villages. The government factors, moreover, were not allowed to give credit in their dealings with the Indians. When cold weather approached, the savages were usually without money or furs, but it was necessary for them to secure many articles, such as guns, ammunition, traps, kettles, and blankets, before they could set out for their wintering grounds. Since these articles could not be obtained at the factories, the Indians were obliged to resort to the private traders, who were more than willing to supply their needs on credit. The obvious result was that the private trader obtained by far the larger share of the returns of the winter's hunt. Furthermore, it is certain that the private traders were able to evade the vigilance of the government agents and make extensive use of liquor in their trading operations, and this gave them a decided advantage over the factors, although it was in the long run injurious to the trade as a whole. The Indian would give up everything he possessed, including furs and even clothing itself, for a little whiskey. In spite of the fact that it was not the intention of the government to derive any profit from the trade, it appears that the goods supplied by the factors usually sold at prices higher than those charged by the

[22] Indian Office Papers, Trade Letter Book, E (1818-20):496.

private traders and were often of inferior quality. Thus, notwithstanding the benevolent intentions of the government in establishing trading houses, the Indians could derive no advantages from dealing with the factories.

Factors and agents alike complained frequently and loudly of the evil influence of foreign traders until one is almost tempted to believe that the British were made the scapegoats for all the misfortunes which attended the efforts of the United States to regulate Indian affairs and to carry on the fur trade. Referring to the Chicago factory in 1820, the superintendent of trade wrote: "The causes [*sic*] which has so successfully prostrated the once flourishing hopes of this establishment, is so notorious, as hardly to need refering to. It lies deep in the influence (principally British,) which is spread so generally over that region; and in the combinations which have been entered into to do away, from amongst the Indians inhabiting that Country, whatever controll the u. s. may essay to acquire over them, either by the Factory or any other system." [23] There is no direct evidence, however, that the British traders were any more active than the American traders in prejudicing the minds of the Indians against the government factories. It was the American Fur Company, in fact, which finally gave the death blow to the factory system.

A most important reason for the failure of the factories to accomplish their purposes is to be found in the attitude of the Indians themselves toward them. Governor Cass, as early as 1814, wrote: "Our trading factories, and our economy in presents have rendered us contemptible to them. The Government should never come in contact with them but in those cases where its dignity, its strength or its liberality will inspire them with respect or fear." [24] In fact, the savages seem to have misconceived entirely the nature of the factory system and the purpose of the government in inaugurating it. Major Marston, who commanded at Fort Armstrong, on Rock Island, revealed the attitude of the

[23] Indian Office Papers, Trade Letter Book, E (1818-20):496.
[24] Indian Office Papers, Michigan Letter Book, 1 (1814-17):7.

Indians living in that vicinity. If mention were made to them of their Great Father, the President, supplying them with goods, they would reply, "You are a *pash-i-pash-i-to,* (a fool) our Great Father is certainly *no trader;* he has sent those goods to be *given* to us, as presents; but his Agents are endeavouring to cheat us, by *selling* them for our peltries." [25] Needless to say, this attitude was fostered by the private traders, who did everything in their power to drive the factories out of existence. In this opposition the lead was taken by the American Fur Company, and its influence was strong enough to nullify all efforts to strengthen the system, and finally brought about its abolition in 1822.

The government factories are of interest chiefly from the political rather than from the commercial point of view, for it was in the hands of the private concerns that the fur industry attained its highest development. The Indian trader in Illinois had a long and varied career and the story of his picturesque wilderness traffic constitutes an alluring phase of the history of the state. For over a century the smooth-flowing streams of Illinois were disturbed by the paddle of the French-Canadian *voyageur* and the hills on either side re-echoed his melodious songs, while during part of that period the prairies and forests recognized the semi-feudal authority of a great fur company. Controlled in turn by the French, the English, and finally by the Americans, the fur trade, as it was carried on in Illinois in 1818, bore traces of both the French and the British regimes. The *engagés* who performed the menial labor connected with the industry, as well as many of the traders who bartered with the Indians, were, in some instances, descendants of the *coureurs de bois* who had come while the *fleur-de-lis* still waved over the region of the Great Lakes and the Mississippi valley. The influence of the British period, on the other hand, may be traced in the business organization of the trade.

It is difficult for the present inhabitants to realize the extent to which wild game once abounded in the state, and the enor-

[25] Blair, *Indian Tribes,* 2:177.

mous quantities of peltry which were annually exported. The valley of the Illinois River was, at the close of the territorial period, one of the important fur-bearing areas of the north-west. In 1816, the furs sent out from the various posts upon the Illinois River included 10,000 deer, 300 bear, 10,000 raccoon, 35,000 muskrat, 400 otter, 300 pounds of beaver, 500 cat and fox, 100 mink. The total value of this peltry was estimated at $23,700. The merchandise imported into the region during the same year was estimated to be worth $18,000. Chicago was an important trade center, and the furs exported thence in the same year were estimated to be worth more than $8,000.[26] In considering the Illinois fur trade, it should be remembered that it constituted only one part of an industry of enormous proportions, covering the Great Lakes region, and extending westward far beyond the Mississippi, an industry which at one time or another has made its influence felt in almost every part of the North American continent.

By far the largest and most important of the trading concerns operating in Illinois and the northwest in 1818 was the American Fur Company. At the close of the War of 1812, a large part of the trade of the Great Lakes region was in the hands of two associations, the Northwest and Southwest companies. The former was a British concern, in which were included a number of the most powerful trading firms of Montreal, but it had several posts south of the boundary line, within the territory of the United States. The Southwest Company was owned by John Jacob Astor and certain Montreal traders, Astor having a two-thirds interest in the trade carried on within the United States.

The act of Congress of 1816 excluding foreigners from the fur trade unless specially licensed made it difficult for the Canadian firms to operate their trading posts upon American territory. Immediately upon the passage of this act, Astor, who cherished the design of obtaining control of the entire fur trade within the limits of the United States, formed a concern which he called the American Fur Company and purchased not only the interest

---

[26] The exports from the Illinois River in 1816 also included 10,000 pounds of maple sugar.

of the Montreal merchants in the Southwest Company but a number of posts of the Northwest Company on American soil as well. Besides the posts, Astor was able to secure the services of a large number of traders and *engagés* formerly attached to them who would otherwise have been thrown out of employment. The act of 1816 was interpreted so as not to exclude foreign *engagés,* and thus it was possible for the new company to make use of the services of these British subjects, without whose assistance, indeed, success in an enterprise of such magnitude as was contemplated would have been almost impossible.[27] In order that the manner of conducting the business might have an appearance of legality, licenses were taken out in the names of young American clerks, while the actual conduct of the trade was in the hands of those who had formerly been in the service of the British merchants, and who possessed the necessary experience.

The American Fur Company began operations in 1817, and in the following year its trade covered a wide range of territory, stretching from the eastern shores of Lake Huron to the Missouri River and from the Canadian boundary to the frontier line of settlements in Illinois and Indiana. Traders supplied by Astor's company were to be found along the shores of Green Bay, in the valley of the Fox and Wisconsin rivers, and also upon the upper reaches of the Minnesota River, then called the St. Peter's; they coasted along the shores of Lake Michigan and Lake Superior, trading with the Indians from such posts as Milwaukee and Fond du Lac; they descended the Mississippi from Prairie du Chien, exchanging goods for furs with the Indians living in Illinois and Missouri territories; and every year their brigades visited the Illinois and Wabash rivers, to reap the rich harvest of peltry in their valleys.[28]

[27] Chittenden, *American Fur Trade,* 1:310, 311; Bancroft, *History of the Northwest Coast,* 1:513. Chittenden says that Astor was largely instrumental in securing the passage of the law referred to.

[28] An idea of the extent of the company's operations may be readily gained from the list of American Fur Company employees, 1818-19, published in the *Wisconsin Historical Collections,* 12:154.

Astor and his agents entered upon the conduct of the north-west trade with the avowed intention of driving all competitors from the field. Such a task necessarily required some time, but the spirit of this undertaking is revealed in the words of Ramsay Crooks and Robert Stuart, agents of the company, who wrote to Astor in the summer of 1817: "Next year our exertions must be more general and efforts must be made to embrace every section of the trade and not leave the[m] [the competitors] a corner to repose in—this summer it was impossible to effect everyth[ing.]" [29] The following season, Stuart was able to report that his colleague had, after much effort, secured the services of nearly every good trader in the whole region in the interests of the company. He added that while their rivals had carried on a vigorous competition in every section of the interior, there was good reason to believe that they were secretly disheartened. In 1819, Astor was considering the advisability of contracting somewhat the range of the company's operations, but Crooks advised against it, pointing out that victory over their rivals was almost within their grasp and that to yield any ground at that particular time would strengthen the opposition by just so much.[30]

The arbiter of the destinies of the American Fur Company was its founder, John Jacob Astor. He directed the general policy of the concern, and superintended the conduct of the business at its headquarters in New York. The management of affairs in the Indian country itself, as well as along the communications to New York and Montreal, was entrusted to the two young Scotchmen already named, Ramsay Crooks and Robert Stuart. These agents gathered merchandise and provisions for use in the trade and arranged for transporting them to Mackinac Island, the general rendezvous of the company in the northwest. It was their business to see that a sufficient number of *engagés* was hired to perform the labor of carrying goods and furs, as well as enough clerks and traders to carry on the busi-

[29] American Fur Company Letter Book, 1816-20, p. 50.
[30] American Fur Company Letter Book, 1816-20, pp. 109, 260.

ness in the interior. They organized the different departments in which the traffic was conducted, assigned the traders and *engagés* to their wintering grounds, and directed the preparation of the outfits. When the peltries came in from the Indian country in the spring, the agents saw to it that they were properly sorted and packed and prepared for shipment to the eastern market. Ramsay Crooks's headquarters were nominally at New York, but he spent a great deal of his time at Mackinac, and occasionally made visits to the interior.

Mackinac was in 1818 the great entrepôt of the northwest fur trade, the place of rendezvous of the traders and *engagés* of the region. When the goods from New York and Montreal arrived, they were made up into outfits, which were supplied to the traders on various terms. Some were turned over to clerks and traders in the regular employ of the concern, who were paid a stipulated wage and instructed to exchange the goods entrusted to their care to the best possible advantage, on the account of the company. Other outfits were traded on shares; that is to say, the company received a certain proportion of the returns and the remainder belonged to the trader who bartered with the Indians. Still other traders purchased their goods outright from the company, which had no interest in them thereafter, save to collect the amount for which they were sold.

The three principal regions of fur-trading activity of Illinois interest were that portion of the Mississippi between Prairie du Chien and St. Louis and the Illinois and Wabash river valleys. In 1817, a clerk named Russell Farnham was sent out from Mackinac with an assortment of goods to be traded along the Mississippi and its tributaries below Prairie du Chien. The goods were to be traded on the account of the company, Farnham being merely a salaried employee. The instructions made it clear that while the outfit was nominally under his charge, the business of dealing with the Indians was to be supervised by one St. Jean, a trader of long experience, to whose judgment was left the choice of a spot in which to spend the winter. Before setting out, Farnham was given a license issued by Major Puthuff, Indian agent at Mackinac, authorizing him to trade in any part of the Indian country. He was instructed to proceed to St. Louis, where he was to obtain a territorial and United States license, which would permit him to sell goods on both the Illinois and Missouri sides of the river, in territory which had been ceded by the natives.[31]

Upon arriving at Prairie du Chien, Farnham and Daniel Darling, another trader who accompanied the outfit, were ordered by Lieutenant Colonel Chambers, who commanded at Fort Crawford, to have no dealings with the Indians until new licenses had been obtained from the governor of Missouri territory. The traders defied Colonel Chambers, who thereupon sent them to St. Louis under military escort. Though this mishap injured the trade to a considerable extent, Farnham succeeded in opening up a traffic with certain Indians lying west of the Mississippi, and did fairly well, considering his handicap. In the following year, 1818, Farnham once more returned to the Mississippi, carrying with him an outfit to be traded with the Sauk, in which he himself had an interest. Though some further difficulties were experienced on this second voyage, the reports indicated that the trade in the department was successful. There was at this time strenuous competition on the Mississippi between the American Fur Company and a group of traders with headquarters at St. Louis, and this spirit of rivalry may have partially accounted for the difficulties which Farnham experienced during the course of his operations in that quarter.[32] The Department of the Mississippi was on the whole quite productive, the Sauk and Fox being the principal nations from which returns were secured.

The commerce of the Department of the Illinois River was under the supervision of Antoine Deschamps, an experienced

[31] American Fur Company Letter Book, 1816-20, p. 47.

[32] Chittenden, *American Fur Trade*, 1:312. The agents of the company made vigorous protests against the interference which their traders met with at the hands of the United States officers. The nominal ground for the interference appears to have been that Farnham's brigade included foreign traders who were excluded from operating in United States territory by the law of 1816.

trader, who selected the sites for the various posts and assigned the clerks and *engagés* to their winter quarters. From a list of the employees of the American Fur Company in 1818 and 1819 it appears that some 30 clerks, traders, interpreters, and boatmen were located upon the Illinois River; the reports of Crooks to Astor show that the trade of the Illinois posts was fairly successful during this period. The number of men engaged in the trade for the company upon the Wabash, according to the same list of employees, was 16 or 17, and it is probable that some of these occasionally penetrated into Illinois. There were also scattered traders of the concern upon the Desplaines and Kankakee rivers, and at least two traders at Chicago in 1818, James Kinzie and Jean Baptiste Chandonnais, were equipped by the American Fur Company. Jean Baptiste Beaubien was transferred from Milwaukee to Chicago about this time. The Detroit firm of Conant and Mack also maintained an establishment at a place known as "Hardscrabble" on the south branch of the Chicago River. A trader by the name of John Crafts was in charge and his strategic position enabled him to intercept the Indians on their way to Chicago from the Illinois, the Desplaines, and the Kankakee rivers. It is said that Crafts also sent outfits to the Rock River and other places within a range of about 100 miles.[33]

The men engaged in the fur trade fell into two distinct classes, the *voyageurs* or *engagés*, who performed the menial labor,[34] and the traders who directed operations—the *bourgeois* of the French regime. Many of the *voyageurs* were halfbreeds, descendants of the *coureurs de bois* who had taken to the wilder-

[33] Andreas, *History of Chicago*, 1:92 *et seq.*; *Wisconsin Historical Collections*, 12:154; American Fur Company Letter Book, 1816-20, pp. 28, 123; Hurlbut, *Chicago Antiquities*, 31.

[34] The terms *engagé* and *voyageur*, as generally used, are almost synonymous, though the former term includes not only the boatmen or *voyageurs*, but also those who performed other forms of labor incidental to the trade. The persons employed in the trade were obliged to sign contracts, or *engagements*, by which they bound themselves to perform certain stipulated services for a definite period of time. There are at the present day a great many of these *engagements* preserved in the archives of the District of Montreal.

ness in the early days of the French occupation of Canada. Others were native-born Canadians and had left wives and children in the little parishes in the neighborhood of far-away Montreal, to come into the wilderness and eke out a difficult and precarious livelihood. All observers agree in describing the *voyageurs* as a happy, carefree lot, cheerfully performing their arduous labors and taking no thought for the morrow with its possible dangers and privations. "These people," wrote Crooks,

are indispensable to the successful prosecution of the trade, their places cannot be supplied by Americans, who are for the most part are [*sic*] too independent to submit quietly to a proper controul, and who can gain any where a subsistence much superior to a man of the interior and although the body of the Yankee can resist as much hardship as any man, tis only in the Canadian we find that temper of mind, to render him patient docile and persevering, in short they are a people harmless in themselves whose habits of submission fit them peculiarly for our business.[35]

The *voyageur* stood in a sort of feudal relation to the trader who was in command of the brigade, whose word was law, both with regard to the property of the company and the persons in its employ. James H. Lockwood, a former employee of the American Fur Company, said of the *voyageurs*: "They are very easily governed by a person who understands something of their nature and disposition, but their burgeois or employer must be what they consider a gentleman, or superior to themselves, as they never feel much respect for a man who has, from an *engagee*, risen to the rank of a clerk." [36]

In spite of the carefree and irresponsible existence which he led, the lot of the *voyageur* was not a particularly happy one. His average salary was less than $100 a year, and his daily ration was a soup made of hulled corn seasoned with tallow. The yearly outfit furnished him by his employer consisted of perhaps two cotton shirts, a triangular blanket, a portage collar, and a pair of heavy shoes. All luxuries, such as pipes and tobacco, he was obliged to furnish himself. The toil to which the

[35] American Fur Company Letter Book, 1816-20, p. 12.
[36] *Wisconsin Historical Collections*, 2:110.

voyageur was subjected was arduous in the extreme. To drive a heavily laden canoe or Mackinac boat through the water was in itself no task for a weakling, but this was a trifle in comparison with the labor which confronted him at the portage or at the rapids or falls which occasionally interrupted the streams. Here the craft must be unloaded, and the merchandise carried to the point where the expedition was to re-embark. The older *voyageurs* were often wrecks, broken down by the labor which they were obliged to perform and the exposure to which they were subjected.

The traders in the employ of the American Fur Company in 1818 were partly experienced hands, many of whom were French-Canadians like Antoine Deschamps, in charge of the Department of the Illinois River, and partly young clerks, most of whom were Americans. These clerks were carefully watched by the agents of the company, for it was upon their initiative and industry that the future prosperity of the concern depended. The advice which Ramsay Crooks gave to Edward Upham, a young clerk located upon the Illinois and Kankakee rivers in 1819, is of interest in this connection. He was told to be industrious, cautious, and enterprising and to spend his time in acquiring a knowledge of the country and its people rather than in dozing away the winter in his hut.[37] The great event in the trader's life was the annual voyage to Mackinac. According to one observer who visited the rendezvous in 1820, "The trader, or interior clerk, who takes his outfit of goods to the Indians, and spends eleven months of the year in toil, and want, and petty traffic, appears to dissipate his means with a sailor-like improvidence in a few weeks, and then returns to his forest wanderings; and boiled corn, pork, and wild rice again supply his wants." [38]

The goods which the wilderness trader carried to the Indians in exchange for their furs included a great variety of objects, and by no means consisted entirely of trinkets designed to satisfy

[37] American Fur Company Letter Book, 1816-20, p. 169.
[38] Schoolcraft, *Narrative of an Expedition*, 69.

the vanity of the savage. The assortment of the trader in the Illinois country in 1818 included such goods as blankets, strouds, handkerchiefs, tools of all sorts, guns, ammunition, and kettles—articles which were really useful or even indispensable to the savage in his everyday life. On the other hand, the outfit usually contained some luxuries, such as ribbons, jewelry, wampum, tobacco, pipes, vermilion, earbobs, and even jew's-harps.

The craft in which the fur traders conveyed their outfits on lakes and streams of the northwest were mainly of two sorts, the bateau, or Mackinac boat, and the canoe. The former was a light boat, some 30 feet long, cut away at both bow and stern. It was navigated by five men, four of whom propelled it with oars, while the fifth steered. The canoe in which one employee of the American Fur Company navigated Lake Michigan in 1818 was made of birch bark and was 33 feet long by 4½ feet broad, tapering toward the bow and stern posts. The bark was sewed with wattap, and pine gum was used for the seams. The canoe was propelled by paddles, with the occasional assistance of a sail. There were eight *voyageurs* to each canoe, those stationed at the bow and stern being men of particular skill, who received double wages. Two or more canoes or boats formed a brigade, which was under the charge of a *guide* or brigade commander. Each man was allowed to carry a sack containing 40 pounds of baggage. The entire cargo of the canoe, including goods, provisions, crew, and baggage, was about four tons. In propelling these boats, the *voyageurs* moved their oars or paddles to the rhythm of their French-Canadian boat songs, in which the *bourgeois* often took the lead. Every five miles or so, the *bourgeois* might shout "Whoop la! à terre, à terre—pour la pipe!" and the whole brigade would pause to rest while the men smoked a welcome pipe of tobacco. Thus distances on the lakes and streams of the interior came to be measured in "pipes" rather than miles.

As the trader advanced into the interior, he gave out goods to the savages whom he passed, the Indians promising to bring in the returns of their winter's hunt in exchange for them. Arrived at the post, the trader unpacked his goods and gave credit to the Indians in the vicinity, who thereupon departed for their hunting grounds. The average value of the goods advanced to each man was about $40 or $50, calculated at cost prices, but the honesty and ability of the individual hunter were taken into consideration. The amounts were carefully entered in the books and the trader aimed to secure in exchange furs valued at at least twice the cost of the goods advanced. Of course, bands came in from time to time with furs to be bartered on the spot, while during the winter the trader usually made occasional visits to the Indians at their hunting grounds. In the wilderness trade, the unit of exchange was the *plus*, originally the value of a pound of beaver skin, but later the equivalent of one dollar. Whiskey, the curse of the fur trade, was used extensively in spite of the vigorous efforts of the United States authorities to keep it out of the Indian country. When the trader and the Indian came together, it was customary to use some liquor to facilitate the traffic, with the result that the proceedings at these meetings were sometimes rather uproarious. Under the stress of competition whiskey flowed more freely and the disorder increased.

The policy of the great company in its dealings with the savages is indicated by the advice which Crooks gave to a young trader in 1819. He was told to bear in mind that with the Indian as with the civilized man, "honesty is the best policy." If the Indian could be convinced that the trader was always just, his own disposition to cheat would gradually disappear, particularly when he discovered that the trader, being just himself, would not suffer others to defraud him. Nevertheless, the Indian trade was not regarded as an appropriate field for the application of idealistic principles. When free from the interference of rival traders the Indians could usually be relied upon to fulfill their contracts but the presence of competition was always a demoralizing factor. Traders would sometimes induce the Indians to steal the credits of their rivals; that is, they persuaded them to give up the furs which they had already pledged to another trader in return for goods advanced to them. There was bound to be more or less uncertainty in the collection of credits so that the traders were obliged to regulate their prices in such a way as to compensate themselves for possible losses. On the whole, however, when the lack of facilities for communication in the Indian country and the roving character of the natives are taken into account, the degree of influence which the trader exercised over his Indian customers was really most remarkable.

One of the young American employees of the fur company, Gurdon Saltonstall Hubbard by name, has left a narrative of his experiences with the Illinois brigade which presents a vivid picture of the fur trade as it existed in northern Illinois in the year in which the state was admitted to the Union.[39] On the morning of May 13, 1818, the brigade which Hubbard accompanied to Mackinac departed from Lachine, a little village just above Montreal, the oars keeping time to the rhythm of the Canadian boat song. Nearly two months later, July 4, the brigade reached Mackinac, where it was warmly welcomed by Crooks and Stuart, the agents of the company, together with a host of *voyageurs* and clerks. At Mackinac Hubbard found all the traders and their *engagés* from the interior gathered on the island, where they added some 3,000 to the population. Indians numbering some 2,000 or 3,000 more lined the entire beach with their wigwams. These Indians, he says, made day and night hideous with the yells they emitted while performing their war dances and other sports. There were also frequent fights between the champions or "bullies" of the various brigades.

After the traders had disposed of the returns of the past season and secured new outfits, preparations were made for the departure of the brigades for the various posts of the interior. "A vast multitude assembled at the harbor to witness their departure, and when all was ready the boats glided from the shore, the crews singing some favorite boat song, while the multitude shouted their farewells and wishes for a successful trip and a safe return; and thus outfit after outfit started on its way for Lake Superior, Upper and Lower Mississippi, and other posts."[40]

---

[39] The narrative was published first in *Incidents and Events in the Life of Gurdon Saltonstall Hubbard* (1888). It is also to be found in *The Autobiography of Gurdon Saltonstall Hubbard* (1911). For the material on which the following paragraphs are based see *Incidents and Events*, 11-67, or the *Autobiography*, 7-64.

[40] Hubbard, *Incidents and Events*, 25.

The Illinois and Wabash outfits were among the last to leave, being followed by the smaller expeditions bound for the shores of Lakes Huron and Michigan. At about noon on September 10, the Illinois brigade left the harbor at Mackinac in 12 boats, with Antoine Deschamps, who was in charge of the outfit, leading the boat song. Many of the traders were accompanied by their Indian wives, and the brigade must indeed have presented a motley appearance. The boats proceeded down the east shore of Lake Michigan, making about 40 miles a day, under oars, but when the wind was favorable, square sails were hoisted by means of which it was possible to make 70 or 75 miles a day.

On the evening of September 30, just 20 days after the departure from Mackinac, the expedition arrived at the mouth of the Calumet River, where it was met by a party of Indians returning from a visit to Chicago. They were drunk and started a fight among themselves in which several of their number were killed, necessitating the removal of the trading party to the opposite side of the river for safety. The members of the brigade spent a portion of the night in preparation for their arrival at Chicago. "We started at dawn," says Hubbard. "The morning was calm and bright, and we, in our holiday attire, with flags flying, completed the last twelve miles of our lake voyage." [41] The brigade spent a few days at Chicago repairing the boats, and then passed up the south branch of the Chicago River into Mud Lake, a sort of marsh, which drained partly into the Chicago River and partly into the Desplaines. The boats were half dragged, half floated, through this marsh to the waters of the Desplaines, while the goods were carried on the backs of the *engagés*. After three days of such labor, the portage was crossed, the boats were reloaded, and the voyage to the Illinois was begun. The water being very low, the progress of the brigade was slow and difficult, and it was three weeks before the expedition reached the mouth of the Fox River. Two days more brought the party to the foot of Starved Rock.

From this point on, the voyage was less difficult, and the bri-

[41] Hubbard, *Incidents and Events*, 31.

gade floated down the river, stopping occasionally to barter powder and tobacco for Indian corn. The first trading house was located at the mouth of the Bureau River near the present site of the town of Hennepin. It was placed in charge of a trader named Bibeau, who, though illiterate, had a wide experience in the Indian trade. Hubbard was assigned to this post to keep the accounts and perform the general duties of clerk. The next post was located three miles below Peoria Lake and was placed in charge of another old trader, who was well acquainted with the Indians in the vicinity. The brigade proceeded on down the river, establishing posts every 60 miles or so, the last one being some 50 miles above the mouth of the stream.

Deschamps proceeded with one boat to St. Louis to purchase certain articles needed in the trade and also to obtain flour and tobacco at Cahokia. Hubbard accompanied him on the voyage. About November 20, they started back, distributing various portions of the cargo at the posts along the river. Hubbard reached his station at the mouth of the Bureau River about the middle of December and was given final instructions concerning the keeping of his accounts. "The accounts," he says, "had heretofore been kept in hieroglyphics by Beebeau [Bibeau], my ignorant master, who proved to be sickly, cross, and petulant. He spent the greater part of his time in bed, attended by a fat, dirty Indian woman, a doctress, who made and administered various decoctions to him." [42] The cabin in which Hubbard spent the winter was of logs and very much resembled the cabin of the pioneer settler. The duties of the young clerk were to keep the books and to be present when sales were made for furs or when credit was to be given. Leisure time was spent in hunting, trapping, making oars and paddles, chatting and joking with the men at the post, and making ready for departure in the spring. During the winter, Hubbard made two trading excursions into the interior, one to the mouth of the Rock River, and the other to the Wabash, the latter being particularly successful.

Early in March, orders were received from Deschamps to have

[42] Hubbard, *Incidents and Events*, 49.

everything in readiness to start for Mackinac on the twentieth. In the forenoon of the day set, writes Hubbard, "we heard in the distance the sound of the familiar boat-song and recognized the rich tones of Mr. Deschamps' voice, and we knew the 'Brigade' was coming. We all ran to the landing and soon saw Mr. Deschamps' boat rounding the point about a mile below; his ensign floating in the breeze. We shouted with joy at their arrival and gave them a hearty welcome." [43] On the following morning, the brigade, consisting of 13 boats, started on the long return voyage to Mackinac. The same route was followed as on the outward trip, and the destination was reached without mishap about the middle of May, the brigade being among the first to arrive from the Indian country. Thus was finished one cycle in the life of an Illinois fur trader.

[43] Hubbard, *Incidents and Events.*

Chapter 2

The Public Lands

No more important and interesting story can be found in the annals of the human race than that of the progress of settlement across the North American continent—the transformation of successive areas of wilderness into highly organized agricultural and industrial communities. The significance of this phase of American history has been widely recognized in recent years, and the region undergoing this transformation at any particular period has come to be known as the frontier. The process is a long one, however, with many different stages that appear simultaneously in different areas so that the frontier at any given time includes a wide belt of territory whose boundaries shade away on one side into the wilderness, on the other into civilization. Using the term as here defined, the whole of Illinois can be said to have been frontier country in 1818. The northern part of the state had passed through the stage of the explorer's frontier and represented the frontier of both the Indian trader and the military post, while the southern part had emerged into the frontier of the pioneer settler.

The expression "frontier" may also be used in another but closely allied sense, as connoting the extreme limit of progress of some phase of the movement. Thus the frontier of exploration is the line between the territory which has been visited by explorers and that which has not, and similarly there are frontiers of Indian land cessions, government surveys, land sales, and actual settlement. The fact that the lines of several of these frontiers run through the Illinois of 1818 adds interest to a study of the region at that time. Progress along some of these lines was always irregular, however; and the frontier in such cases can be indicated only approximately, by drawing a line to connect up the extreme points. Considering the nation as a whole, these frontiers were, in the main, north and south lines; but various factors, principally geographical, resulted in their running in Illinois from east to west across the state.

The southern limit of the Indian country in Illinois in 1818 was a line drawn east from the mouth of the Illinois River to a point about ten miles west of the Wabash and then northward bearing slightly to the east to the Vermilion River. The location of this line was determined by a series of treaties between the United States and the various Indian tribes. By a treaty negotiated at Vincennes in 1803, the Kaskaskia surrendered to the United States all their claims to land in Illinois covering an immense tract stretching from the Mississippi on the west to the divide between the Kaskaskia and the Wabash on the east, and from the Ohio on the south, northward to a line running in a northeasterly direction from the mouth of the Illinois River. Previous to this the United States had secured, at the Treaty of Greenville of 1795, which was participated in by most of the tribes of the northwest, a recognition of grants made by the Indians during the French and British periods of a tract of land about Vincennes, part of which lay west of the Wabash. In 1803 the limits of this grant were defined by another treaty at Fort Wayne. Two years later the small tribe of the Piankashaw ceded to the United States their claims to the land between the Kaskaskia cession on the west and the Wabash River and Vincennes tract on the east, extending north a short distance beyond the thirty-ninth parallel.[1]

In 1809 a narrow strip of land along the boundary between Illinois and Indiana, stretching from the Vincennes tract to the Vermilion River, was acquired by treaties negotiated by Governor William Henry Harrison with various tribes of Illinois and Indiana Indians, including the Potawatomi and Kickapoo. The purpose of this cession was to open the way for the advance of settlement up the Wabash River. When the Illinois tribes had

---

[1] The cessions are listed chronologically, with the essential data, and excellent colored maps, in Royce, *Indian Land Cessions*. The treaties can be found in full in Kapper, *Indian Affairs, Laws, and Treaties*, vol. 2. The two volumes of *American State Papers, Indian Affairs* contain many documents relating to the negotiations.

been driven out from northern and central Illinois, the territory
had been occupied by a stream of northern tribes, the Sauk and
Fox, Kickapoo, Winnebago, and Potawatomi. Mingled with the
latter were also fragments of the Ottawa and Chippewa. Newcomers in the region, these various tribes had illy defined holdings, and a large number of overlapping cessions had to be secured before their claims were extinguished. In 1804 a treaty
was made with certain members of the allied Sauk and Fox tribes
by which the United States claimed to have acquired from these
tribes the vast stretch of country lying between the Mississippi
on the west and the Illinois and Fox rivers on the east and extending northward into what is now Wisconsin. The validity of
this cession was denied by the Indians, however, on the ground
that it was made by men who had no authority to represent the
tribes; and in 1815 and 1816, when peace was made with the
Sauk and Fox respectively, after the War of 1812, the United
States secured confirmations of this grant. The Indians retained
the privilege of living and hunting on the land so long as it remained the property of the government. The region between the
Mississippi and Illinois rivers having been selected for military
bounty land, the United States was desirous of perfecting its
title in order that the surveys might proceed. For this purpose
it was necessary to secure a relinquishment from the associated
Potawatomi, Ottawa, and Chippewa. By a treaty negotiated at
St. Louis in August, 1816,[2] these tribes gave up their claims to
the Sauk and Fox cession south of a line drawn due west from
the southern extremity of Lake Michigan to the Mississippi
River, while the United States in turn relinquished to them its
claim to the part of the cession lying north of that line. By the
same treaty, these Indians also ceded a strip about 10 miles wide
from the Fox River to the Kankakee along the north side of the
Illinois and about 20 miles wide from the mouth of the Kankakee
on both sides of the Desplaines River and the portage to Lake

---

[2] Such tracts, not to "exceed the quantity that would be contained in five
leagues square" as the President might reserve, were excepted. It was expected that these would be so located as to include the Galena lead mines.
See *Wisconsin Historical Collections*, 13:286.

Michigan. The purpose of this cession was to make possible the construction of a canal from Lake Michigan to the Illinois River, and the Indians were allowed to continue to hunt and fish on the ceded land.

The title of the United States to the military tract having been cleared up, it was expected that settlement would follow rapidly, and the desirability of securing a cession of the area between that tract and the Kaskaskia cession of 1803 was realized. In 1817 commissioners were appointed and instructions issued, and on September 25, 1818, representatives of all the remnants of the Illinois tribes met Governor Edwards and Auguste Chouteau, United States commissioners, at Edwardsville and agreed to a treaty. The remnant of the Peoria had not been a party to the treaty of 1803, and so, in order to quiet any claim which they might have, the cession here made included the whole of the earlier cession as well as all the land beyond that cession and south of the Illinois and Kankakee rivers. A week later the Potawatomi ceded their claim to a tract northwest of the Wabash, lying mostly in Indiana but including a small triangle in Illinois between the Vermilion and the state line. Neither of these treaties, however, gave the United States undisputed claim to any additional territory in Illinois, for the Kickapoo, a numerous and powerful tribe, for many years claimed by right of conquest and possession the whole of central Illinois including not only all the new area covered by the treaty of 1818 but also all the original Kaskaskia cession and the Piankashaw cession north of an east and west line through the mouth of the Illinois River. Not until July 30, 1819, were the Kickapoo induced to give up their claim and to agree to move west of the Mississippi. By this cession of 1819 the land claimed by Indians in Illinois was reduced to the region north of the canal cession and of an east and west line through the southern extremity of Lake Michigan, and a smaller tract along the Indiana line extending south from the canal cession and the Kankakee River to the Vermilion. Not until the years 1829, 1832, and 1833 were these claims given up by the Potawatomi, Ottawa, Chippewa, and Winnebago.

When Illinois was admitted to the Union in November, 1818,

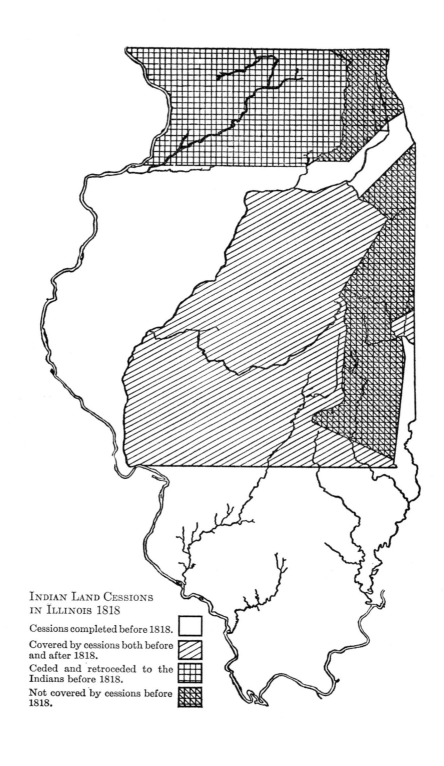

INDIAN LAND CESSIONS
IN ILLINOIS 1818

Cessions completed before 1818.

Covered by cessions both before
and after 1818.

Ceded and retroceded to the
Indians before 1818.

Not covered by cessions before
1818.

therefore, the land in the state upon which all Indian claims had been extinguished, or, more accurately, of which no further cessions were made, lay in two detached areas. The first included all south of the east and west line through the mouth of the Illinois and also a narrow strip along the eastern border of the state extending as far north as the Vermilion River; the second consisted of the military tract and the strip connecting it with Lake Michigan.

After the Indian title to the land was extinguished, it was government land, and the first step in the transition to private property was its survey into the familiar rectangular townships and sections. By an act of 1804 the surveyor general in charge of this work in the northwest was authorized to arrange for the survey of all the land north of the Ohio and east of the Mississippi to which the Indian titles had been extinguished.[3] The system of rectangular surveys based on a principal meridian and a base line had already been worked out for the land in Ohio; but the tracts to be surveyed in Indiana Territory were widely separated from this land, and it was necessary to select a new point of departure. For the second principal meridian, therefore, the surveyor general established a line running due north and south through the northeast corner of the Vincennes tract, as confirmed by the Indians in 1803; and this meridian governed most of the surveys in Indiana and those in Illinois east of a line running north from the mouth of the Wabash. In the rest of Illinois south of the Illinois River the surveys were governed by the third principal meridian, which was run north from the mouth of the Ohio. For both of these systems an east and west line, selected because it ran through the westernmost corner of Clark's grant on the Ohio, served as the base line. Ranges were numbered east and west from the principal meridians and townships north and south from the base line. Each township was divided into 36 sections one mile square.[4]

[3] *Statutes at Large,* 2:277.
[4] Treat, *National Land System,* ch. 8; *Niles' Weekly Register,* 12:97-99; 16:362.

While the work of locating the main township lines in Illinois was begun in 1804, the same year in which the surveys were authorized, the principal work of the surveyors for a number of years was the marking out of the numerous private claims. Not until about 1810 was the detail work in the townships taken up in earnest, and then it progressed so slowly that much was uncompleted when the sales began in 1814. With the close of the War of 1812, however, the surveys proceeded more rapidly; in 1816 a surveyor general for Illinois and Missouri territories was appointed; and at the close of the territorial period most of the land to which the Indian titles had been extinguished was surveyed.[5] The frontier of government survey then, in 1818, started on the Mississippi near Alton and ran east to the third principal meridian, then south 30 miles to the base line, east again to the southwest corner of the Vincennes tract, and then northeastwardly along the boundaries of that tract and the Harrison purchase to the Indiana line near the boundary between the present Vermilion and Edgar counties. West of the meridian, the line was only a few miles below the frontier of Indian cessions, but between the meridian and the Vincennes tract the two frontiers were 36 miles apart.[6]

In this statement of the extent of surveys, the triangle between the Mississippi and the Illinois rivers has been left out of consideration. When this land was purchased from the Indians in 1804, it was apparently intended that it should be disposed of in the ordinary way, for an act of Congress of March 3, 1805, attached it to the Kaskaskia land district. At the beginning of the War of 1812, however, Congress, by the act of May 6, 1812,

[5] Land records, auditor's office, Springfield; *Statutes at Large*, 3:325.

[6] Additional surveys were frequently urged by the land officers, and during the late summer of 1818, 36 townships above township 5 north, and west of the third principal meridian were surveyed. This land was not offered for sale, however, until 1819, and the line described above is for convenience referred to as the "frontier line of survey in 1818." Orders were issued September 26, 1818, for the survey of the tract north of the base line and east of the meridian, and the work was completed the following year. Land records, auditor's office, Springfield; *Intelligencer*, October 21, 1818.

directed that 2,000,000 acres of this land with like quantities in
Michigan and Louisiana territories be reserved for the purpose
of satisfying the bounties of land promised to soldiers—160 acres
to each—by acts of December 24, 1811, and January 11, 1812.
The surveys of the "military tracts," as they were called, were
delayed by Indian hostilities, but they were under way in the
summer of 1815. As the work progressed, the officials reached
the conclusion that the Michigan lands were not suitable for the
purpose, and so Congress was induced to pass the act of April 29,
1816, substituting for the Michigan lands an additional 1,500,000
acres in Illinois and an additional 500,000 acres in Missouri.[7]
This increased the amount of bounty land in Illinois to 3,500,000
acres, and carried the northern boundary of the tract to a line
from the Illinois River at the mouth of the Vermilion due west
to the Mississippi. As this region was wholly separated from the
other surveys in Illinois, it was necessary to run a fourth principal meridian, fixed by the mouth of the Illinois River, with a
base line run due west from the point where the meridian crossed
the Illinois in the vicinity of the site of Beardstown.

The survey of the Illinois bounty lands progressed rapidly
during the winter of 1816-17; and on September 25, 1817, the
commissioner of the General Land Office announced that the surveys had all been received and that the distribution of the land
by lot as provided by law would begin on the first Monday in
October. Warrants had been issued to the soldiers entitled to
bounties, or to their heirs, and between October 6, 1817, and
January 28, 1819, some 18,000 of these warrants were exchanged
at the General Land Office for patents to quarter sections of land
in Illinois, covering the greater part of the military tract. While
the warrants were non-transferable there was no requirement
that the patentee settle upon the land and nothing to prevent
him from disposing of the patent as soon as received. As a matter of fact the title to most of this land passed at once into the
hands of eastern speculators; and no settlement appears to have

[7] *American State Papers, Public Lands,* 3:162-164; *Statutes at Large,*
2:344, 669, 672, 728; 3:332; *Niles' Weekly Register,* 9:15.

resulted from this wholesale distribution of land until after the admission of the state to the Union.[8]

The regular procedure in the disposition of the public lands at this time was sale by the government without distinction between settlers and speculators. To facilitate its sale, the region in which the land was located was divided into districts, in each of which was established a local land office. In 1818 there were three such land offices with their corresponding districts wholly in Illinois, while the strip along the eastern border north of the base line was included in the Vincennes district, the greater part of which lay in Indiana. Land offices had been established at Vincennes and Kaskaskia as early as 1804; but their only work for many years was the settlement of claims, of which there were a large number, based on the rights of the old French inhabitants and on various donations by Congress to the early settlers. It was obviously desirable that the validity of each of these claims and the location and limits of those which stood the test should be determined before the remainder of the land was offered for sale. The process of settlement dragged on from year to year, however, and it was not until 1814, only four years before the state entered the Union, that land could be purchased from the government in Illinois. In the meantime another land office had been authorized at Shawneetown in 1812, the boundary between the two Illinois districts being the third principal meridian. With the beginning of sales and the progress of the surveys the need for another land office in the west, north of Kaskaskia, was apparent, and in 1816 one was established at Edwardsville for the sale of the land north of the base line and west of the meridian. This left in the Kaskaskia district the triangle between the Mississippi, the meridian, and the base line. While the acts establishing the Shawneetown and Edwardsville districts had not definitely fixed their northern boundaries, these coincided in practice with the frontier of survey; that is, the base line for the

[8] "Lands in Illinois to soldiers of the late war," *House Documents*, 26 Congress, 1 Session, no. 262; Illinois State Historical Society, *Transactions*, 1910, p. 151; Chicago Historical Society Manuscripts, 52:29, 177; 53:59; *Intelligencer*, November 6, 1817.

Shawneetown district, and a line five townships or 30 miles farther north for the Edwardsville district. The Kaskaskia district, then, contained approximately 2,188,800 acres or 95 townships, the Shawneetown, 3,018,240 acres or 131 townships, and the Edwardsville, 1,059,840 acres or 46 townships.[9]

The system of public land sales in operation in Illinois in 1818 was that inaugurated by the act of Congress of May 10, 1800, with some modifications by later acts. The land was first offered at public sales on dates fixed by proclamations of the President; all land for which two dollars or more an acre was offered was sold to the highest bidder. After land had once been offered at public sale without finding a purchaser, it could then be bought at private sale for the minimum price. Under the act of 1800 all the land was to be sold in half sections or 320-acre tracts; but in 1804, the sale of quarter sections was authorized and an act of 1817 permitted six specified sections in each township to be sold in half-quarter sections or 80-acre tracts. Of the purchase money, one-twentieth had to be paid down to hold the land, and enough more to amount to 25 per cent was due in 40 days. The remainder was due in three equal installments at the end of two, three, and four years from the date of entry. No interest was charged if payments were promptly made; but if not, they drew 6 per cent from the date of sale. A discount of 8 per cent was allowed, however, on all advance payments, which reduced the minimum cash price to $1.64 an acre. If the installments were not all paid at the end of five years from the date of entry, the land reverted to the United States and was offered at public auction. Should it then bring more than the amount still due with interest, the balance went to the original purchaser. As a rule, in Illinois, only a small proportion of the land offered was disposed of at the public sales, and the bulk of that brought only the minimum price. It was possible, therefore, for anyone with $80 to enter a quarter section of land, "looking to the land to reward your pains with the means of discharging the other three-fourths as they

[9] *Statutes at Large*, 2:277, 684; 3:323; *American State Papers, Public Lands*, 3:312.

become due," as Morris Birkbeck expressed it.[10] From the records of land sales in Illinois it appears that practically all the purchasers took advantage of the credit system and most of them bought only the minimum amount.

The protracted delay in the opening of the land sales resulted in a situation which is well described in a memorial addressed to Congress by the first territorial legislature in 1812. This declared that,

from the establishment of a land office in the Territory several years ago, a general opinion prevailed that the public land would shortly thereafter be offered for sale, whereby the great majority of the citizens now residing in the Territory were induced to move into it and settle themselves, hoping that they would have an opportunity of purchasing the land they occupied before they had made such ameliorations thereon as would tempt the competition of avaricious speculators, in which reasonable expectation they have been hitherto disappointed in consequence of the unexampled postponement of the sales owing to causes which are well understood and which it is unnecessary to detail . . . those good people have made valuable and permanent improvements on the land they thus occupied (at the same time that they have risked their lives in defending it against the barbarous savages who invaded it), but are now in danger of losing the whole value of their labor by competition at the sales or by the holders of unlocated claims being permitted to locate on their improvements.[11]

In the eyes of the law these settlers on the public domain were intruders with no legal rights to their "improvements," and Congress had in the past usually refused to recognize the claim of such settlers, on the ground that to do so would encourage illegal settlement. The sales in Illinois had been so long postponed, however, that the justice of some measure of relief was obvious, and on February 5, 1813, Congress passed an act of great importance to the people of that territory. By the terms of this measure, settlers who had "actually inhabited and cultivated a tract of land, lying in either of the districts established for the sale of public lands, in the Illinois territory" before the passage

[10] Birkbeck, *Letters from Illinois*, 97; *Statutes at Large*, 2:73, 277; 3:346; *Niles' Weekly Register*, 12:99.

[11] James, *Territorial Records*, 109.

of the act, were granted a pre-emption right to not more than
the quarter section on which they had located; that is, they were
allowed to purchase the tract at the minimum price at any time
up to within two weeks of the opening of the public sales in the
district. The terms were the same as for other purchases at private sales, but the settler was relieved from any danger of having
to bid against others for the land which he had occupied. About
a year later, before any sales had been made in the Kaskaskia

OLD FRENCH HOUSE AT PRAIRIE DU ROCHER

district, Congress passed another act, dated April 16, 1814, which
enlarged and extended pre-emption rights in that section of the
territory. The greater part of the Kaskaskia district, including
what was later set off as the Edwardsville district, was designated as a reserved tract in which the numerous confirmed unlocated claims must be located. Settlers within this tract who
had established themselves before February 5, 1813, the date
of the original pre-emption law, were allowed pre-emption rights
to not less than a quarter or more than a whole section, application to be made on or before October 1, 1814. Settlers holding

confirmed unlocated claims were allowed to use them as payments for the land to which they had pre-emption rights, while other holders of such claims might locate them within the tract between October 1, 1814, and May 1, 1815. It was expected, apparently, that the situation would thus be cleared up by May 1, 1815, so that the public sales could take place; but another act of February 27, 1815, extended the time for pre-emptions to May 1, 1816; and an act of April 27, 1816, made a further extension in certain cases to October 1, 1816. By this last act, also, holders of unlocated confirmed claims were allowed to locate them in the tract up to the same date.[12]

These various acts relating to pre-emption rights created distinctions in different parts of Illinois, the reasons for which are not apparent. Thus in the Shawneetown district those who had settled on the land before February 5, 1813, were given the preference in the purchase of a quarter section only, while within the reserved tract, the preference was extended to a whole section. Especial provision was made in the Kaskaskia district, moreover, for settlers on fractional sections; but the law was so interpreted as to allow such settlers no pre-emption rights in the Shawneetown district, with the result that a few had to pay advanced prices for their lands at the public sales. The worst discrimination, however, was with reference to that part of Illinois within the Vincennes district. The act of 1813 was interpreted as not applying to this tract at all and the settlers there were left to compete with speculators in the public sales for the lands on which they had made improvements. The legislature of Illinois Territory, at its session of 1816-17, after the sales had taken place, forwarded to Congress a long memorial devoted to proving that the pre-emption act had not been correctly interpreted in this particular, and asking for some measure of redress for those settlers who had lost their land or had been forced to pay advanced prices for it. This memorial, together with a petition from the settlers themselves drawn up in 1818, was referred and

[12] *Statutes at Large*, 2:797; 3:125, 218; Treat, *National Land System*, 382-385.

re-referred to the House Committee on Public Lands until finally
Congress passed the relief act of May 11, 1820. By this act all
settlers who would have been entitled to pre-emption rights, had
the act been interpreted to apply to the part of the Vincennes
district in Illinois, were given credit certificates for the sums
above the minimum price which they had paid; or, if they had
not purchased, they were allowed to exercise a pre-emption right
on any land in Illinois which might be surveyed before September 1, 1820.[13]

The first government sales of land in Illinois took place, as
has already been stated, in 1814. During the year ending September 30, 1814, the only sales were 8,837 acres in the Shawneetown district; these were all made to settlers in accordance with
the pre-emption act of 1813, and consequently at the minimum
price. The first public sale in the territory took place in the
same district in October of 1814 and included the sale of town
lots in Shawneetown, which had been laid out for that purpose
by the government surveyors under acts of April 30, 1810, and
March 28, 1814. Only a part of the land in the district could be
offered at this sale because the surveys were incomplete, and
only a little over 50,000 acres were sold in the district in the
year ending September 30, 1815. Sales under the pre-emption
acts began in the Kaskaskia district in the fall of 1814, and
about 30,000 acres were disposed of during the fiscal year. During the year ending September 30, 1816, the sales were still
smaller, amounting to less than 34,000 acres in the Shawneetown
and less than 13,000 in the Kaskaskia districts. The bulk of the
Shawneetown sales must have been of land which had been offered in 1814 and which was now available at private sales at
the minimum price, while at Kaskaskia land could still be purchased only by pre-emptioners.

The largest offerings of land at public sales in Illinois, prior

[13] Legislative memorial in *Intelligencer*, January 22, 1817; petition of
James McFarland and others, November, 1818, and petition of inhabitants
of Crawford County, December 25, 1818, in House Files; *Statutes at Large*,
3:573.

to the admission of the state to the Union, took place in October
and November, 1816, when sales were held at all three of the
offices in the territory.[14] The intention was that the government
land in the respective districts, not hitherto offered and not
reserved for schools or other special purposes, should be offered
at these sales; but the officers at Kaskaskia reported that certain
townships could not be sold because descriptions had not been
received from the surveyor general, while certain sections in 15
townships in the Shawneetown district were not actually offered
until October, 1818. Nineteen townships and fractional townships, comprising about two-thirds of the part of the Vincennes
district in Illinois, were offered at public sale in September of
the same year. So much of the best land in the Kaskaskia and
Edwardsville districts had been covered by private claims and
pre-emption rights that only small amounts were disposed of at
these sales. In Edwardsville the bidding could not have been
very brisk for none of the 60 or 70 tracts sold brought more than
the minimum price, while at Kaskaskia only five or six tracts
which were located near the mouth of the Ohio, and were bought
up by town-site speculators, sold for an advanced price, the

[14] The following table gives the acreage of land sales in the three Illinois
districts for the periods indicated, with amounts of reversions deducted from
the sales. It is compiled from statistics in *Reports of the Secretary of the
Treasury*, 1:550; 2:68, 97, 135, 137, 157; *American State Papers, Public
Lands*, 3:312; *Executive Documents*, 16 Congress, 2 Session, no. 8:19.

Years ending Sept. 30	Shawnee-town	Kaskaskia	Edwards-ville	Total
1814	8,837	....	....	8,837
1815	51,735	31,005	....	82,740
1816	33,975	12,765	....	46,740
1817	67,084	78,508	104,073	249,665
1818	239,011	160,446	193,259	593,316
1819	161,654	124,303	97,398	383,355
Total	562,296	407,027	394,730	1,364,053
Total to Sept. 30, 1818	400,642	282,724	297,332	980,698
Est. total to Dec. 31, 1818	440,000	320,000	320,000	1,080,000
Area of districts	3,018,240	2,188,800	1,059,840	6,266,880
Proportion sold Dec. 31, 1818	14½%	14½%	30%	17%

See also *Statutes at Large*, 2:591; 3:113; President's proclamation, April
5, in land records, auditor's office, Springfield.

highest being five dollars an acre.[15] The significance of the public sales, however, lay not in the amounts of land disposed of
but in the fact that after they were over, extensive tracts of land
in all parts of Illinois below the frontier line of survey were
available for purchase at private sale at the minimum price.

With the return of peace on the frontier after the War of 1812,
immigrants poured into the territory, and the sales increased by
leaps and bounds. During the year ending September 30, 1817,
almost 250,000 acres of land were sold in the three districts
wholly within Illinois, Edwardsville leading with over 100,000
acres. This was nearly twice as much as had been sold in all the
previous years, but the amount was again doubled in the next
fiscal year, the total being nearly 600,000 acres. This time the
Shawneetown district led with about 240,000 acres. The fiscal
year ending September 30, 1819, shows a falling off in the total
sales to less than 400,000 acres, due in part to the fact that the
choicest tracts had already been selected, and in part to the financial panic of 1819. The total sales of public land in these
districts to September 30, 1818, amounted to 980,698 acres.
Approximately the sales to the end of 1818 amounted to about
1,080,000 acres, of which 440,000 were in the Shawneetown,
320,000 in the Kaskaskia, and 320,000 in the Edwardsville districts. Thirty per cent of the Edwardsville district had been sold
but only 14½ per cent of the Shawneetown and Kaskaskia districts. Taking the three districts together, only about 17 per cent
of the available land had passed out of the possession of the
government.[16]

The actual location of the land in Illinois which had become
private property by the end of 1818 is indicated on the accompanying map.[17] From this it appears that the largest solid blocks

---

[15] President's proclamations in *Intelligencer*, June 12, 1816; August 5,
1818; Letter Book A, 109-111, 115, and land record, Palestine district,
auditor's office, Springfield; *Intelligencer*, November 20, 1816; *House Documents*, 15 Congress, 2 Session, no. 46:6.

[16] See table in note 14.

[17] Compiled from records in the auditor's office at Springfield, and in the
General Land Office in Washington.

Tracts in the Edwardsville district have been taken from the Tract Book, those in the Kaskaskia district from the Application Books, and those in the Shawneetown district from the Tract Book and Entry Books. These records are in the auditor's office, Springfield, Illinois. Entries in the Illinois part of the Vincennes district have been plotted from the Entry Books in the General Land Office, Washington, D. C. Lands included in the old surveys have been plotted from copies of the plats in the surveyor's office, St. Louis, made for and certified by F. R. Conway, surveyor of the public lands in the states of Illinois and Missouri, February 7, 1848 (bound volume in the auditor's office, Springfield). The boundaries of the Wabash saline reservation have been taken from *American State Papers, Public Lands.* 3:270.

Land office districts and reservations. ─────────

Present county boundaries. ─ ─ ─ ─ ─ ─ ─ ─ ─ ─ ─ ─

Townships.

Tracts entered prior to January 1, 1819.

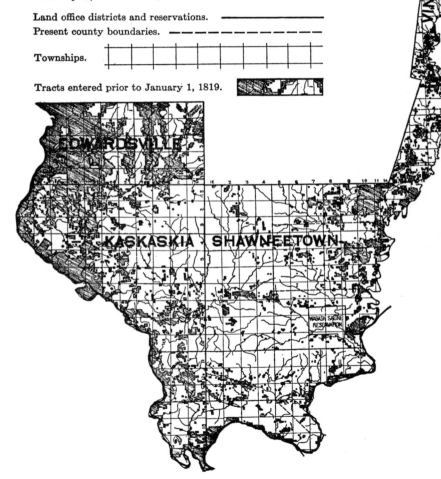

of private holdings were in the present Madison and St. Clair counties. In the American bottom, also, stretching along the Mississippi above Kaskaskia, practically all the land had been taken up. On the opposite side of the territory a tract equivalent to about two and a half townships had been entered in Edwards County, where the English settlement was located. There was a smaller block in the neighborhood of Shawneetown, and along the lower Ohio an extensive tract had been purchased by firms of speculators who hoped that great commercial cities would spring up on their holdings. The map brings out in a striking way the importance of streams in giving value to land in their vicinity. Along the Kaskaskia River and its tributaries, as far as the surveys extended, along the Big Muddy in Jackson County, and the Cache in Union County, extended ribbons of purchased land. On the eastern side of the state, the land along the Saline River was all in the United States reservation, but the influence of the Little Wabash is clearly seen. Another factor in giving value to land was its location along the main roads which crossed the state. Thus the lines of the roads from Shawneetown to Carlyle, Shawneetown to Kaskaskia, and Golconda to Kaskaskia are clearly indicated by the holdings, although these are more broken than those along the streams. Between these roads in the interior of the state were tracts containing ten or a dozen townships, in each of which scarcely a single section of land had been sold.

Significant as is the distribution of purchased land, it is not a definitive index of the progress of settlement for two reasons; in the first place much land was purchased for speculation rather than for settlement, and in the second place many settlers lived on land which still belonged to the government.

Before land could be purchased from the government, the speculators had been obliged to confine their operations to the field of private claims; but many of the original French and American holders of these claims were readily induced to dispose of them to the more enterprising men with capital, and as a result thousands of acres passed into the possession of such men as John Edgar and William Morrison. When the government land sales began, speculators were always on hand to pick

up the choice tracts, which, because of their supposedly favorable
location, were expected to rise in value rapidly. As has already
been noted, much of the land along the lower Ohio was purchased in large tracts by firms of eastern men. The resident
speculators wisely devoted themselves largely to land in the
Edwardsville district, which was settling up rapidly, while on
the eastern side of the territory, Morris Birkbeck entered 26,400
acres of land in Edwards County during 1817 and 1818. Birkbeck's purchases were made in part to secure the land for the
English immigrants whom he was inducing to come to Illinois,
but it is undoubtedly true that he and the other leaders in the
English settlement hoped for great personal returns from the rise
in value of the land. The effects on settlement of the extensive
purchase of land by speculators were very great. Desirable tracts
in the neighborhood of settlements were held at prices too high
for most of the immigrants to pay, and consequently they were
forced to go farther afield or take up less desirable land. The
result of this and of the uniform price of government land, regardless of quality, was a widespread scattering of the settlers
over a vast extent of territory instead of an orderly progression
along a definite frontier.[18]

The occupation of the public lands by settlers long before they
could purchase and the measures which were taken for their relief have already been noted. The pre-emption acts did not entirely solve the problem, however, for no provision was made for
those who settled after February 5, 1813; and many who had
established themselves before that were too poor to exercise their
pre-emption rights. Nor were these people inclined to surrender
the land when it was purchased by others. The situation is well
described in a letter written by the register of the Shawneetown
land office to his superior in Washington in 1815. "Several persons," he wrote,

have called on me as the public Agent, to give them peaceable possession of their Lands—persons who are residing on them now, & were

[18] Thwaites, *Early Western Travels*, 11:277; Birkbeck, *Letters from Illinois*, 37, 81, 85, 120; Dana, *Geographical Sketches*, 143; *Intelligencer*, November 20, 1816.

previously to the sale, refuse to give them up—a[n]d the rightfull owner is kept out of possession, who thinks his case a very hard one to be compelled after paying the Government for a tract of land to be reduced to the necessity of commencing a suit at Law to obtain his just right—There are nearly a thousand improved places in this district that are not located, and if the Government does not adopt some energetic measures to nip this conduct in the bud it will retard the Sale of all those places which are or may be improved hereafter I hope this subject will present itself forcibly to your mind as it will materially affect the public sales.[19]

The situation was so serious that the matter was taken up with the Secretary of State, and the President issued a proclamation directing that after a certain day in March, 1816, all squatters on the public lands should be removed. Against the execution of this proclamation, Benjamin Stephenson, the delegate from Illinois Territory, protested vigorously. "Should this order be inforced," he wrote to the Secretary of State, "it [wi]ll . . . be distressing to many Citizens and not beneficial to the interest of the government, My object in addressing you, is, to solicit that a time may be set for the removal of the above settlers one or two months after they shall have an oppertunity [*sic*] of purchasing the land on which they have sett[l]ed and made improvements." The marshal of Illinois Territory actually made preparations to remove the intruders; but the Secretary of the Treasury wrote him on May 11, 1816, recommending "a prudent and conciliatory course"; and nothing seems to have been accomplished. Two months earlier Congress had passed an act authorizing the land officers to issue to settlers on unsold public lands permits to remain as tenants at will on condition of their agreeing to "give quiet possession" whenever required to do so; but very few applications for such permits appear to have been received.[20]

The situation in Illinois at this time is typical of the history

[19] Extract from Sloo to Meigs, March 11, 1815, in United States State Department, Bureau of Indexes and Archives, Miscellaneous Letters.

[20] Stephenson to Monroe, January 19, 1816, Dallas to Fouke, May 11, 1816, Fouke to Pope, January 5, 1817, in United States State Department, Bureau of Indexes and Archives, Miscellaneous Letters; *Statutes at Large*, 3:260; *Intelligencer*, June 5, 1816; correspondence in auditor's office, Springfield.

of the American frontier. Although large quantities of government land were on the market, the attraction of the wilderness and the desire to secure the choicest locations regularly led to settlement in advance of the purchase of the land; and this was true regardless of whether or not the land sales were delayed. Often, indeed, the frontier line of settlement was beyond the line of survey and even beyond that of the Indian cessions.

Chapter 3

Extent of Settlement

The historian rarely has the aid of written records when he undertakes to determine the spread of population in a primitive region. In America, for instance, it is only with great difficulty that the location of the aborigines can be traced, because they migrated frequently and left very few records of their stay in any district. With the advent of Europeans, however, the problem assumes a very different aspect. From the first, their settlements had a permanency beyond the dreams of the savages; and the settlers, products of a mature civilization, kept definite written records of their activities. Instead of an evolution from a nebulous origin in prehistoric times, therefore, the settlement of the white race in America has been a well-documented and comparatively orderly progress, like the advance of multitudinous chessmen across a gigantic board.

Just how far the game had progressed into Illinois by the year in which the state was admitted to the Union it is possible to determine with considerable accuracy from the records available. In 1818 the legislature of the territory ordered a census to be taken, in order to substantiate the claim that the population was large enough to be organized as a state. The original law required the enumeration to be made between April 1 and June 1, but a later act allowed the commissioners to draw up supplementary schedules listing settlers who came in after June 1. That there was some padding of the lists is certain, but the greater part of this was probably in the supplementary schedules; most of these appear to have been lost.[1]

Commissioners appointed for the purpose canvassed each of the 15 counties, recording the names of the heads of families and the number of individuals in each household. The commissioner for Franklin County was the only one who noted loca-

---

[1] For an abstract of the census of 1818, see appendix, p. 319.

tions of settlers; but since as a rule the other commissioners appear to have gone through the county from settlement to settlement, entering the information in the order in which they received it, the arrangement of names furnishes a good clue; having learned from county histories and similar sources the location of a few of the settlers, it is easy to fix, at least roughly, the location of the rest.[2] It is chiefly on the basis of the results thus worked out that the accompanying map of settlement has been constructed.[3]

The frontier of extreme settlement, it will be noted, may be roughly indicated by a line drawn from outpost to outpost across the state. Starting at the Indiana boundary in the southeastern part of Edgar County, the line runs in a southwestern direction to the northeastern corner of Jasper County, then drops down to the Vincennes road, and follows that west to the third principal meridian. From there it curves back to take in the settlements on the Kaskaskia in northern Fayette County, crosses Hurricane Creek in the southeastern part of Montgomery, and Shoal Creek in the vicinity of Hillsboro, and then drops back to the settlements on Silver Creek in northern Madison County. Curving northward again to the settlements of Macoupin County, it crosses the northeastern corner of Jersey, takes in the southwestern part of Greene, and crosses Calhoun to the Mississippi River. Doubtless there were unrecorded establishments above this line in some places, but in general it can be taken to indicate the extreme limit of the progress of settlement in 1818. Not all the region below the line, however, can be considered as settled territory. "In the year 1818," writes Ford, "the settled part of the State extended a little north of Edwardsville and Alton; south, along the Mississippi to the mouth of the Ohio; east, in

[2] This procedure has been impossible in the case of St. Clair and Crawford counties, the names for which are arranged alphabetically. The schedules for Randolph and the principal part of Edwards have not been found.

[3] No attempt has been made to give specific references to the many county histories and biographical collections which have been consulted. A bibliography of these and a discussion of their value will be found in Buck, *Travel and Description of Illinois*, 253-382.

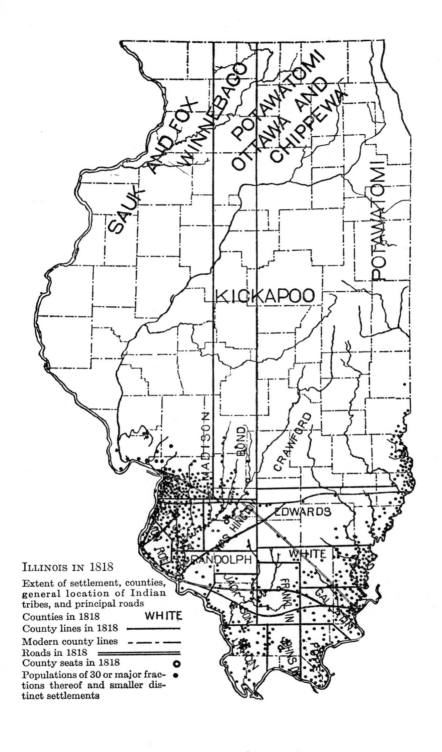

SAUK AND FOX

WINNEBAGO

POTAWATOMI

OTTAWA AND

CHIPPEWA

POTAWATOMI

KICKAPOO

MADISON

BOND

CRAWFORD

EDWARDS

RANDOLPH   WHITE

FRANKLIN

JACKSON

JOHNSON

ILLINOIS IN 1818

Extent of settlement, counties,
general location of Indian
tribes, and principal roads

Counties in 1818   WHITE

County lines in 1818   ————

Modern county lines   –·–·—

Roads in 1818   ════

County seats in 1818   ○

Populations of 30 or major frac-   ●
tions thereof and smaller distinct settlements

the direction of Carlysle to the Wabash; and down the Wabash
and the Ohio, to the mouth of the last-named river. But there
was yet a very large unsettled wilderness tract of country, within
these boundaries, lying between the Kaskaskia river and the
Wabash; and between the Kaskaskia and the Ohio, of three days'
journey across it." [4]

From a study of the census schedules, it appears that what
may properly be termed the settled area lay in two widely separated tracts. The larger of these was in the west and consisted
of the triangle bounded by the Mississippi and Kaskaskia rivers,
Shoal Creek, and the frontier line of survey. In this region of
less than 2,000 square miles dwelt about 15,000 people, more than
a third of the population of the state, and the average density
was not far from eight to the square mile. The other settled district lay along the Wabash River on the eastern side of the state,
extending from the site of York in southeastern Clark County to
Saline Creek and having an average width of about 15 miles.
Nearly another third of the population, approximately 12,000,
dwelt in this region of some 1,500 square miles, thus giving it a
density about equal to that of the settled area in the west. Between these two districts and north of the one on the Mississippi
lived the remaining third of the inhabitants in an immense area
of at least 7,000 square miles. The density of the population in
this region averaged less than two to the square mile, the number used by the United States Census Bureau in delimiting the
frontier of settlement.

Despite the multitude of town-site projects in the state, there
were only two places of sufficient size and importance to justify
their being termed towns—Kaskaskia, the capital, and Shawneetown, the port of entry. These were located at the southern ends
of the western and eastern settled districts, respectively, and
each had an office for the sale of public lands. Edwardsville, the
third land office town, though destined to grow rapidly in the next
few years, was a mere village in 1818, while Cahokia, the former
rival of Kaskaskia, was declining in population. Each of the 15

[4] Ford, *History of Illinois*, 38.

counties, with the exception of Franklin, had a county seat; but these towns as a rule contained little more than a courthouse, jail, and tavern, and possibly a general store. That they depended for their existence on the county business is evident from the number of them which failed to survive the loss of their position as county seat: Palmyra, Brownsville, Covington, Perryville, and even Kaskaskia are now to be found only in the records of the past.

The distribution of the people in 1818 can be indicated more fully by a survey of the population, location of settlements, and towns and villages in each of the 15 counties.

The largest county in Illinois in 1818 was Crawford, which included the whole northeastern part of the state east of the third principal meridian and north of a line cutting across the modern Marion, Clay, Richland, and Lawrence counties 18 miles above the base line, to the Embarras River and down that stream to the Wabash. In this immense area of over 20,000 square miles there were living 2,839 people, according to the final report of the census of 1818. The figures do not quite agree, however, with returns on the schedules. For the first census, these show a population of 2,069, of whom 78 were free negroes and 20 servants or slaves. There were 397 families averaging about five members each. For the supplementary census the commissioner was able to list 121 additional families with 877 souls. The two schedules together, therefore, show a total population of 2,946. The greater part of the Crawford County of 1818 was still Indian land, and the only part in which the land had been surveyed and offered for sale was a strip in the southeast averaging about ten miles in width which extended along the Wabash and the eastern boundary of the state to near the southern boundary of Vermilion County. In this restricted region of about 700 square miles lived nearly all of the population, making an average density of about four to the square mile.

Beyond the survey, there was at least one settler in the southeast corner of Jasper County, and there may have been others who had pushed into the interior from the east. On the opposite side of the county, in what is now Fayette, a few settlers are

said to have been located on the Kaskaskia above the site of
Vandalia, but they were too far away to be listed by the census
commissioner. Within the surveyed tract settlers had pushed
as far north as the present Edgar County, where about a dozen
families were established in Hunter and Stratton townships. In
Clark County settlement was confined principally to the three
eastern townships and was densest in the southeastern parts.
Similarly in the modern Crawford, practically all the settlers
whose location can be determined were in the three townships
along the Wabash, with considerable concentration in La Motte,
the middle of the three. The part of Lawrence County which
was then included in Crawford was across the Wabash from
Vincennes, and a considerable number of allotments under old
grants were located opposite the town, but there seems to have
been no settlement here except such as was connected with the
ferry. Some Frenchmen and a few American pioneers established themselves in the district at the beginning of the century,

WOODEN BEAM PLOW

and after the War of 1812 was over settlers pushed in rapidly, so
that by 1818 they were scattered over all the townships east of
the line of survey. On the site of Russellville in the southeastern
part of Lawrence County a little frontier fort had been built at
the beginning of the Indian troubles, and in this vicinity settlement had progressed most rapidly. A ferry was established at
this point in 1818. The county seat and only town of Craw-

ford County was Palestine, located a mile and a half from the Wabash, on La Motte's Prairie. Settlement began here in 1811, and as soon as the war was over the town was laid out in anticipation of the organization of the county in 1816, but this town appears to have been very small until after the establishment of a land office there in 1820.

South of Crawford and, like it, stretching from the Wabash to the third principal meridian, lay Edwards County. With its southern boundary on a line with the southern boundaries of the present Wayne and Edwards, the dimensions of the county were 33 miles from north to south and 75 on an average from east to west. Its area, therefore, was approximately 2,475 square miles, and within its boundaries were all of the present Wabash, Edwards, and Wayne counties, and parts of Lawrence, Richland, Clay, Marion, and Jefferson. Within this area, according to the census of 1818 as reported to the convention, there were only 2,243 inhabitants, an average of less than one to the square mile. The original schedule made by the census commissioner for Edwards County has not been found, but the secretary of the territory reported on June 17, 1818, that it listed a population of 1,948. This appears to have covered only the eastern part of the county, however, for later in the summer the commissioner for Washington County crossed over into the western part of Edwards, "the detached part," he called it, and listed 42 additional families containing 298 souls. No supplementary count appears to have been made in the eastern section, although the population there, especially on the English prairie, increased rapidly during the summer months.

Through the center of the county, east and west, ran the base line, north of which none of the land was surveyed and open to purchase, except that in the Vincennes tract along the Wabash. Across this unsurveyed region ran the newly laid-out road from Vincennes to St. Louis, and on this road were located a number of tavern keepers at points about 20 miles apart, and also a few other settlers. In the present Richland County, it is doubtful if there were more than two or three families, while in Clay there may have been five or six including three tavern keepers on the

road. In Marion County, however, a little settlement of ten or a
dozen families had sprung up in and around the site of Salem,
and there were three or four families located about Walnut Hill
where the "Goshen Road," from Shawneetown to Carlyle, crossed
the trail branching from the Vincennes–St. Louis road. Scattered
in the southern part of Marion County were possibly five additional families. In the limits of the present Jefferson County were
about 14 families, most of whom lived along the Goshen road.
Included in this number were at least two tavern keepers; there
was also the nucleus of a settlement at Mt. Vernon. East of these
settlements in Marion and Jefferson counties and south of the
Vincennes road lay a wide stretch of country apparently without
any inhabitants.[5]

Fully two-thirds of the population of the Edwards County
of 1818 lived in the triangle between the Wabash and Bon Pas
Creek, the present Wabash County and the southern part of
Lawrence. Settlement was begun in this region as early as 1800
by a number of Frenchmen who came over from Vincennes to
locate their allotments on the west side of the river. The first
American settlers made their appearance a few years later but
there was little advance into the interior until after the War of
1812 was over, and even in 1818 the bulk of the settlers lived
within six or eight miles of the Wabash or the Embarras. Between Bon Pas Creek and the Little Wabash in the part of the
modern Edwards County below the base line was located the
famous English settlement. American backwoodsmen began to
establish their isolated settlements in this region immediately
after the close of the War of 1812, and by the end of 1817 there
were perhaps 25 families located on the edges of the prairies in
the district. Some of these moved away as the English came in,
but others took their places, and it is probable that there were
more American than English families in the region when Illinois
became a state. The English settlement, which in October, 1818,

[5] No attempt has been made to include in the footnotes all the material
on which this survey of local conditions is based. For further information
regarding any particular locality the reader is referred to the bibliography,
p. 321, and to the lists in Buck, *Travel and Description of Illinois.*

numbered about 200, had doubled by August of the following year, but there were then about 700 Americans in the region.[6] The greater number of the settlers in 1818 lived in the central and southern parts of the modern Edwards County, but there were settlements as far north as the base line, with possibly two or three families above the line. In the modern Wayne County lived some 20 or 30 families, mostly in the southeastern part on or near the Little Wabash.

The oldest town in Edwards County, and the county seat, was Palmyra, which had been laid out in 1815. The site selected, a low and swampy spot on a sluggish bend of the Wabash, proved to be unhealthful; and in 1818 the town of Mt. Carmel was started about three miles farther down the river. In October of

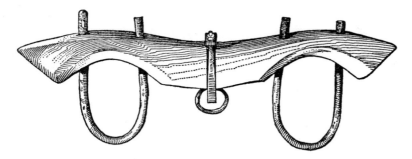

HANDMADE OX-YOKE

the same year Albion was laid out in the center of the English settlement; and in 1821 it became the county seat, after which Palmyra soon disappeared from the map. It is doubtful if any one of these embryo towns contained a dozen houses at the end of the year 1818.

South of Edwards lay White County, covering the territory

[6] Ogg, *Fordham's Personal Narrative*, 236; Thwaites, *Early Western Travels*, 10:104; see map in Fearon, *Sketches of America*, 443, and in Ogg, *Fordham's Personal Narrative*, 113; for Palmyra see Thwaites, *Early Western Travels*, 10:328.

included in the present White and Hamilton counties and a strip
nine miles wide of the southern part of Jefferson running west
to the third principal meridian. Its area was approximately 1,150
square miles and its population, according to the final report of
the census of 1818, was 3,832. The density was thus between three
and four to the square mile. Before the supplementary census
was taken the population was reported as 3,539, and the schedule
shows 572 families with an average of a little above six to a
family. Eleven free people of color and 57 servants or slaves
were noted in the schedule. Although all the land in White
County, except the usual reservations, was open for entry, only
a small proportion of it had been taken up, and settlers were few
and far between in the western section. Apparently the only settlement in the area of the present Jefferson which was included
in White was in the southeastern township, Moore's Prairie,
where some 20 families had established themselves. Through
Hamilton County, diagonally from northwest to southeast, ran
the Goshen road, which was a good drawing card for settlers;
but it is doubtful if there were 100 families in the county. The
principal settlements appear to have been in the central township, in which McLeansboro is now located, and in Knight's
Prairie, the township directly west; but there were isolated settlements scattered throughout the county.

At least three-fourths of the inhabitants of the White County
of 1818 lived within the territory of the modern White County,
and here the region of densest settlement was along the Wabash,
on both sides of the Little Wabash, and between the two streams.
In the southwestern part of the county there was a considerable
number of settlers, but the northwestern townships were practically unoccupied. On the Little Wabash near the center of the
modern White County was located the county seat, Carmi, the
second largest town on the eastern side of the territory. According to George Flower it was "a very small place" in 1818, and
the statement is doubtless correct, for three years before there
had been nothing but a mill on the site. The town was laid out
in 1816 and in the same year a store was started and a ferry
established. The sale of lots was advertised for July 15, 1816;

and in December the county officials were advertising for bids for the construction of a two-story brick courthouse, 30 by 36 feet in size. By 1818 two doctors had located in Carmi and a traveler who passed through the town the next year reported that it "conducts rather lively trade in wares." [7]

The oldest county on the east side of the state is Gallatin, established by executive proclamation in 1812. By 1818, through the formation of other counties, it had been reduced to an area of about 800 square miles, including the present Galatin and Saline counties and the northeastern half of Hardin. The schedule of the first census of 1818 for Gallatin County lists 541 families with a total of 3,440 souls including 83 free negroes and 218 servants or slaves, the largest number of each of these classes to be found in any of the counties. The additional census, taken during June and July, added 511 to the roll, of whom 8 were free negroes and 81 servants or slaves. These were grouped in 75 families. According to the schedules, therefore, the total was 3,951, while the total reported to the convention was 3,849. Inasmuch as this latter figure is larger by 694 than the population reported for Gallatin County, with the same area, by the United States census of 1820, it becomes apparent that the census of 1818 is not reliable. From a study of the schedules it is evident that many who were passing through to locate elsewhere in the state or even in Missouri were counted; and the permanent population in the fall of 1818 was probably less than 3,000.

A most important factor in the development of Gallatin County was the salt works on Saline Creek and the government reservation which surrounded them. A rectangle, 10 by 13 miles in the center of the county, together with an irregular strip of land extending from the southeastern corner of the rectangle along the creek to its mouth, had been set aside by the United States government for the support of the salt works. No land could be sold in the reservation, but it is not to be inferred that

[7] Flower, *English Settlement*, 109; *Intelligencer*, June 12, December 4, 1816; Illinois State Historical Society, *Transactions*, 1903, p. 150.

there was no settlement there. The operation of the salt works gave employment to a considerable number, including probably a majority of the slaves in the county. These were, of course, entitled to reside on the reservation, and there they formed a little settlement which later became the town of Equality. There were others living on the reservation, however, who had no connection with the salt works but who refused to be deterred by the impossibility of purchasing the land. As early as 1816 the manager of the saline complained to the General Land Office that "the intruders on this tract increase, and experience convinces me that their improvements must be destroyed before they will leave it. In fact, if one set leaves it, another comes on it immediately, and they no longer pay any attention to a threat from me.[8] Had the land covered by the reservation been open to entry, the settlements upon it would undoubtedly have been much more extensive, for it was located near the land office, and through it ran the road from Shawneetown to Kaskaskia. In December, 1816, a number of inhabitants of the county, in a petition to Congress, complained that "there has been none but temporary nor is there encouragement for buildings and improvements, within the reservation for a public House for the accommodation of Travellers, and persons who have to resort to that place on business." They pointed out that "the road is much travelled and from the great emigration to the westward must increase every year" and requested that the tavern keeper might be allowed to enter a quarter section of land which he would improve "with permanent and convenient buildings. Grass Lotts &c so as to make it a public convenience."[9] Congress rejected the petition, however, and when the state was admitted to the union the reservation was turned over to it intact.

In what is now Saline County, outside the reservation, there were probably not more than 90 families, a considerable proportion of whom, to judge from the land entries, lived along the road to Kaskaskia. There were scattered establishments in vari-

[8] *American State Papers, Public Lands*, 3:273.
[9] Petition, December 10, 1816, in House Files.

ous parts of the county, as well as in the part of Hardin then included, and in the northwestern and southwestern parts of the modern Gallatin. There was some concentration of settlement in the vicinity of the ferry over the Little Wabash in the northeastern part of the county—the beginnings of New Haven; but certainly a half and probably two-thirds of the permanent population of Gallatin County lived in the region between the Ohio River and the reservation and within a radius of six or eight miles of Shawneetown.

The first white settlement in this region is said to have been made in 1800; it is certain that Shawneetown contained a few scattered houses in 1804. Cuming, a traveler who visited the place in 1809, reported: "The town now contains about twenty-four cabins, and is a place of considerable resort on account of the saline salt-works about twelve miles distant, which supply with salt all the settlements within one hundred miles, and I believe even the whole of Upper Louisiana. . . . There were several trading boats at the landing, and more appearance of business than I had seen on this side Pittsburgh." [10] When Gallatin County was established, Shawneetown became the county seat; a jail was erected in 1810 and a courthouse in 1815. Until 1814 the land on which the town was located belonged to the United States, but in that year the lots were sold at auction. The bidding appears to have been brisk and the lots sold for good prices. Two years later, however, the bubble had collapsed. The purchasers of lots then drew up a petition to Congress which brings out the serious disadvantages of the town as well as the principal cause of its development. The petitioners, having purchased lots "at an excessive high price," set forth:

That within a few months after the sales of the said lots, our town was visited by a most destructive epidemic, which nearly depopulated the place; and immediately after in the same winter the whole of the town on the River was inundated, the water being from 10 to 20 feet over the whole of that part of the town. . . . That alarmed and disheartened many persons have ceased to improve, and have abandoned the place, and others have been detered from settling here.—That under these

[10] Thwaites, *Early Western Travels*, 4:271.

unfortunate combinations the improvements have languished, and at length appear to have ceased entirely, the lots have depreciated so much in value, that very few of your petitioners can venture to make the remaining three payments into the land office. . . . That at the time the sales of lots in Shawneetown took place, in consequence of the War, salt was commanding a very high price, and the Saline was in extensive operation.—Peace has brought down the price of salt, mismanagement has made the Saline of little comparitive value, and consequently cut off the best branch of the trade which heretofore has centered at Shawneetown.—That the *then* promising prospects of our town, drew to the sales of lots a vast number of distant adventurers, which together with an unhappy spirit of opposition amongst ourselves combined to run up the lots to the astonishing prices for which they were sold; prices far *greater* than they would now bring if again offered for sale.

In view of this doleful situation, the purchasers asked to be relieved from further payments; but Congress, needless to say, rejected the petition.[11]

Besides the salt works, there were two other factors of importance in the development of Shawneetown. It was the principal port of entry for emigrants whose destination was farther north in White and Edwards counties, and also for the even greater numbers bound for western Illinois and Missouri. Closely connected with this was the fact that the land office for the southeastern part of the state was located here. These factors, however, contributed to the transient rather than to the permanent population of the town, which even in 1818 was described by one traveler as "a handful of log cabins." Another visitor pictured it "an inconsiderable place . . . [containing] several taverns, a bake-house, and a few huts." A more definite writer counted "about 30 houses (log.) The chief occupation of the inhabitants is the salt trade. There is here a 'United States' Land-office,' and a *log* bank is just established. The *chief cashier* of this establishment was engaged in cutting logs at the moment of my arrival."[12] William Tell Harris, who passed

[11] Petition referred December 24, 1816, and committee report, December 30, 1816, in House Files.

[12] Thwaites, *Early Western Travels*, 8:291; 13:70; Fearon, *Sketches of America*, 258.

through Shawneetown in September, 1818, on his way from the English settlement to Kentucky, after commenting on the annual floods and the unhealthfulness of the site, noted "considerable business being done here, as it is on the road from the southern States to St. Louis, and the Missouri, and the land-office is here. The number of waggons, horses, and passengers crossing, and waiting to cross the Ohio, was so great, that a great part of the morning was spent in waiting for my turn; at length I grew impatient, and taking the opportunity of a skiff, turned my back on Illinois, and landed in the State of Kentucky." [13] Such was the metropolis of eastern Illinois and the chief town on the Ohio below Louisville in 1818.

Pope County included, besides the present county of that name, the southwestern half of Hardin and the part of Massac east of the western boundary of the modern Pope extending south to the Ohio River. In this territory of about 600 square miles according to the final census figures there lived 2,069 people, an average of a little above three to the square mile. The schedule of the first census totals 1,944, including 64 servants or slaves. There were 322 families with an average of six members. Little information is available as to the location of these people, but it is probable that most of them lived along or near the road leading west from Golconda to Kaskaskia or along the Ohio. Golconda itself, the county seat, consisted of only a handful of houses and a tavern clustered about the ferry near the mouth of Lusk Creek. About 25 miles farther up the Ohio a promoter had laid out a paper town to which he gave the breezy name of Hurricane, and the sale of lots was advertised for the last Thursday in May, 1818. There is no evidence of any special settlement here; but there may have been a ferry, for the place was announced as on the "great crossway from the southern and western states, to the principal towns upon the Mississippi river." [14]

West of Pope lay Johnson County, embracing the present

---

[13] Harris, *Remarks Made During a Tour*, 139.
[14] *Intelligencer*, April 15, 1818.

Johnson and the parts of Pulaski and Massac between it and the Ohio River. With the exception of Monroe, Johnson was the smallest county in the state, having an area of only about 400 square miles; and its population was less than that of any other county. Only 678 people including 1 free negro and 24 servants or slaves, grouped in 117 families, were counted in the first census report of 1818. To these the supplementary census added 89, making a total of 767. Circling through the western part of the county ran the Cache River with tributaries flowing in from the north, and along these streams and the Golconda-Kaskaskia road which crossed them, in the precincts of Elvira, Bloomfield, and Vienna, were located the bulk of the settlers. The county seat was at Elvira until Union County was set off in January, 1818; it was then changed to Vienna. Very few settlers appear to have located along the Ohio, although much of the land there had been bought by speculators, and lots in "Waterloo . . . on the western bank of the Ohio . . . nine miles below the mouth of Tennessee river" were advertised to be sold on April 10, 1818.[15] This location must have been at or near the present site of Metropolis, a town which was not started until 1839.

Franklin County, one of the two counties which nowhere touched the boundaries of the state, included the modern Franklin and Williamson, an area of about 860 square miles. It was one of the three new counties established in January, 1818. The census in Franklin, which was not completed until July 11, shows a population, according to the schedule, of 1,228, or less than two to the square mile.[16] The number of families was 171. There were 15 slaves and 52 free negroes, the latter including five whole families living near together on Saline Creek. The modern Franklin County is drained principally by the Big Muddy and its forks, while through Williamson flows Crab Orchard Creek, a branch of the Big Muddy, and Saline Creek,

[15] *Intelligencer*, February 11, 1818. Another Waterloo in Monroe County, which is still in existence, was laid out the same year. See pp. 83, 84.

[16] The final report to the convention was 1,281. There was no supplementary census, however, and the discrepancy was probably caused by an error in addition.

the waters of which reach the Wabash through the Saline River. Across the southern tier of townships of the modern Franklin ran the new road from Shawneetown to Kaskaskia, which was under construction in 1818, while the route of the old road between the same places crossed Williamson. The people appear to have located principally in the vicinity of these streams and roads, with some concentration in Frankfort precinct. There was nothing in the county that could be called a town; and the county records, until 1826, were kept at the tavern of Moses Garrett on the old road about three miles east of the site of Frankfort.

Union County was another of the three established in January, 1818. At that time its boundaries were fixed exactly as they are now, but the region south from these boundaries to the Mississippi and Ohio, including the modern Alexander and the greater part of Pulaski, was "attached to" and made "a part of" Union County until it should be formed into a separate county. This whole area, comprising about 800 square miles, had a population of 2,709 according to the final report of the census of 1818. This made an average density of between three and four to the square mile. The schedules of the census as first taken show 2,492 inhabitants grouped in 392 families. There were 33 servants or slaves but no free negroes. At least two-thirds of these settlers were located within the modern Union County, and of these the greater number lived some eight or ten miles back from the Mississippi River on the divide separating the creeks flowing into the Mississippi from those that entered the Cache. There were a few settlers along the Mississippi, however, and in the eastern part of the county, especially in Stokes precinct, through which passed the road from Golconda to Kaskaskia. The few families living in Alexander County and the part of Pulaski contained in Union were located along or a few miles back from the Ohio and on or near the Cache.

Although Union County was liberally supplied with paper towns in 1818, of real towns there was only a beginning. The principal concentration of settlement appears to have been near the center of the modern Union; and here in March, 1818, the commissioners located the county seat, to which was given the name of Jonesboro. The first sale of lots took place in July, and some of them are said to have brought over $100. On the Mississippi 12 miles above Cape Girardeau, a group of speculators had laid out the town of "Hamburg," named doubtless with a view to attracting the trade of the "Dutch settlement," an industrious community located in the northeastern part of Meisenheimer precinct.[17] There was a ferry here and lots were advertised to be sold at auction on September 1, but no town has ever developed on the site. It was along the Ohio that town-site projects flourished most luxuriantly. The greater part of the land here was purchased by speculators as soon as it was offered by the government, and about 1817 a town called Trinity was laid out just above the mouth of the Cache. No lots appear to have been sold but a joint tavern and store was established; and the place was a point of transshipment for river traffic for a few years, until a growing sand bar put an end to its prosperity. Several of the men connected with Trinity were also interested in a town six miles farther up the river, called America, "which was laid out with much pomp and parade as the future great metropolis in 1818." In advertising a sale of lots to take place on the third Monday in November, the proprietors modestly observed that "the obvious advantages of its local situation . . . and its general notoriety, are such as to render all comment on its merits, superfluous." The first house appears to have been built by Dr. W. M. Alexander in the winter of 1818-19; and when Alexander County was established America became its county seat. The county business kept the town alive for a few years.[18]

The most interesting of all the schemes for towns in Union

[17] Perrin, *History of Alexander, Union, and Pulaski Counties*, 287, 358, 435. W. M. Alexander, one of the proprietors of America, proposed to build a bridge across the Cache "so as to draw the trade of the Dutch in Union county." *Ibid.*, 270. None of the names of members of this settlement given in the county history are to be found in the census schedule. Possibly they were included in the supplementary census.

[18] Perrin, *History of Alexander, Union, and Pulaski Counties*, 67-72, 269, 448-453; *Intelligencer*, October 21, 1818.

County was "The City and Bank of Cairo," which was incorporated by an act of the territorial legislature on January 9, 1818. Five months earlier John G. Comegys of Baltimore had entered about 1,800 acres of land on the narrow peninsula between the Ohio and Mississippi rivers, but not including the extreme point. This land was now deeded to the company, of which Comegys was the moving spirit; an elaborate plat was prepared; and plans were laid for the sale of lots and the establishment of the bank, which was to be located temporarily at Kaskaskia. The act of incorporation provided for 2,000 lots which were to be sold at $150 each. One-third of the proceeds was to be used in constructing levees to protect the city from floods, and for other improvements. The remaining two-thirds was to constitute the capital stock of the bank, one-half of which should belong to Comegys and his associates and one-half to the purchasers of the lots. The death of Comegys in 1819 was followed by the collapse of the entire scheme; the land reverted to the government, and Cairo remained unborn for another 20 years.

Advancing up the Mississippi, the next county above Union was Jackson, which, in 1818, included the territory of the present Jackson and a strip six miles wide off the south of Perry—about 730 square miles in all. The population of the county according to the final report of the census of 1818 was 1,619, making the density only a little above two to the square mile. There were 240 families, and 53 of the inhabitants were servants or slaves. The first census report gave the population as 1,295, but 38 additional families were discovered by the supplementary census. The principal attractions to settlement in the county were the Big Muddy River and its tributaries flowing in from the north. Along these streams and the Mississippi, and to a smaller extent along the several roads which crossed the county, were located the greater number of settlers, although there were isolated establishments throughout the county. The largest groups of settlements were on the Big Muddy near the center of the modern Jackson County. Here were located the salt works of Dr. Conrad Will and the county seat, Brownsville. This town, which has now entirely disappeared, was situated on the north bank of the river about four miles west of the site of Murphysboro. It was laid out by Dr. Will when the county was organized in 1816, the sale of lots being advertised for July 15. By 1818 it had a frame courthouse and log jail, a store, and a blacksmith shop. For a number of years Brownsville was a flourishing town, but the closing of the saline and the removal of the county seat to Murphysboro in 1843 sealed its fate.

Randolph County, lying north of Jackson and stretching from the Mississippi to the third principal meridian, included, besides the present Randolph, the northern two-thirds of Perry County —a total area of about 875 square miles. Unfortunately the schedule of the first census of 1818 for Randolph County has not been found, but the population as reported by the secretary of the territory in June was 2,939. The supplementary census added 16 families with 45 souls, which would make a total of 2,984, but the final report to the convention was 2,974. The average density in the county, therefore, was between three and four to the square mile. The population was very unevenly distributed, however, for it is doubtful if there were 200 people living in the part now included in Perry County and the western tier of townships in Randolph. The region of densest settlement was in the American bottom along the Mississippi and up the Kaskaskia River, and nearly half the population of the county was to be found in the two towns of Kaskaskia and Prairie du Rocher.

Although Kaskaskia was over 100 years old and had been for many years the metropolis of the upper Mississippi valley, it impressed a visitor in 1819 as "not very important." From 1765 on, Kaskaskia had declined steadily in population until in 1807 it was reported to consist of not more than 50 families.[19] In 1809, however, it became the capital of the new territory of Illinois, and that event, together with the acquisition of the land office, gave it a new lease on life. Its population in 1810

[19] Illinois State Historical Society, *Transactions*, 1903, p. 152; Schultz, *Travels*, 2:74.

was reported as 622. By the close of the territorial period it must have had nearly 1,000 inhabitants, and Governor Edwards had sufficient faith in its future to announce his intention of applying to the court for an order to add to the town an adjoining tract of 34¾ acres.[20] Samuel Brown in his *Western Gazetteer* (1817) describes the town as

situated on the right shore of the river of the same name, eleven miles from its mouth, and six from the Mississippi, in a direct line. It is at present the seat of the territorial government and chief town of Randolph county—contains 160 houses, scattered over an extensive plain; some of them are of stone. Almost every house has a spacious picketed garden it its rear. The houses have a clumsy appearance; it is 150 miles south-west of Vincennes, and 900 from the city of Washington. The inhabitants are more than half French, they raise large stocks of horned cattle, horses, swine, poultry, &c. There is a postoffice, a land office for the sale of the public lands, and a printing office, from which is issued a weekly newspaper entitled the *"Illinois Herald."* This place was settled upwards of 100 years ago, by the French of Lower Canada. The surrounding lands are in a good state of cultivation.

Dana, in his *Geographical Sketches* (1819), waxes enthusiastic over Kaskaskia: "Placed near the mouth of a river extensively navigable, and in the vicinity of some of the richest lands of the western country, connected with a convenient position for commerce, this place assumes that degree of importance which must eventually attract wealth and numbers. It has a good harbor for boats, contains a land office, a printing-office, and a bank, and is now in a flourishing condition." An eastern traveler who visited the town in November, 1819, presents quite a different picture: "Remained in this inconsiderable village this day. Much disappointed in the appearance of the long-talked-of-Kaskaskia. It is situated on the Okaw or Kaskaskia river, three miles from the Mississippi. It never can be a place of much business. The land office is kept at this place. There are some neat buildings, but they are generally old, ugly and inconvenient. Their streets are irregular and of bad widths. The inhabitants are all generals, colonels, majors, land speculators or adventurers, with now and then a robber and a cutthroat."

[20] Darby, *Emigrant's Guide*, 213; *Intelligencer*, April 1, 1818.

Nevertheless Kaskaskia must have been a place of considerable commercial importance in 1818, for its weekly newspaper contained advertisements of nine general stores, an establishment for the manufacture and sale of hats, and three tailor shops. There was only one tavern, however, the famous Bennett's, and its accommodations were severely taxed by the constitutional convention of 33 members. John Mason Peck, the Baptist missionary, who stopped there while the convention was in session, was informed that "every room was occupied, and every bed had two or more lodgers." [21] Kaskaskia was not in a position to profit by the immigration which was surging through Shawneetown and up the Mississippi to the northwestern counties, and with the removal of the capital and the newspaper to Vandalia in 1820 it began to decline again. Following a flood in 1844, the county seat was removed to Chester, and during a subsequent inundation the Mississippi cut a new channel to the Kaskaskia just above the town, so that all there is left today of the first capital of Illinois is a building or two on an island in the Mississippi.

Fifteen miles farther up the American bottom, near the northwestern corner of the county, was the old French village of Prairie du Rocher, nestling under the bluffs which gave it the name. Schultz found about 40 Catholic families there in 1807. Brown's *Western Gazetteer* (1817) reported "sixty to seventy French families; the streets are narrow—there is a catholic chapel." The village was on the road from Kaskaskia to St. Louis, and in 1816 Archibald M'Nabb advertised the opening there of a "house of private entertainment." The best-known tavern, however, was that of Pierre La Compte, which, after his death in 1818, was carried on by his widow. There were no other towns in Randolph County when Illinois became a state, although a couple of speculators were advertising the town of Blenheim, "situated about thirteen miles from the town of Kas-

[21] The descriptions of Kaskaskia from which quotations have been made are found in Brown, *Western Gazetteer*, 27; Dana, *Geographical Sketches*, 154; Mason, *Narrative*, 56; Babcock, *Memoir of Peck*, 97.

kaskia, at the junction of Horse creek and the Kaskaskia river
. . . it lies immediately on the direct line from Kaskaskia to
Belleville, Edwardsville and St. Louis, on a road exempt from
the unavoidable inconveniences connected with the present route
to those places." [22]

The smallest county in Illinois in 1818, and the only one
which is larger today than it was then, was Monroe, situated on
the Mississippi just above Randolph. Its boundaries at that
time did not include the township which now projects to the
eastward. With an area of about 340 square miles, Monroe
County had a population of 1,371 according to the schedule of
the first census of 1818. The number of families was 227, and
there were 41 servants or slaves and 6 free negroes. After the
supplementary census was taken, the total population was reported as 1,517, giving the county an average density of nearly
six to the square mile. While there were settlers in all parts of
the county, the regions of greatest density were the Mississippi
bottom and the higher lands in the north central part extending
from the New Design settlement near the center beyond the site
of Waterloo. From New Design southward, John Mason Peck
traveled in 1818 "for sixteen miles, without a house, to the
French village of Prairie du Rocher," while Mason, the following year, "saw only three houses" from Waterloo to Prairie du
Rocher.[23] When the county was organized in 1816 the seat of
justice was fixed at Harrisonville on the Mississippi about mid-
way between the northern and southern boundaries, and a dinner was held at M'Clure's tavern in celebration of the event. A
few months later M'Night and Brady were advertising a sale
of lots in Carthage, "formerly Harrisonville," but the latter
name was restored by legislative enactment in December, 1816.
In 1818 the county commissioners advertised the sale of a number of lots in the town. There were probably about 50 families
in Harrisonville and its vicinity when the census was taken.
Waterloo, the present county seat, was laid out in 1818 by

[22] *Intelligencer,* October 2, 1816; April 22, May 13, 1818.
[23] Babcock, *Memoir of Peck,* 97; Mason, *Narrative,* 55.

Daniel P. Cook and George Forquer "at the well known stand of Mrs. Ford, on the road leading from Kaskaskia to St. Louis, 36 miles from the former, and 24 from the latter place. It is surrounded by a beautiful and fertile country and a population of 50 families within 5 or 6 miles." The public sale of lots took place at Harrisonville on the first Monday in April, after which the "few lots" remaining unsold were to be purchased from Forquer "on the premises." There is no evidence, however, of any influx of settlers before the census was taken, and as late as November, 1819, a traveler reported that he "lodged at Waterloo, a town without houses. Only two families in the place. Every land speculator produces one or more of these dirt-cabin villages." [24]

St. Clair, the oldest county in Illinois, had been reduced by 1818 to its present boundaries with the exception of Prairie du Long precinct, which has since been transferred to Monroe County. Within this area of about 725 square miles there dwelt 5,039 people, according to the final report, making the density about seven to the square mile, higher than that of any other county. The schedule of the first census has been burned in part while that of the supplementary census, which added 520 to the original figure of 4,519, has not been found, but it is evident from what is available that the families averaged between six and seven members. Even in this most densely populated part of the state, therefore, there was only about one family to each square mile, and as part of the population lived in the villages the statement of the county historian that "the settlements were so sparse that seldom did neighbors live nearer than two miles to each other" is probably not far from the truth. St. Clair County was one of the first regions to attract the American pioneers in considerable numbers, and some years before the close of the territorial period settlements had been established in all parts of the county. The metropolis of the county was the old French village of Cahokia, which at one time had rivaled

[24] *Intelligencer*, June 12, October 2, 1816; February 4, March 11, May 13, 1818; *Laws of Illinois Territory*, 1816-17, p. 3.

Kaskaskia, the capital. Schultz found "about a hundred and thirty houses" there in 1807, "one dozen of which may be inhabited by Americans." The county seat was at Cahokia at that time, and after this was removed in 1814, there was probably a decline in population. Brown in his *Western Gazetteer* (1817) describes the village as "situated on a small stream, about one mile east of the Mississippi, nearly opposite to St. Louis. It contains about 160 houses, mostly French." Dana's *Geographical Sketches* (1819) also mentions 160 houses but in another place gives the population as about 500. Mason, a pessimistic traveler who passed through in 1819, speaks of it as "a small village called Cahokia, a miserable, dirty little hole" and again as "a small and unimproving village." [25]

As the American settlers in the interior of the county increased in numbers, the desire grew to have the county seat in a more central location, and in 1813 commissioners were appointed by the legislature to select a new site. In March, 1814, the commissioners decided in favor of the cornfield of one George Blair, and in accordance with the usual practice in such cases Blair agreed to donate to the county an acre of land for the county buildings and one-fifth of the lots in the town, to be laid out in the adjoining 25 acres. The survey was made at once and the June term of court was held at Blair's house. The plat was not recorded, however, until a few years later, when Governor Edwards had become the proprietor. In December, 1817, he was offering lots at $60 until the end of the year, after which date they were to be $100 each. By the time Illinois became a state Belleville had a courthouse, jail, general store, one or two taverns, and possibly other establishments. Dana described it as "a flourishing new town" but it is doubtful if it had 150 inhabitants.[26]

A still smaller place was Illinoistown, though now, under an-

[25] Schultz, *Travels*, 2:39; Brown, *Western Gazetteer*, 27; Dana, *Geographical Sketches*, 150, 154; Mason, *Narrative*, 53, 62.

[26] *History of St. Clair County*, 183-185; *Intelligencer*, May 22, 1816; December 11, 1817; Dana, *Geographical Sketches*, 154.

other name, it has become the largest city in the county. As early as 1815 the advantages of the site directly across the Mississippi from St. Louis were observed and it was platted as a town with the name of "Jacksonville." The property soon changed hands and was replatted as the "Town of Illinois," the lots being sold at auction in St. Louis on November 3, 1817. The following March, Simon Vanorsdal gave notice of his intention to apply "for an order to establish a Town . . . on a tract of land containing 100 acres, lying on the Mississippi river, opposite St. Louis." Whether this was to be a rival or an addition to Illinoistown does not appear. A tavern and a store existed near the east end of the ferry to St. Louis as early as 1815, and a traveler who passed that way in November, 1819, speaks of "the town of Illinois, on the Mississippi, a little village opposite St. Louis." [27]

Before 1818 St. Clair County had extended east to the third principal meridian, but in January of that year the eastern part including the modern Washington and all of Clinton except the northern tier of townships was set off as Washington County. In this area of 900 square miles, there dwelt, according to the final report, 1,819 people, an average of about two to the square mile. There were 265 families, 16 with 113 souls having been added by the supplementary census. The number of free negroes was 19 and there were 28 servants or slaves. This small population was very unevenly distributed over the county, however, probably nine-tenths being in what is now Clinton County. Settlement had progressed eastward and northward up the Kaskaskia and the streams flowing into it from the north until by the close of 1818 there were a few inhabitants in each of the townships of this region. The northeastern township, however, being mostly prairie, had only two or three families of settlers. South of the Kaskaskia and of Crooked Creek, in the modern Washington County, it is doubtful if there were 200 people. A few families were living along the river, there were the beginnings

[27] *History of St. Clair County,* 298; *Intelligencer,* April 1, 1818; Mason, *Narrative,* 51.

of a settlement in Plumb Hill precinct near the center, and two
or three families had established themselves on the road from
Vincennes to Kaskaskia. Most of the precincts of the county,
however, did not receive their first settlers until near the middle
of the next decade.

When Washington County was organized there was no town
within its boundaries, and the county seat was fixed at a place
on the south side of the Kaskaskia near the center of the county
where an old trail from Kaskaskia to Peoria crossed the river.
The town of Covington was immediately platted on the site "on
a very extensive and liberal plan," and an attempt was made
in the convention to have it selected for the capital of the state.
The advantages of the place were advertised in glowing terms
in the *Intelligencer* of July 1, and on July 29, the county commissioners gave notice of a public sale of lots on the first Monday in September. The town appears to have had very few settlers, however, and with the division of the county and the removal of the county seat it disappeared from the map. A more
promising venture was Carlyle, "beautifully situated on the
west bank of the Kaskaskia river, at the well known crossing
of *Hill's Ferry* . . . having the great United States road from
Vincennes to St. Louis, the roads from Shawneetown, the Saline
and the Ferries on the lower Ohio, to the mouth of Missouri
and the great Sangamo country passing thro' its principal
street." The town was "laid off in squares of two acres, having
its mainstreet 75 and its other streets 66 feet in width, each
square having an alley 20 feet in width passing through its
center.—A public square, church lots, &c." [28] The public sale
of lots was advertised to begin on September 29, 1818, and the
following year Dana reported the town "in a flourishing condition." A sale of lots in the rival "Town of Donaldson" laid
out on the opposite side of the river "just at the point where the
two leading roads from the east to the west, unite" was advertised for the first Monday in November, 1818; but Donaldson

[28] *Intelligencer*, September 9, 1818.

appears to have been stillborn. Carlyle and Donaldson, like Covington, aspired to become the capital of the new state.

North of St. Clair lay Madison County, with its present southern and western boundaries; the west line, however, extended to the northern boundary of the state. All the immense region between this line and the Mississippi River was nominally a part of the county, but in only the three southern tiers of townships, about 570 square miles, was land available for purchase before 1819. The schedule of the first census of 1818 lists 717 families in Madison County with 4,516 souls, of whom 34 were free negroes and 77 servants or slaves. This is only three less than the population of St. Clair as reported in June; and including the supplementary census of 847 as compared with 520 for St. Clair, Madison becomes the most populous county in the state. The final report to the convention was 6,303, but this includes 980 reputed residents at the forts in the Indian country. The part of this population residing south of the line of survey may be placed conservatively at 4,500, which would give to that region a density of about eight to the square mile, slightly more than that of St. Clair County. While settlers were to be found in all parts of these townships, the areas of greatest density were along the Mississippi, and southwest of Edwardsville where the so-called Goshen settlement was located. Toward the eastern boundary settlers were less numerous and were located mainly in the vicinity of Silver Creek and its branches and along the road to Shawneetown.

Of special interest are the settlements above the line of survey, for these illustrate the way in which the frontier population pushed out and squatted on land which was not yet in the market and which in some cases had not yet been cleared of the Indian title. The census schedules indicated that about 70 families were living in this region in the early summer of 1818, but the number was probably doubled before the end of the year. As usual on the extreme frontier, the settlers were to be found principally along the rivers and creeks. Even the military tract between the Mississippi and Illinois had a few inhabitants on the southern point, extending north to about the middle of Cal-

houn County, though it is doubtful if any of them had secured
title to the soil. Major Stephen H. Long, on a trip down the
Mississippi, "took an excursion" across this peninsula in August,
1817, and reported: "There are five settlements at this place,
including two immediately upon the Mississippi at Little Cape
Gris." [29] This point was about 20 miles up the river from the
mouth of the Illinois.

On the eastern side of the Illinois adventurous spirits had
pushed as far north as Apple Creek in Greene County and also
up the tributaries flowing in from the east, Macoupin Creek
with Phill's Creek, its branch, and Otter Creek in Jersey County.
The census schedule indicated several families on Macoupin
and Phill's creeks in the southeastern part of Greene and the
northeastern part of Jersey counties and at least one settler on
the headwaters of Macoupin Creek in what is now Macoupin
County. There was probably a considerable increase during the
summer; and, if local tradition is reliable, Macoupin County
contained ten families when Illinois became a state. Edmund
Dana, who visited this region in the late summer of 1818, speaks
of finding 60 families in the tract drained by Macoupin, Apple,
and Otter creeks "in the sickly months of 1818." In another
place, referring to the whole region from Piasa Creek, which enters the Mississippi near the boundary between Madison and
Jersey counties, to and including Macoupin County, he states
that "nearly 120 families had settled here before the lands were
surveyed," which would be before the spring of 1819.[30] On
Wood River, which enters the Mississippi a couple of miles below Alton, the settlements had extended north only a mile or
so above the line of survey, and there appear to have been no
establishments on the branches of Cahokia Creek above this
line when the census schedule was compiled. Farther east, however, on Silver Creek, there were settlers within a mile or two
of the present northern boundary of Madison County.

[29] *Minnesota Historical Collections*, 2:82. On the location of Cape au
Gris see *Wisconsin Historical Collections*, 2:209.

[30] Dana, *Geographical Sketches*, 139-144. For another statement on the
settlements in this region in 1819, see Babcock, *Memoir of Peck*, 155.

When Governor Edwards issued the proclamation establishing Madison County in 1812, he appointed "the house of Thomas Kirkpatrick to be the seat of justice of said county." Not until 1816 was a town laid out and given the name of Edwardsville. The establishment of a land office there in the same year made it an important place, but its population probably did not exceed 200 when the census was taken in the early summer of 1818. The 18 households listed which can definitely be assigned to Edwardsville comprised 166 souls. The composition of this population indicates something of the character of the place and the influence of the land office. There were 74 men, only 71 women and children, including all under 21, 17 servants or slaves, and 4 free negroes. Eight of the slaves belonged to Benjamin Stephenson, register of the land office, and four to Governor Edwards, who had established his residence in the town named for him. At least three of the households, and probably four, were taverns at which dwelt over half of the men. The town grew rapidly during the summer; and Edmund Dana, whose name appears in the Edwardsville group in the census schedule, wrote of it the following year as a "flourishing town, containing 60 or 70 houses, a court house, jail, public bank, printing office, which issues a weekly newspaper, and a United States land office." The bank and the printing office did not exist in 1818, however. In November, 1819, a traveler described the place as "a small but flourishing little village." [31]

The city of Alton also had its beginnings during the territorial period, these being in the form of some four or five town-site projects. Alton proper was laid out in 1817 by Colonel Easton, a St. Louis speculator; but Reverend Thomas Lippincott found there in December, 1818, only one cabin besides the ferryhouse. About the same time Upper Alton was laid out on the bluff and soon afterward "Alton on the river," or Hunterstown, was platted, all now parts of the city of Alton. Larger than any of these in 1818, however, was Milton, about three miles back from the

[31] *History of Madison County*, 333; Dana, *Geographical Sketches*, 143; Mason, *Narrative*, 63; James, *Territorial Records*, 26.

Mississippi on Wood River. Here were to be found a store, two
sawmills, a gristmill, and a distillery. John Mason Peck, who
visited Upper Alton in February, 1819, in search of a location
for a boarding school, found "between forty and fifty families,
living in log-cabins, shanties, covered wagons, and camps.
Probably not less than twenty families were destitute of houses;
but were getting out materials and getting up shelters with industry and enterprise." Mason, who was here in December, 1819,
was struck by the fact that "within five miles there are five
towns, as they are called, but all insignificant and improperly
placed. Their names are Milton, Alton, Middle Alton, Lower
Alton and Sales." In another place, however, he refers to Milton
as "a flourishing little village only one and a half years old."
Dana, in his *Geographical Sketches* (1819), writes of Alton, not
specifying which village he meant: "Nearly 100 decent houses
are already erected. The spirit of enterprise displayed by the
settlers, who are mostly from the eastern states, and the natural
advantages attached to the place, point out this town as a stand
where small capitals in trade may be profitably vested." Milton
he describes as containing "about 50 houses, and although it
seems to flourish, it is considered an unhealthy situation. The
creek here drives both a grist and saw mill; each of which do
great business." [32]

Filling in the gap of 24 miles between Madison and Crawford
counties was Bond County, which stretched like a ribbon from
six miles south of the modern Bond County northward to the
state line. Here also only the three southern tiers of townships,
an area of 432 square miles, were within the line of survey. The
number of families living in the county in the early summer of
1818, according to the census schedule, was 212, and the total
population was 1,384, of whom 15 were servants or slaves. No
supplementary census appears to have been taken, but the final
report to the convention was 1,398. Nearly all these people
were living along the southward-flowing streams in the southern

[32] Lippincott, "Early Days in Madison County," nos. 2-4; *History of
Madison County*, 374-376; Babcock, *Memoir of Peck*, 154; Mason, *Narrative*, 64, 66; Dana, *Geographical Sketches*, 142.

part of the county. About four-fifths of them appear to have been within the surveyed district, which would make the density of this tract less than three to the square mile. Above the line of survey from 40 to 50 families established themselves, mainly on Shoal and Hurricane creeks. Up the former the settlers had pushed as far north as the vicinity of Hillsboro in Montgomery County, and on Hurricane Creek there was a group of settlements in what is now Fayette County and another in the southeastern part of Montgomery.

When Bond County was established in 1817, a site "on the Harricane [sic] Fork of the Kaskaskia river, one mile from its junction, and 2¼ miles from Pope's Bluff" was selected for the seat of justice. This was in the southeastern corner of Fayette County. In October, according to the *Intelligencer*, the county commissioners advertised a sale of lots at the proposed town of Perryville, but there was probably no settlement there at the time, for the sale was to take place "at Hill's Station on Shoal creek." Pope's Bluff was projected at a site on the Kaskaskia a mile or two above the mouth of Hurricane Creek and aspired to be the capital of the state. Another paper town was Ripley, "situated on Shoal creek, a navigable stream of the Kaskaskia river, and about 33 miles from the great river Mississippi. . . . There is [sic] near this town several valuable mills, a grist mill and saw mills, which will do business nearly the whole year." The sale of lots was to take place May 30, 1818. Ripley was also a candidate for the location of the state capital. None of these places had enough settlers in 1818 to justify its being termed a village. There may have been a log courthouse and a jail and a few houses in Perryville but the establishment of Fayette County in 1821 necessitated the removal of the county seat, and the town faded away.

Chapter 4

The Pioneers

The first settlers within the limits of the present state of Illinois were Frenchmen, mainly from Canada, who, about the beginning of the eighteenth century, established themselves in a number of villages on the American bottom along the Mississippi River. During the French regime these people consisted of two classes, the *habitants*, ignorant and improvident, engaged largely in the fur trade as *voyageurs*, and the gentry, as George Rogers Clark called them, many of whom had come from the better classes in France and Canada, who had acquired considerable property, either before or after coming to Illinois, and who lived lives of refinement despite their wilderness surroundings. The disordered conditions in the Illinois country from the time of the British occupation in 1765 until about the close of the century caused nearly all the more enterprising among the French to cross the Mississippi to Spanish territory. It is doubtful if there were more than 1,500 people of French descent living in Illinois in 1818 and practically all these belonged to the *habitant* class. Most of them were natives of the country, for there had been very little immigration of Frenchmen after 1760. Besides those living in and about the towns of Cahokia, Prairie du Rocher, and Kaskaskia, there were a few on the eastern side of the territory, in what is now Lawrence County, who had crossed over the Wabash from the Vincennes settlement.[1]

A traveler from Philadelphia, who visited the villages in the

---

[1] Alvord, *Cahokia Records*, xv-xxi; Alvord, *Illinois: The Origins*, 9-12, 18. The estimates of the number of French in Illinois are usually exaggerations. One reminiscent writer states that in 1818 they comprised "nearly a fourth part of the inhabitants." Brown, "Early History of Illinois," in *Fergus Historical Series*, no. 14:82. Daniel Pope Cook asserted in 1817, however, that they made up only a tenth of the population, which would be between 3,000 and 4,000 (*Intelligencer*, November 27, 1817), while Governor Ford estimates them at "some two thousand" (*History of Illinois*, 35).

American bottom in 1819, described the residents of Cahokia
as "half French, half Indian, retaining part of the manners of
both." To him the French in general appeared "to be a wretched
set of beings. Their great-coats are made out of a blanket, with
a cap or hood out of the same piece. Then moccasins and leggins
complete the suit. Uncover a Frenchman's head and his friends
are immediately alarmed for his health. The pig pens in Pennsylvania are generally as clean and much better built than the
miserable huts occupied by these lazy people. In a state of almost starvation they hold their Gumbo balls twice a week. For
nimbleness of foot and lightness of heart the French have never
been surpassed." In Prairie du Rocher, the traveler found the
houses of

the most antique and mean appearance, built of the barks of trees
and puncheons, slabs, etc., often without doors. Their windows are
without sashes, but small pieces of broken glasses of all shapes pasted
ingeniously together with paper serve to admit the light upon a motley
family, between white, red and black. Many of those wretched hovels
are ready to tumble down on the heads of starving Indians, French and
negroes, all mixed together. Negro-French is the common language of
this town. Indeed, unless you can speak some French it is with much
difficulty you can find any person who can understand you.

The writer was given to looking on the dark side of the picture,
and in concluding his narrative, he felt it necessary to add:
"When I have expressed an opinion which appears not to have
been liberal, it is intended to apply to the lower class, of whom
there is a large majority . . . although some of the French are
rich, liberal and gentlemanly men, yet this memorandum is
strictly correct when applied to the general mass." [2]

Governor Ford, who lived in Monroe County from 1805 on,
and who was thus in a position to observe the French inhabitants, has left an excellent picture of these people as he remembered them. "The original settlers had many of them in-
termarried with the native Indians," he writes,

and some of the descendants of these partook of the wild, roving disposition of the savage, united to the politeness and courtesy of the

[2] Mason, *Narrative*, 53-56, 74.

Frenchman. In the year 1818, and for many years before, the crews of keel boats on the Ohio and Mississippi rivers were furnished from the Frenchmen of this stock. Many of them spent a great part of their time, in the spring and fall seasons, in paddling their canoes up and down the rivers and lakes in the river bottoms, on hunting excursions, in pursuit of deer, fur, and wild fowl, and generally returned home well loaded with skins, fur, and feathers, which were with them the great staples of trade. Those who stayed at home, contented themselves with cultivating a few acres of Indian corn, in their common fields, for bread, and providing a supply of prairie hay for their cattle and horses. No genuine Frenchman, in those days, ever wore a hat, cap, or coat. The heads of both men and women were covered with Madras cotton handkerchiefs, which were tied around, in the fashion of night-caps. For an upper covering of the body the men wore a blanket garment, called a "capot," (pronounced cappo) with a cap to it at the back of the neck, to be drawn over the head for a protection in cold weather, or in warm weather to be thrown back upon the shoulders in the fashion of a cape. Notwithstanding this people had been so long separated by an immense wilderness from civilized society, they still retained all the suavity and politeness of their race. And it is a remarkable fact, that the roughest hunter and boatman amongst them could at any time appear in a ballroom, or other polite and gay assembly, with the carriage and behavior of a well-bred gentleman. The French women were remarkable for the sprightliness of their conversation and the grace and elegance of their manners. And the whole population lived lives of alternate toil, pleasure, innocent amusement, and gaity.

Their horses and cattle, for want of proper care and food for many generations, had degenerated in size, but had acquired additional vigor and toughness; so that a French pony was a proverb for strength and endurance. These ponies were made to draw, sometimes one alone, sometimes two together, one hitched before the other, to the plough, or to carts made entirely of wood, the bodies of which held about double the contents of the body of a common large wheel-barrow. The oxen were yoked by the horns instead of the neck, and in this mode were made to draw the plough and cart. Nothing like reins were ever used in driving; the whip of the driver, with a handle about two feet, and a lash two yards long, stopped or guided the horse as effectually as the strongest reins.

The French houses were mostly built of hewn timber, set upright in the ground, or upon plates laid upon a wall, the intervals between the upright pieces being filled with stone and mortar. Scarcely any of them were more than one story high, with a porch on one or two sides, and sometimes all around, with low roofs extending with slopes of different steepness from the comb in the centre to the lowest part of the porch.

These houses were generally placed in gardens, surrounded by fruit-trees of apples, pears, cherries, and peaches; and in the villages each enclosure for a house and garden occupied a whole block or square, or the greater part of one. Each village had its Catholic church and priest. The church was the great place of gay resort on Sundays and holidays, and the priest was the adviser and director and companion of all his flock.

Unlike the American settlers, most of whom lived on isolated farms, the French lived close together in their village communities, where they could enjoy the society of their fellows and the privileges of their religion. Despite the abundance of land, the common field system of agriculture had been transplanted from France, and outside each village was to be found the commons of woodland and pasture for the whole village and the common field with its long narrow strips of arable land allotted to the individual inhabitants of the village. Originally the conduct of agricultural operations had been regulated by village assemblies, held usually on Sundays before the door of the church and presided over by a syndic elected by the inhabitants. By 1818, however, the influx of Americans in some of the villages and the purchase by them of allotments had introduced an element of confusion, and legislative enactments were necessary to adjust the system to the changed conditions.[3]

Forming as they did so small a proportion of the population, it is not to be expected that the French would play any considerable part in the political and economic development of Illinois. The conflict between the two elements, French and American, for the control of the Illinois country had ended a generation before 1818; and the unprogressive French, who remained in the American bottom after that contest was over, understood little of American ideals and took practically no part in the successive territorial governments.[4] Only one French name is to be found in the lists of officeholders during this period,

[3] Brown, "Early History of Illinois," in *Fergus Historical Series*, no. 14: 83; Thorpe, *Constitutions*, 2:981-982; *Laws of Illinois*, 1819, p. 122; *American State Papers, Public Lands*, 3:432; Ford, *History of Illinois*, 36-37.

[4] Alvord, *Cahokia Records*, introduction; Dunn, *Indiana*, 270.

that of Pierre Menard; and he was a recent arrival from Canada. Although their influence upon the development of the state was so slight that it may be disregarded, the French continued to form for many years a picturesque element in the population of Illinois.[5]

The American occupation of Illinois may be said to have begun with the advent of traders and land speculators from the eastern colonies during the British regime, 1765 to 1778. The occupation of the French villages by George Rogers Clark and his troops during the Revolution introduced a new element, for a number of Virginians became permanent settlers in the country. It was only very slowly that emigrants drifted in from the east during the last decade of the eighteenth century; and while there was a decided increase in population from 1800 to 1810, 2,458 to 12,282, the outbreak of Indian hostilities in 1811, followed by the War of 1812, almost completely checked immigration to the whole northwestern frontier. With the advent of peace in 1815 and the opening of the land sales in 1814 and 1816, immigration received a great impetus, and Illinois experienced her first real "boom." By this time the choice locations in Ohio, Indiana, and Kentucky had either been filled by settlers or bought up by speculators, and consequently Illinois and Missouri became a veritable promised land for immigrants. From a population of approximately 15,000 in 1815 Illinois had by midsummer of 1818 increased to a population of about 35,000, and by the end of the year she had almost if not quite 40,000. The Illinois of 1818 was, then, a very new community. Less than half the inhabitants had lived there three years, and not quite a third had been in the region as long as ten years. For only four years had it been possible to purchase government land in the territory and for only two years had such land been available to newcomers outside the Shawneetown district.[6]

Who were these people who flocked to southern Illinois in

[5] For a description of the French villages and their inhabitants in 1836, see Thwaites, *Early Western Travels*, 27:19-121.

[6] Boggess, *Settlement of Illinois*, chs. 3, 4. On the land sales see above, pp. 53-59.

such numbers in the last years of the territorial period? Where did they come from and what manner of people were they? Why did they leave their former homes and why did they select Illinois for their new home? To none of these questions can simple definite answers be given, but some evidence can be brought to bear upon them. From the schedules of the census

FLAX AND SPINNING WHEELS

of 1818, supplemented by poll lists, petitions, and other reliable records, it has been possible to compile a list of the names of 6,020 people resident in Illinois in the year 1818, nearly all of whom were heads of families.[7] From county histories and all other available sources, information about the birthplace or

[7] [See Margaret C. Norton (ed.), *Illinois Census Returns, 1810, 1818* (Illinois State Historical Library, *Collections*, vol. 24. Springfield, 1935).]

former residence of 716, or nearly 12 per cent of those thus
listed, has been secured. Generalization based upon so small a
proportion cannot be altogether reliable, but it is believed that
the figures throw some light on the antecedents of the people who
were living in Illinois in the year in which it became a state.

Combining data as to nativity with that for earliest known
residence when birthplace is unknown, it appears that 273, or
38 per cent, of those of known antecedents came from the southern states, Virginia being credited with 94, North Carolina with
84, South Carolina with 40, Georgia with 29, and Maryland with
26. Almost the same number, 267, or 37 per cent, were from the
western states. One hundred and fifty, or over half of them, came
from Kentucky; this is a larger number than is credited to any
other state. Tennessee contributed 82, Ohio 23, Indiana 9, and
Illinois 3.[8] From the middle states came 91, or 13 per cent; 47
from Pennsylvania, 36 from New York, 6 from New Jersey, and
2 from Delaware. Only 19, or 3 per cent, were from New England, Massachusetts and Vermont being credited with 6 each,
Connecticut and New Hampshire with 3 each, and Rhode Island
with 1. The remaining 66, or 9 per cent, were foreign born, 40
coming from England, 10 from Ireland, 5 each from Germany
and Canada, 4 from France, and 2 from Scotland. Including
Kentucky and Tennessee with the southern states, the totals
show that 505, or 71 per cent, came from south of Mason and
Dixon's line and the Ohio River, as compared with 142, or 20
per cent, who came from the north and northwest.

A study of the movements of individual immigrants discloses
the fact that a surprisingly large number had made one or two
other moves before coming to Illinois. If there are added to those
counted above as coming from the western states those who came
to Illinois from these states but are known to have been born
elsewhere, the total becomes 385, or 54 per cent. Of this number
only 60 are known to have been born in the west; 118 are known

[8] Obviously the proportion of 3 to 716 is too small for the native-born
if the French are taken into consideration. Very few of them are included
in the list, however, because specific information about individuals is lacking.

to have been born elsewhere: 89 in the southern states; 16 in the north; and 13 abroad. Assigning the remaining 207, whose birthplace is unknown, to the respective sections in the same proportions produces the following revised figures: from the old south, 53 per cent; from the west, 18 per cent; from the north, 18 per cent; and from abroad, 11 per cent. This may be taken as representing roughly the nativity of the 716 inhabitants of known antecedents, and therefore as an indication of the sources of the population of Illinois in 1818.

The outstanding conclusions from this investigation are: first, that about half the heads of families in Illinois in 1818 had been born in the five states of Maryland, Virginia, North and South Carolina, and Georgia; and second, that about the same proportion had come to Illinois directly from the four western states of Ohio, Indiana, Kentucky, and Tennessee, principally from the latter two. Most of the immigrants from Kentucky and Tennessee who had been born there, moreover, were descendants of natives of the old southern states. It would probably be a safe generalization, therefore, to say that two-thirds of the people of Illinois at this time belonged to southern stock, while the numbers with New England or middle states antecedents only slightly exceeded those of foreign birth. This coincides with the impression to be gained from contemporary and reminiscent writers. Two of the correspondents to the *Intelligencer* during the convention campaign indicate that, in their opinion, immigration up to that time had been principally from the southern states.[9] William H. Brown states that "the early inhabitants of Illinois were composed of the French Canadians . . . and immigrants from Kentucky, Tennessee, and North Carolina," while Governor Ford speaks of the American inhabitants as "chiefly from Kentucky, Virginia, and Pennsylvania." Reynolds states that they "were almost entirely emigrants from the Western States; Tennessee, Kentucky, Virginia, and some from Pennsylvania and Maryland." According to Robert W. Patterson, "the families in the country, were generally of Southern origin, many of them having come originally

[9] "A republican," Daniel P. Cooke, in *Intelligencer*, April 1, 1818, and "Caution," in *ibid.*, April 15, 1818.

from Virginia and the Carolinas to Tennessee, Kentucky, and Ohio, and thence to Illinois." [10] Later writers, also, have reached the same conclusion, adducing as evidence, in addition to the testimony of contemporaries, the fact that most of the political leaders during the territorial period and the early years of statehood were natives of the south.[11]

It is not a sufficient identification of these people, however, to say that they came from the south, for the south was far from being a homogeneous section. Westward of the tidewater and plantation area along the Atlantic coast was a region of uplands and mountain valleys stretching across state boundaries from Pennsylvania to Georgia, the population of which differed materially in origin and characteristics from the occupants of the tidewater section; it was from this stock that the bulk of the "southern" people in Illinois came. The evidence for this is to be found not only in the biographical and genealogical data available in the county histories, but also in the names of heads of families in the schedules of the census of 1818. A large proportion of these names are typically Scotch-Irish, Welsh, or German, with Scotch-Irish predominating; and thus they are indicative of the connection of the people with that stream of non-English immigrants which poured into Pennsylvania during the eighteenth century and thence up the valleys and through the gaps to the back country of Virginia, the Carolinas, and Georgia. By the time of the Revolution, the occupation of this region had been completed and the stream began to flow into Kentucky and Tennessee. In the early decades of the nineteenth century it progressed into southern Indiana, Illinois, and Missouri.

A striking characteristic of these people was their love of the frontier. From the time it appeared on the continent their strain had been in the vanguard of settlement. As frontier conditions

[10] Brown, "An Historical Sketch of the Early Movement in Illinois for the Legalization of Slavery," in *Fergus Historical Series*, no. 4:9; Reynolds, *My Own Times*, 65; Patterson, "Early Society in Southern Illinois," in *Fergus Historical Series*, no. 14:105.

[11] *Johns Hopkins University Studies*, 1:pt. 3, p. 9; Illinois State Historical Society, *Transactions*, 1903, p. 75; Boggess, *Settlement of Illinois*, 145; Mathews, *Expansion of New England*, 206-207.

passed away in one place, they packed up their few possessions and pushed farther into the interior. Few sons were born in the same locality that their fathers had been; few men died near where they had been born. Probably a majority of those in Illinois in 1818 had made at least one move before coming to the territory, and many, located near the border of settled area, had advanced from more southern locations within the territory. These people were true pioneers; they had become experts in grappling with frontier conditions. As Morris Birkbeck wrote of them, "to struggle with privations has now become the habit of their lives, most of them having made several successive plunges into the wilderness." [12] They blazed the trail for the more permanent settlers who were to follow; always, of course, a part of them dropped out of the procession and became permanent settlers themselves. Essentially, then, these people were westerners rather than southerners.

Neglecting to make this distinction, various writers have sought for the causes of this migration from the south to the northwest in the social and economic conditions of the south. Opposition to slavery, the pressure of the plantation system on the small farms, and the desire for social equality have been assigned as causes; and doubtless these were factors which prompted many individuals. But in general the real explanation is to be found in the irresistible attraction which the wilderness exerted upon these people. They were essentially frontiersmen; they preferred life in the woods to that in the busy haunts of men; and they felt themselves cramped and crowded in any except the most thinly populated regions. Then, too, they had a restless hope of finding something better a little farther on; they were always ready to take a sportsman's chance on the unknown. As Morris Birkbeck, the Englishman, wrote: "They are also a migrating people; and even when in prosperous circumstances, can contemplate a change of situation, which under our old establishments and fixed habits, none, but the most enterprising, would venture upon, when urged by adversity." [13] It was not

---

[12] Birkbeck, *Notes on a Journey*, 121.
[13] Birkbeck, *Notes on a Journey*, 36.

so much positive dissatisfaction with conditions existing in their old communities, then, as the force of habit and the hope of bettering themselves economically, that prompted the migration.

No description of these pioneers from the south can be adequate unless it takes into account the existence of different types among them. Although possessing some characteristics in common, even these varied in degree; and statements of contemporary writers who have a particular class in mind can not be applied indiscriminately to all the pioneers. Among the best observers of pioneer settlers were some of the leaders of the English settlement, who were careful to discriminate between the different types. Fordham divided the people on the frontier into four classes, "not perfectly distinct yet easily distinguishable." [14] To the first two of these classes belonged the bulk of the element under consideration.

1st. The hunters, a daring, hardy, race of men, who live in miserable cabins, which they fortify in times of War with the Indians, whom they hate but much resemble in dress and manners. They are unpolished, but hospitable, kind to Strangers, honest and trustworthy. They raise a little Indian corn, pumpkins, hogs, and sometimes have a Cow or two, and two or three horses belonging to each family: But their rifle is their principal means of support. They are the best marksmen in the world, and such is their dexterity that they will shoot an apple off the head of a companion. Some few use the bow and arrow. I have spent 7 or 8 weeks with these men, have had opportunities of trying them, and believe they would sooner give me the last shirt off their backs, than rob me of a charge of powder. Their wars with the Indians have made them vindictive. This class cannot be called first Settlers, for they move every year or two.

2d class. First settlers;—a mixed set of hunters and farmers. They possess more property and comforts than the first class, yet they are a half barbarous race. They follow the range pretty much; selling out when the Country begins to be well settled, and their cattle cannot be entirely kept in the woods.

The description and classification of these people by George Flower is especially interesting. "These original backwoodsmen," he writes, "look upon all new-comers as obtruders on their especial manorial rights. The old hunters' rule is: when you hear

[14] Ogg, *Fordham's Personal Narrative*, 125.

the sound of a neighbor's gun, it is time to move away." He found "all of this class of men, who live in solitude and commune so much with nature, relying on their own efforts to support themselves and their families, to be calm, deliberate, and self-possessed whenever they are sober. The best breeding in society could not impart to them more self-possession or give them greater ease of manner or more dignified and courteous bearing." Flower acknowledges the services of representatives of this class to the English settlers: "Dextrous with the ax, they built all our first log-cabins, and supplied us with venison. In a year or two, they moved into less-peopled regions, or to where there were no people at all, and were entirely lost to this part of the country." These men derived their means of livelihood principally from hunting, and devoted very little attention to farming. Some, however, says Flower, "follow a different destiny. Their little corn-patch increases to a field, their first shanty to a small log-house, which, in turn, gives place to a double-cabin, in which the loom and spinning-wheel are installed. A well and a few fruit-trees after a time complete the improvement. Moderate in their aspirations, they soon arrive at the summit of their desires." [15]

A more systematic account of the classes of settlers in the west is given by James Flint, a Scotch economist with keen powers of observation and analysis, who traveled in the west during 1818, 1819, and 1820:

All who have paid attention to the progress of new settlements, agree in stating, that the first possession of the woods in America, was taken by a class of hunters, commonly called backwoodsmen. . . . The improvements of a backwoodsman are usually confined to building a rude log cabin, clearing and fencing a small piece of ground for raising Indian corn. A horse, a cow, a few hogs, and some poultry, comprise his livestock; and his farther operations are performed with his rifle. The formation of a settlement in his neighbourhood is hurtful to the success of his favourite pursuit, and is the signal for his removing into more remote parts of the wilderness. In the case of his owning the land on which he has settled, he is contented to sell it at a low price, and his establishment, though trifling, adds much to the comfort of his successor. The next class of settlers differ from the former in having considerably less

---

[15] Flower, *English Settlement*, 67-72.

dependence on the killing of game, in remaining in the midst of a growing population, and in devoting themselves more to agriculture. A man
of this class proceeds on a small capital; he either enlarges the clearings
begun in the woods by his backwoodsmen predecessor, or establishes
himself on a new site. . . . The settler of the grade under consideration,
is only able to bring a small portion of his land into cultivation, his success, therefore, does not so much depend on the quantity of produce
which he raises, as on the gradual increase in the value of his property.
When the neighbourhood becomes more populous, he in general has it
in his power to sell his property at a high price, and to remove to a new
settlement, where he can purchase a more extensive tract of land, or
commence farming on a larger scale than formerly. The next occupier
is a capitalist, who immediately builds a larger barn than the former,
and then a brick or a frame house. He either pulls down the dwelling of
his predecessor, or converts it into a stable. He erects better fences, and
enlarges the quantity of cultivated land; sows down pasture fields, in-
troduces an improved stock of horses, cattle, sheep, and these probably
of the Merino breed. He fattens cattle for the market, and perhaps
erects a flour-mill, or a saw-mill, or a distillery. Farmers of this description are frequently partners in the banks; members of the State assembly, or of Congress, or Justices of the Peace. . . . The three conditions
of settlers described, are not to be understood as uniformly distinct;
for there are intermediate stages, from which individuals of one class
pass, as it were, into another. The first invaders of the forest frequently
become farmers of the second order; and there are examples of individuals acting their parts in all the three gradations.[16]

While it is true that some of the backwoodsmen or their descendants occasionally became men of prominence and of influence in the community, as a rule the leaders in the movements
for the political and economic development of the territory belonged to a different class. The majority of them were southerners also, but their antecedents went back usually to the planter
class of the tidewater region. As was the case with the frontiersmen, many of them had lived in Kentucky, Tennessee, or Indiana, before locating in Illinois. A few migrated because of a dis-
like of the institution of slavery, many were brought in to fill
appointive offices during the territorial period, others sought opportunity for political advancement and the practice of their
professions in a new country, while all of them expected to make

[16] Thwaites, *Early Western Travels*, 9:232-233, 235-236.

fortunes by speculating in land. A smaller number of the leaders were from the middle states and New England and their influence was slowly increasing. These men of influence were usually fairly well educated and possessed of a moderate amount of property; but, above all, they were ambitious for themselves and for the country. They formed the third group of Fordham's classifi-

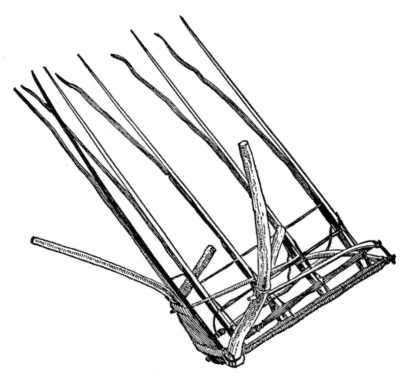

GRAIN CRADLE

cation—"composed of enterprising men from Kentucky and the Atlantic States. This class consists of Young Doctors, Lawyers, Storekeepers, farmers, mechanics, &c., who found towns, trade, speculate in land, and begin the fabric of Society." [17] Most of them lived in or near one of the land office towns, Kaskaskia, Shawneetown, or Edwardsville, but a few were to be found located in the smaller settlements.

Besides the settlers of German antecedents who had come to Illinois by way of the south, there were a number of Germans who had come directly from Pennsylvania. One early writer, indeed, classified the settlers as "French, Pennsylvania Dutch and native American." As a matter of fact the French and the "Dutch" were practically all native-born Americans, but the classification is a rather significant commentary on those Germans who, by isolating themselves, kept for so long their peculiar characteristics. Even when they migrated to Illinois they manifested a tendency to keep together. The principal settlement of Pennsylvania Germans was in and near Brownsville in Jackson County, where Dr. Conrad Will, their leading representative, established himself in 1815. A number of families from Somerset County, Pennsylvania, came under the leadership of Singleton Kimmel in 1817; and John Ankeny, a relative of Kimmel, brought out eight or ten families early in 1818. Of these people, the writer before referred to says: "They were industrious, though not enterprising people, usually farmers of moderate means, who lived comfortably, and kept their associations mainly among themselves." [18] As for the real foreigners, there were a few scattered in all parts of the settled area. With the exception of the English, who will be considered later, they had

[17] Fordham lists a fourth class, also, not clearly distinguishable from the third: "old settlers, rich, independent, farmers, wealthy merchants, possessing a good deal of information, a knowledge of the world, and an enterprising spirit. Such are the Ohio men, Western Pennsylvanians, Kentuckians and Tennessee men. . . . They undertake with facility, and carry on with unconquerable ardour, any business or speculation that promises great profit, and sustain the greatest losses with a firmness that resembles indifference." Ogg, *Fordham's Personal Narrative*, 126.

[18] Patterson, "Early Society in Southern Illinois," in *Fergus Historical Series*, no. 14:104; Illinois State Historical Society, *Transactions*, 1905, pp. 351-377; P. Kimmel to Pope, December 22, 1817, in United States State Department, Bureau of Indexes and Archives, Miscellaneous Letters.

generally been in America for some time before coming to Illinois; and being mainly Scotch-Irish and Germans, they were scarcely distinguishable from the frontiersmen already described. Robert Reynolds, for example, emigrated from Ireland to Pennsylvania in 1785, moved to Tennessee in 1788, and from there to Illinois in 1800. George Barnsback came from Germany to America in 1797, and had lived in Philadelphia and in Kentucky before moving to Illinois in 1809.[19]

The closing years of the territorial period saw the beginning of a settlement of foreigners that was unique not only in Illinois but in the whole west—the English settlement in Edwards County. The men who planned this enterprise, selected the site, directed the emigration, and established the settlement were George Flower and Morris Birkbeck. Men of education and means, their purpose was partly philanthropic—to provide better opportunities for English laborers. Economic and political conditions in England following the close of the Napoleonic wars were such that emigration to the United States began to assume large proportions and these men planned to point the way for their countrymen and to assist them in establishing themselves in the new world. The reasons which led them, after a careful survey of the United States, to select the prairie land between Bon Pas Creek and the Little Wabash River for their place of settlement are of considerable interest.

When Morris Birkbeck arrived in the United States in May, 1817, he had made up his mind to locate in western Pennsylvania, Ohio, Indiana, or Illinois; farther north he would not go because of the climate, and the south had no attractions for him because of his abhorrence of the institution of slavery.[20] In Richmond, Virginia, Birkbeck was joined by Flower, who had been traveling in the United States for about a year; and the two men, accompanied by Birkbeck's family, started on a tour of

[19] Reynolds, *My Own Times*, 6-7, 24, 31; *Illustrated Encyclopedia of Madison County*, 47.

[20] Birkbeck, *Notes on a Journey*, 6-7.

exploration to the west.[21] The rough conditions of the frontier had no such attraction for the English emigrants as they had for the American pioneers, but the opportunity to purchase land in unlimited quantities at a low price appealed to them very much. Land ownership was the measure of social and political position in England; and, to Birkbeck and Flower, who although men of considerable means had in England only been tenants of their farms on long-time leases, the possibility of possessing large estates of their own had been one of the principal reasons for their coming to America. The prospect of more liberal political institutions held forth considerable attractions, especially to Birkbeck, but the leading motive in the formation of the settlement was the desire to enjoy not so much the political liberty of the United States as the liberty to be "found in its great space and small population. Good land dog-cheap everywhere, and for nothing, if you will go far enough for it." [22]

The part which the land situation played in inducing Flower and Birkbeck to select a site on the frontier in Illinois instead of in one of the more settled states to the eastward is explained by Birkbeck in a letter written in November, 1817, a few months after the decision had been made. "Had we remained in the state of Ohio," he wrote,

we must have paid from twenty to fifty dollars per acre for land which is technically called "improved," but is in fact deteriorated; or have purchased, at an advance of 1000 or 1500 per cent. unimproved land from speculators: and in either case should have laboured under the inconvenience of settling detached from society of our own choice, and without the advantage of choice as to soil or situation. We saw many eligible sites and fine tracts of country, but these were precisely the sites and the tracts which had secured the attachment of their possessors.

It was in fact impossible to obtain for ourselves a good position, and the neighbourhood of our friends, in the state of Ohio, at a price which

[21] For accounts of this tour, see Birkbeck, *Notes on a Journey*; Flower, *English Settlement*, ch. 3. Elias Pym Fordham, a cousin of Flower, joined the party at Cincinnati. Ogg, *Fordham's Personal Narrative*, 94-99.

[22] Flower, *English Settlement*, 29. See also Birkbeck, *Letters from Illinois*, 46-50; Ogg, *Fordham's Personal Narrative*, 122, 226; Thwaites, *Early Western Travels.* 9:174; 11:231.

common prudence would justify, or indeed at *any* price. Having given up the Ohio, we found nothing attractive on the eastern side of Indiana; and situations to the south, on the Ohio river bounding that state, were so well culled as to be in the predicament above described; offering no room for us without great sacrifices of money and society. The western side of Indiana, on the banks of the Wabash, is liable to the same and other objections. The northern part of Indiana is still in possession of the Indians.

But a few miles farther west opened our way into a country preferable in itself to any we had seen, where we could choose for ourselves, and to which we could invite our friends; and where, in regard to communication with Europe, we could command equal facilities, and foresee greater, than in the state of Ohio, being so much nearer the grand outlet at New Orleans.[23]

The amount and cheapness of available land was a motive in bringing American settlers as well as the English to Illinois; but there was another motive, more idealistic, which influenced the English much more than the Americans—the desire to locate on prairie land. George Flower was especially attracted by the prairies. When traveling in the west in 1816 he sought diligently for information about them. "I had read of them in Imlay's work," [24] he says,

and his vivid description had struck me forcibly. All the country that I had passed through was heavily timbered. I shrank from the idea of settling in the midst of a wood of heavy timber, to hack and hew my way to a little farm, ever bounded by a wall of gloomy forest. . . . It was at Governor Shelby's house [in Kentucky] that I met the first person who confirmed me in the existence of the prairies. It was Mr. Shelby's brother. He had just come from some point on the Mississippi, across the prairies of Illinois to the Ohio River, about Shawneetown.

This was enough; I felt assured of where they were, and that, when sought for, they could be found. It was then too late in the season for me to go to explore them.[25]

The following spring when Flower met Birkbeck, he led the party without hesitation or deviation toward the prairies of his vision. Romantic as it may appear, this longing of Flower's for the open

[23] Birkbeck, *Letters from Illinois*, 18-19.

[24] The first edition of Imlay's *Topographical Description of the Western Territory of North America* was published in London in 1792.

[25] Flower, *English Settlement*, 36, 38.

prairies which he had never seen was to have a very practical effect on the development of Illinois. The American settlers had shunned the prairie partly because of their belief that the best land was to be found where the tallest timber grew and partly because of a number of real obstacles such as the lack of water, lack of wood for buildings, fences, fuel, and difficulties of transportation. These men, with their larger means, were able to overcome some of these difficulties and to demonstrate the value of prairie land for farming.

Knowing how his imagination had been stirred, one can share with Flower the adventure of his first sight of the prairies in reality. Having established the rest of the party temporarily at Princeton in Indiana, Birkbeck, Flower, and one of the former's sons "mounted again, determined to find these ever-receding prairies." Crossing the Wabash near New Harmony, they came first to "the settlement of the Big-Prairie. . . . It was being settled exclusively by small corn-farmers from the slave-states. This prairie, not more than six miles long and two broad, was level, rather pondy, and aguish. Its verdure and open space was grateful to the eye, but it did not fulfil our expectations." Inquiring "the way to the Boltenhouse Prairie, so-called from the name of a man who had built a small cabin on its edge, near the spot where his brother had been killed by the Indians the year before," they were directed to follow a light trail through the woods, which they did

for seven mortal hours . . . in doubt and difficulty.

Bruised by the brushwood and exhausted by the extreme heat we almost despaired, when a small cabin and a low fence greeted our eyes. A few steps more, and a beautiful prairie suddenly opened to our view. At first, we only received the impressions of its general beauty. With longer gaze, all its distinctive features were revealed, lying in profound repose under the warm light of an afternoon's summer sun. Its indented and irregular outline of wood, its varied surface interspersed with clumps of oaks of centuries' growth, its tall grass, with seed stalks from six to ten feet high, like tall and slender reeds waving in a gentle breeze, the whole presenting a magnificence of park-scenery, complete from the hand of Nature, and unrivalled by the same sort of scenery by European art. For once, the reality came up to the picture of imagination. Our station was in the wood, on rising ground; from it, a descent of

about a hundred yards to the valley of the prairie, about a-quarter of a
mile wide, extending to the base of the majestic slope, rising upward
for a full half-mile, crowned by groves of noble oaks. A little to the left,
the eye wandered up a long stretch of prairie for three miles, into which
projected hills and slopes, covered with rich grass and decorated with
compact clumps of full-grown trees, from four to eight in each clump.
From beneath the broken shade of the wood, with our arms raised above
our brows, we gazed long and steadily, drinking in the beauties of the
scene which had been so long the object of our search.

After spending several days exploring the prairies, they started
on the return journey to Princeton. "Before leaving Illinois, night
overtook us," continues Flower.

We halted by the side of a fallen log, at a point of timber that stretched
into the prairie. A fire being kindled, we sat down on the grass, talked
over and decided what was to be done. . . . The result of our decision
was this:—After clubbing together all the money we could then command, Mr. Birkbeck was to go to Shawneetown and enter all the woodland around the Boltenhouse Prairie. We had not money enough with
us to purchase the whole prairie. I was to return to England to remit
him money as soon as possible, take with me and publish the manuscript
of his book containing the record of our journey from Richmond to the
prairies; bring out my father's family; and spread the information;
point out the road to it; and facilitate emigration generally. He was on
the home department to purchase more land and make the necessary
preparations in building. I on the foreign mission, to bring in the people.
As will be seen hereafter, he did his duty and I did mine.[26]

The first purchase of land for the settlement was made at
Shawneetown before Flower left for England; the tract bought
consisted of about 3,000 acres. During 1817 and 1818 Birkbeck
entered 41¼ sections, or 26,400 acres in all; and Flower, after
his return, also made additional purchases. Not having sufficient
funds available at first to enter all the land desired for the settlement, and fearing extensive purchases by speculators, which
would defeat the purposes of the project, Birkbeck determined to
apply to Congress for a "grant by purchase" of a large tract of
land in the unsurveyed district beyond the base line, which ran
only six miles north of the first purchases. His memorial, dated
November 20, 1817, set forth "that a number of his Countrymen,

[26] Flower, *English Settlement*, 60-74.

chiefly Yeomen, Farmers, Farming labourers, and rural Mechanics are desirous of removing with their families And Capital into
this Country, provided that, by having situations prepared for
them, they might escape the wearisome & expensive travel in
quest of a settlement which has broken the Spirits & drained the
purses of many of their emigrant brethren, terminating too frequently in disappointment." No reference was made in the memorial to amount of land or terms of purchase, but it appears
from correspondence between Birkbeck and Nathaniel Pope, the
territorial delegate, that what was desired was the privilege of
purchasing so much as might be needed for the purpose, "not exceeding twenty, thirty, or forty thousand acres," at the minimum
price and with "such an extension of time of payment as might
preclude embarrassment or disappointment." The proposition
failed to meet with the approval of Congress, however, for it was
felt that such grants would be "liable to be abused by speculators," and that it was not desirable "to encourage the settlement
of foreigners in distinct masses." The leaders were obliged to
content themselves, therefore, with making plans for the reception of their countrymen "on a contracted scale." [27]

In the spring of 1818 Birkbeck moved his family from Princeton to the new home on the prairie. His *Notes on a Journey* had
been published in Philadelphia as well as in London, and coming
to the hands of a number of English people already in this country, induced them to join him. By June the colony contained,
according to Fordham, "between 40 and 50 persons, besides
American settlers in the neighbourhood"; and Birkbeck was having difficulty in getting cabins erected by the backwoodsmen
rapidly enough to supply the demand.

Flower started his first party from England in March, 1818.
It consisted of

forty-four men and one married woman. . . . The men were chiefly farm-
laborers and mechanics from Surrey. Many of them had for years

[27] The chief authorities for the English settlement of Edwards County
are Flower, *English Settlement*, Ogg, *Fordham's Personal Narrative*, Birkbeck, *Letters from Illinois*, and land records, auditor's office, Springfield.
The memorial is in Birkbeck, *Letters from Illinois*, 147-149.

worked for Mr. Birkbeck, others were from his neighborhood, and were either personally acquainted or knew him by reputation. This party was under the especial care and leadership of Mr. Trimmer. Another party, of about equal number, composed of London mechanics, and tradesmen from various parts of England formed another party that sailed in the same ship. These were under the guidance and direction of Mr. James Lawrence, merchant tailor, of Hatton Garden, London. Neither Mr. Lawrence nor any one of his party had any personal acquaintance with either Mr. Birkbeck or myself, but received their impulse from our published expositions.

According to Flower's account these parties arrived at Shawneetown in August, but it must have been late in July for the names of both Trimmer and Lawrence appear in the schedule for the additional census of Gallatin County, which was closed July 28. Trimmer appears in the schedule as the head of a family of 50, 30 of whom were entered as men over 21. Only eight men are credited to Lawrence, which may indicate that some of the mechanics and tradesmen had remained in the east, although some of them may have been entered under their own names.

These first parties, says Flower, included only three women, but his own party of "three score and more," which sailed in April in a chartered ship, contained a number of families. All the spare room on the deck of the ship was occupied by Flower's "live-stock of cows, hogs, and sheep, of the choicest breeds of England." This was doubtless the party referred to in the following item from a New York paper: "We learn that a gentleman has lately arrived in this city from England, whose object is to settle in the Illinois territory—that his family and settlers brought over with him amount to fifty-one persons—that he has furnished himself with agricultural instruments, seeds of various kinds, some cows, sheep and hogs, for breeding, and about 100,-000 pounds sterling in money." [28]

In October, Fordham wrote: "We have now 200 English on our Settlement. Many are discontented; but the strong-minded regret that they did not come out sooner." In August, when the first shipload arrived, "the village of Wanborough was laid off by Mr. Birkbeck in five-acre lots. On these were built cabins, rented

[28] Flower, *English Settlement*, 95-102; *Niles' Weekly Register*, 14:256.

by some, bought by others. A good ox-mill and blacksmith's-shop were soon after added to the village." Flower gives a graphic description of the development of the settlement and of the founding, in October, of a village which grew into a town:

Emigrants were continually flowing in. They first visited Mr. Birkbeck, who had but small accommodations; then came to me, who, at that time, had still less. At this stage, we were experiencing many of the inconveniences of a population in the wilderness, in advance of necessary food and shelter. Do as you will, if you are the very first in the wilderness, there are many inconveniences, privations, hardships, and sufferings that can not be avoided. My own family, one day, were so close run for provisions, that a dish of the tenderest buds and shoots of the hazle was our only resort.

Mr. Lawrence and Mr. Trimmer, who led the first shipload, made their settlement in the Village Prairie, a beautiful and extensive prairie, so-called from the Piankeshaw Indians, there formerly located. It was situated due north of my cabin in the Boltenhouse Prairie, about three miles, the intervening space covered by timber and underbrush, untouched by the hand of man. Emigrants kept coming in, some on foot, some on horseback, and some in wagons. Some sought employment, and took up with such labor as they could find. Others struck out and made small beginnings for themselves. Some, with feelings of petulence, went farther and fared worse; others dropped back into the towns and settlements in Indiana. At first, I had as much as I could do to build a few cabins for the workmen I then employed, and in erecting a large farm-yard, a hundred feet square, enclosed by log-buildings, two stories high; also in building for my father's family a house of considerable size, and appointed with somewhat more of comforts than is generally found in new settlements, to be ready for their reception on the following summer. I had as yet done nothing in erecting buildings for the public in general, as there had been no time. One evening Mr. Lawrence, Mr. Ronalds, and I think, Mr. Fordham, called at my cabin, and, after their horses were cared for and supper over, we discussed the measures that should be taken to form some village or town, as a centre for those useful arts necessary to agriculture. Every person wanted the services of a carpenter and blacksmith. But every farmer could not build workshops at his own door. Daylight ceased, darkness followed. We had no candles, nor any means of making artificial light. On a pallet, mattress, or blanket, each one took to his couch, and carried on the discussion. After much talk, we decided that what we did do should be done in order, and with a view to the future settlement, as well as our own present convenience. The tract of forest lying between Mr. Lawrence's settlement in the Village Prairie, on its southern border, and mine at the north of the Boltenhouse Prairie, was about three-and-a-half miles through. Somewhere in the centre of this tract of woodland seemed to be the place. To the right of this spot, eastward, lay, about a mile distant, several prairies running north and south for many miles, and others east and west to the Bonpas Creek, from three to five miles distant. North-eastward from Mr. Lawrence's cabin, prairies of every form and size continued on indefinitely. About two miles west, and beyond Wanborough, were numerous small and fertile prairies, extending to the Little Wabash, from six to ten miles distant. On the south was my own beautiful prairie. Thus the spot for our town in a central situation was decided upon. Now for a name. We were long at fault. At last we did what almost all emigrants do, pitched on a name that had its association with the land of our birth. Albion was then and there located, built, and peopled in imagination. We dropped off, one by one, to sleep, to confirm in dreams the wanderings of our waking fancies.[29]

The English settlement in 1818 was too young and too much occupied with its own problems to exert any considerable influence upon the affairs of the territory and state, but its influence was destined to be very considerable in later years. The leaders were men of superior intelligence and education and took an active share in public life. Especially in the struggle over the admission of slavery in 1823 and 1824 their influence was to be felt on the side of freedom. The settlement was destined to promote also the agricultural development of the state. The leaders were well instructed in the theory and practice of agriculture, and the farmers whom they brought over were "accustomed to continuous labor." Their capital enabled them to carry on operations on a scale hitherto unknown upon the frontier, and the blooded stock which they introduced was a valuable asset to the community. The English settlement, moreover, was to give to Illinois unlimited advertising, not only in England, but on the continent and in the United States as well.

Eleven editions in English of Birkbeck's *Notes on a Journey* were issued during 1817, 1818, and 1819 in Philadelphia, London, Dublin, and Cork, while a German translation was published at Jena in 1818. His *Letters from Illinois* were published in seven

[29] Ogg, *Fordham's Personal Narrative*, 236; Flower, *English Settlement*, 100, 124-126, 130.

editions in English in 1818, and the following year were trans-
lated into both French and German. Birkbeck wrote a number
of other pamphlets containing advice to emigrants, and several
of the other members of the settlement published accounts of
their experiences. Nearly all the foreign travelers who made
tours of the United States during the years 1818 to 1820 visited
the settlement and published accounts of it in their books. Some
of these were unfavorable, and an extensive literary controversy
followed in which the leading English and American reviews
participated.[30] All this served to call attention not only to the
settlement itself but to Illinois and the west as a whole, and undoubtedly helped to promote emigration both from abroad and
from the eastern states.

[30] See Buck, *Travel and Description of Illinois*, 58-91 *passim*, for biblio-
graphical notes on these publications.

Chapter 5

The Economic Situation

The industrial development of a region on the frontier has always depended to a very large extent on its facilities for transportation. In recent times the settlement of the western plains has followed the lines of the pioneer railroads, usually resisting every attempt to deflect it to regions not traversed by them. When the Mississippi valley was first settled, however, the railroads had not yet begun to play their part as a major economic factor; and accordingly it was the waterways, as offering an obvious and easy means of communication, which exerted the most decisive influence upon the early settlement and development of the middle west.

Illinois in particular owed much to her abundance of navigable streams. With an easy means of communication between the Great Lakes and the Gulf of Mexico by way of the Illinois River and its tributaries, and in touch with the east by way of the Ohio, the Illinois country occupied a strategic position in relation to the outside world. In the interior, the Illinois, the Wabash, and the Kaskaskia, with their numerous tributaries, afforded unusually good transportation facilities; even such lesser streams as the Little Wabash, the Embarras, the Big Muddy, and some of the so-called creeks could be navigated by the barges, flatboats, arks, and keelboats in use on the western waters. As has already been indicated, the first settlers naturally located along these waterways; had it not been for the considerable number of streams, the country could never have been developed as rapidly as it was.

The era of the steamboat, destined to bring about a great increase in the speed and reduction in the cost of transportation, was just beginning at the time when Illinois became a state. The first steamboat trip down the Ohio and Mississippi was in 1811, but not until four years later was the first trip up the river to Louisville accomplished, while August 2, 1817, was the date of the first arrival at St. Louis. The following January, however, Morris Birkbeck reported: "Steam-boats already navigate the Wabash: a vessel of that description has this winter made its way up from New Orleans to within a few miles of our settlement. They are about building one at Harmony." Two months later he wrote to a prospective emigrant: "Your voyage up from New Orleans, by steam, will be about a month. Steam-boats are passing continually. A gentleman who is just come down the Ohio, saw ten new ones on the stocks at different ports of the river." [1]

Important as was river transportation, especially as regards connection with the outside world, the improvement of facilities for travel and transportation on land was also necessary for the development of the territory and state. Often the distance from point to point by water was several times as great as that by land, while much of the most desirable land lay in the interior between the streams. From early territorial times travelers and emigrants had made their way overland from various points on the Ohio to the settlements on the Mississippi, and by 1818 a number of main lines of travel were clearly marked out. The earlier route from Fort Massac, a short distance below the mouth of the Tennessee, to Kaskaskia had been largely superseded by the roads leading from Golconda and Shawneetown to the capital. From Kaskaskia northward an old road wound up the American bottom through Prairie du Rocher and Cahokia to Illinoistown opposite St. Louis and to the mouth of the Wood River. The rapid growth of the country north of Kaskaskia, in St. Clair and Madison counties, led to the development of a direct route of travel from Shawneetown through Carlyle to Edwardsville and Alton, to which was given the name "Goshen Road." From Vincennes to St. Louis ran another trail which joined the Goshen road near Carlyle and coincided with it for a few miles; and a branch of this Vincennes road, leaving the main line near the center of the state, led southwestwardly to Kaskaskia. Other important lines of travel were from Shawnee-

---

[1] Birkbeck, *Letters from Illinois*, 55, 113; Preble, *History of Steam Navigation*, 66-72.

town northward through Carmi to the English settlement and from Kaskaskia by way of Belleville to Edwardsville.

Although there was considerable travel on these main routes during certain seasons of the year, they were in the main little more than trails worn by use. They were made, as George Flower expresses it, "by one man on horseback following in the track of another, every rider making the way a little easier to find, until you came to some slush, or swampy place, where all trace was lost, and you got through as others had done, by guessing at the direction, often riding at hazard for miles until you stumbled on the track again." To guide the traveler through the wilderness, "the tracks or roads from one settlement to another in the woods, are marked by one notch in the bark of the trees for a foot-path, two for a bridle-road, and three for a waggon route." [2]

The need of improvement was obvious, but efforts directed toward making better roads had many practical difficulties to overcome. At the very first session of the territorial legislature in December, 1812, Congress was appealed to for an appropriation "to open a road from Shawneetown on the Ohio river to the Saline and from thence, the most direct way, to Kaskaskia." [3] Two years later an attempt was made in the lower house of the legislature to provide for the laying out of a number of main highways at the expense of the territory. Although the bill for this purpose was "postponed untill next Session of the Legislature," it is significant for the information which it contains as to prevailing conditions and as to the roads desired.[4] It reads:

Whereas it is essential to the prosperity of this Territory that Roads should be laid out & established thro' the same in such directions as will tend most effectually to facilitate & render more safe the intercourse between the two populous extremes of the same.

And whereas a Road from the Ohio Saline to Kaskaskia the nearest & best rout and one from this to begin at a point on the West side of Little Muddy & to run the nearest and best rout to the Court-House

[2] Flower, *English Settlement*, 120; Harris, *Remarks Made During a Tour*, 139; see also Thwaites, *Early Western Travels*, 10:260.

[3] James, *Territorial Records*, 119.

[4] Original in Miscellaneous Assembly Papers, secretary of state's office.

of S'Clair County at Bellville & also one from Lusk's Ferry [5] on the Ohio to intersect the Road leading from the Saline to Kaskaskia at a point to be ascertain'd & fix'd upon by the Viewers would be of the utmost importance to the Country & greatly advantageous to the People of the Territory & those moving to & through the same.

The many advantages resulting from this measure are obvious— Instead of a Wilderness of nearly one hundred Miles thro' which the present intercourse is carried—of the bad roads which in the wet season of the year are rendered impassable—Rafting or swimming the several turbulent streams which often extend some miles beyond their Beds—of being obliged to encamp for Weeks in woods, wanting often the necessary Sustenance for Man & Horse—these several established routs would ere long be found crouded with Farms on each side—Ferrys & Toll Bridges established—provisions for Travellers in abundance—& all the difficulties & obstacles greatly lessened or entirely removed and would render the conveyance of the mails—the marching of Troops from one populous extreme of the Terr^y to the other—the conveyance of Salt more safe easy & less expensive—To the end therefore that the best ground may be selected on or as near these several Routs as the ground will admit of & to the end also that these may be permanently established & opened either as Turnpikes or otherwise by the proper authority   Be it Enacted that Philip Trammil Enock Moore & Thomas Jordan be and are hereby appointed viewers with Power & authority to proceed to view & select the ground most suitable, & cause a survey to be made of the same & to note the obstacles that may present themselves on the several Routs which, together with their opinion of the probable sum necessary for opening the said Roads, the said viewers shall report to the Legislature at the Commencement of their next Session.

Nothing further is heard of this territorial project, but in April, 1816, Congress passed "An Act to authorize the surveying and making a road in the territory of Illinois," which led ultimately to a material improvement of the facilities for travel between Shawneetown and Kaskaskia. Commissioners were to be appointed by the President to "explore, survey, and mark in the most eligible course, a road" between these two places, and $8,000 was appropriated for the expense of opening and marking the road in such manner as the President might direct. On February 5, 1817, the *Intelligencer* reported that the commissioners had completed their survey of the road.

[5] Golconda.

They have taken it from where it at present runs for the longest part of the distance, by doing which they have formed as they state themselves an infinitely better road and have shortened the distance about eighteen miles. At the crossing of all those streams between the Saline and Kaskaskia in the neighborhood of which, so many difficulties were presented in consequence of the marches and quagmires, the present rout will be entirely exempt from them. . . . It is expected that the road will be opened in the spring—and so soon as there are houses of entertainment established on it, it will no doubt be traveled by every person.

The expectation that the new road would soon be opened was not fulfilled. The summer and autumn of 1817 passed without further developments and on November 6 the *Intelligencer* declared:

It is to be regretted very much that the road has not been opened, or the old one improved,—families coming to the country have been detained a week by high water and muddy roads, which is extremely discouraging to emigrants. Had not the $8,000 better be laid out in erecting bridges and improving the old road? That sum properly expended on the old road would make it one of the best roads in the western country. Unless the new road is completed or the other improved, it will almost be impossible for waggons to travel it, as it is becoming worse and worse every day, and especially at this season of the year.

Finally in the following April, two years after the passage of the act, announcement was made that the survey had received the approval of the President, and in August proposals were invited "for Cutting and Clearing out the road as laid out by the commissioners, from Kaskaskia to Demint's[6] a distance of about 50 miles. The road to be cut 33 feet wide and all the timber taken off, the stumps to be very low." The progress of the work during the fall and winter is described by Governor Bond in a communication to the legislature delivered March 4, 1819. "It has been ascertained," he wrote,

that the appropriations made by congress for laying off and completing a road from Shawneetown to Kaskaskia, will not be sufficient for the completion of that object.

[6] This was where the road crossed the Big Muddy in the southwestern part of what is now Franklin County. *Intelligencer*, August 5, 1818.

The road has been cut out, and the timber removed from a part thereof. And it is believed that with the money yet remaining, the road can be made passible, with this exception; the principal creeks and rivers between Kaskaskia and Muddy river, cannot be bridged without an additional appropriation.

From the information I have received, it is not probable that a further grant of money will be made by Congress for the purpose.

I therefore, recommend the propriety of passing a law authorising the building of toll bridges over such creeks and rivers by individuals.

The legislature decided that no legislation was necessary as the county commissioners already had authority to grant such privileges.

Particular interest attaches to the road from Vincennes to St. Louis because for a considerable distance it lay beyond the frontier of survey and itself marked the frontier line of extreme settlement. This was just becoming an established route of travel in 1818. Three years earlier Edward Coles had been "assured at Vincennes that there were no houses of accommodation on the way, and moreover, that it was not safe from Indian massacre, to go from there directly west to St. Louis, but that I would have to go by way of Shawneetown and Kaskaskia." [7] By 1817, however, there was a "trace" across the prairies but "to ride that alone was then thought to be a perilous affair." [8] Two years later it was still considered "a perilous affair" to travel the route alone but the danger appears to have been less from Indians than from white men. There were at that time some six or more road houses along the way between the Embarras River on the east and the Kaskaskia on the west, the limits of settlement; but the hospitality of some of these appears to have been of a very dubious character. An eastern tenderfoot, who made the trip in 1819, gives an account of his experiences, which were so startling that it would be difficult to regard his story as anything but pure fiction, were it not for corroborative evidence.[9]

[7] Illinois State Historical Society, *Journal*, 3:no. 3, p. 62.

[8] Flower, *English Settlement*, 53.

[9] Mason, *Narrative*, 40-50; *History of Wayne and Clay Counties*, 428; Dana, *Geographical Sketches*, 310.

This traveler, Richard Lee Mason by name,

obtained a list of cutthroats and murderers, whose names are as follows on the list: Gatewood, Rutherford, Grimberry, Cain, Young, Portlethwaite, etc. This chain of villains extended for eighty miles through all the dreary and lonesome prairies. We were informed that when they were not engaged in robbing or murdering they were very industriously employed in manufacturing bank notes, which they imposed on travelers at every opportunity. It may be worthy of remark that all the country for forty miles around where these banditti have taken possession belongs to the United States. For the convenience of travelers, a new road has been made through this country, instead of going by Shawneetown, and those villains have posted themselves along the road under the name of tavernkeepers, watching for their prey whenever it may pass. Indeed, I conceive it impossible for any man who has cash enough to make him worth killing to travel this road alone. Called to see Gatewood, the first man on the list of cutthroats. He was from home. Saw his wife, a handsome, young dejected-looking woman, who appeared very uneasy at her husband's being inquired for by a man almost as well armed and not much out of the style of Robinson Crusoe. Saw a bloody cravat on the end of the log of which his house was built. We intend to call and see the balance of the fraternity out of curiosity. . . . Crossed a prairie twelve miles broad and arrived at the house of Rutherford, the second man on the cutthroat list. We had time enough to pass this house, but having a list of desperados, and being disappointed in seeing Gatewood, curiosity induced us to spend the night. This was a piece of comedy for information which was near ending in tragedy. Our traveling party consisted of four persons, Dr. Hill, myself and two young men, strangers, from Kentucky. As we traveled in a little carriage, and with a pair of horses, we placed our fellow-travelers' baggage with our own, which made a considerable show. On our arrival a man dressed like a Quaker pretended to be hostler until he ascertained the quantity of our baggage. I recognized him as an engraver from Philadelphia, who had been a candidate for the penitentiary for forgery. We called for the landlord, and were informed by Mrs. Rutherford that he was from home, but we could be well entertained and made comfortable in every way. . . . We were suddenly startled by the shrill Indian warwhoop, which proceeded from a thicket near the house. . . . We were not kept long in a state of suspense. Rutherford and three sturdy fellows, armed, entered the house, all half-drunk. They took no notice of us, but eyed our baggage, which was heaped on the floor. They drank freely of whisky, and appeared in fine spirits. As one of our companions was passing a small log house, in which food was kept, he heard men whispering, which he informed me of. I immediately got a candle. Searched the house, but did not see any person. However, as I was returning, I found two tall men hid in the chimney, who, on being spoken to, went into the house, making six altogether, and most of them very tall. They were armed with rifles and butcher knives, without coats or hats, their sleeves rolled up, their beards long and their faces smutted, such as the bravos are represented in the play of "The Foundling of the Forest." We had been anxious to see some of these banditti, but we did not contemplate seeing so large a company or having so full a visit from the fraternity. Rutherford disguised himself and denied that he was landlord, or that he lived at the place. It was not long before we were informed of the business of those devil-like looking visitors. Some of their private consultations were overheard. Robbery and murder was contemplated. They would frequently whisper and pinch each other, wink, eye us, then hunch each other and give a number of private signals which we did not understand. One observed "the trap door was too open," "that the boards were too wide apart," in a loud tone of voice. The reply was: "By G——, it should be screwed up tight enough before morning!" They often mentioned the names of the cut-throats we had on our list as their particular friends and associates. They also spoke of the two men who had been murdered the day before, and acknowledged that they ate their last meal in the house we were in. Laughed at the manner in which the throats of one of these unfortunate men was cut, and many other circumstances which would swell this memorandum too much. Convinced us beyond a doubt they were of the banditti that had been described to us. Our own safety now became a matter of serious consideration, and our party of four held a consultation after the robbers' consultation was over (which was held in the dark a little way from the house). . . . The hour of 9 o'clock had now arrived, the night uncommonly dark and cloudy. On our going into the house one of the strangers went into the yard and gave the Indian warwhoop three times very loud. About 10 o'clock they took their six rifles, went into the yard with a candle and shot them off one by one, snuffing the candle at forty yards every shot. They then loaded afresh, primed and picked their flints. A large horn was then taken from the loft and blown distinctly three times very loud. All those signals (which we had been told of) brought no more of the company. They then dispatched two of their own party, who were gone until 12 o'clock. They stated to their comrades "they could not be had." It may be readily imagined, after what we had overheard, seeing such preparations and observing many of their private signals, being warned of our danger previous to stopping at the house, together with the recent and cruel murders which had been committed, in a strange country, where every man made and executed his own law to suit himself—I say it cannot be a matter of wonder that our situation began to put on a character of the most unpleasant kind. However, we were well armed, having pistols, dirks, knives and a gun, and were determined, if necessity should require, to be murdered in the house, and not to be dragged into the woods, there to have our throats cut. It being a little after 12 o'clock the bravos proposed to take a drink and lie down on the floor to rest, which they did, and upon their arms. The house being very small they almost covered the floor of one room. The small back room was intended for us. There was no door to the partition, and the logs were about six inches apart. We were under some apprehension that in case of an attack they would be able to fire on us through the logs. After they were all still, myself and companions lay down in reach of each other, our clothes on, our dirks unsheathed, the guards off our pistols and three extra bullets in our gun, and agreed if a signal was given to fight the good fight. . . . Knowing those fellows were expert at cutting throats, from their conversation on that subject, I determined to put them to as much trouble as possible. Took off my cravat and twisted my silk handkerchief and tied it round my neck. In this situation we spent the night. We lay on our arms ready for the word. But little sleep. When they would move we did the same. If they coughed we followed the example. In this dreadful way the night was spent. I have no hesitation of declaring that if we had not been well armed or kept a strict watch we should have been robbed and murdered, and nothing but the fear of our killing a part of them kept their hands off. Could they have added to their numbers by their signals, our fate would have been certain. It is probable the balance of their party was engaged in some other enterprise. About the break of day the signal of rising was given by our visitors. We were on our feet in a minute, and our hands upon our arms. Three of them examined their rifles, and, after having some conversation with their comrades, proceeded up the road we had to travel. I presumed to place themselves behind trees and fire upon us without the risk of being killed. We lost no time in placing our baggage in our carriage and getting ready to leave this robbers' den. After paying our bill and being ready for a start, one of the brotherhood begged I would take my saddlebags into the house again; that he wanted a dose of medicine for one who was very sick. This I declined doing, suspecting his object, and advised him to call on some person with whom he was better acquainted. We then bid adieu to Mr. Rutherford, his family, the banditti and the edge of the twelve-mile prairie. We had not traveled more than half a mile when we fell in with four travelers going to St. Louis, which increased our number to eight persons, and placed us out of danger. In making a memorandum of this unpleasant transaction, many important circumstances and some facts have been omitted. To have given a full detail would have taken more time than is in my power to devote at this time.

Besides the main highways crossing the state there were, of course, numerous local lines of travel radiating out from the towns through the surrounding country or connecting the settlements with the through roads or with navigable streams. "Most of the settlements," it was reported in 1817, "are connected by practicable roads, at least for packers and travellers on horseback." [10] Jurisdiction over these local roads rested with the county courts. Whenever anything more than a natural trail was desired, viewers were appointed to select a route. That having been accomplished, overseers or supervisors of each road were appointed to see that it was opened up and maintained. A certain amount of work on the roads or the payment of a tax in lieu thereof was an obligation imposed upon all the adult male inhabitants. In some cases the overseers were given "power to call out all the hands on each side of said road within six miles of it, to cut it out and keep it in repair"; but the more usual procedure appears to have been for the county court to compile a "list of persons subject to road labor," in which each individual would be assigned to a specific road.

The provision of means for crossing the many streams was the most difficult problem which these pioneer road makers had to face. Whenever possible a ford was used but there were many streams which could not be forded. The problem was usually solved by granting to some individual the right to establish a ferry or erect a toll bridge. Charges for the use of these conveniences were fixed by the county court, and the proprietor was usually protected in his monopoly of the business. It is doubtful if many of the proprietors had as much confidence in the traveling public as one John Flack, who, in December, 1818, advertised his "Boucoup Bridge" in the *Intelligencer* as follows: "I have opened a road from my house, 4 miles west of Boucoup, on a straight line to the old crossing of Little Muddy, at Jackson's

---

[10] Brown, *Western Gazetteer*, 28; see also *History of Gallatin, Hamilton, Franklin, and Williamson Counties*, 53-58; *History of Madison County*, 82.

bridge, and have erected an excellent bridge across Boucoup—this is the direct route from Kaskaskia to Shawneetown; and the way opened by my bridge is three miles nearer, and much better than the old road. I have not yet established a toll house at the bridge, but any person may cross, and in that case, I will thank them to call at my house and make me some compensation *if they please.*"

Another essential accommodation for travelers making journeys of any considerable length was the road house or tavern, and establishments of this sort were to be found at frequent intervals on all the main highways. From the many descriptions of these taverns which have been preserved it is evident that the accommodations were usually very crude even in the best of them. A tavern establishment in Harrisonville, for example, which was offered for sale in 1818, was described as consisting of "the house containing Four commodious Rooms, a Kitchen, Smoke-House, Corncrib and a Stable, and a Garden attached thereto, at present under cultivation." A good-natured German who was in Illinois in 1819 reports that

after a journey of 22 miles through these prairies we reached the tavern; it was full of travelers. Nevertheless each one was served well enough, the horses were well cared for, and only with respect to the lodgings was the comfort not great. Each one had to prepare his own bed upon the floor as well as he could, and even here the American shows a peculiar ease which is the result of his noble freedom. Everything is done without ado and without ceremony. This manner of living, which was to me at first very strange and disagreeable, soon received my entire approval—little by little one feels himself free among free, honest people.[11]

An English traveler recounts his experience in the tavern at Albion in the same year as follows: "I supped and went to bed in a hog-stye of a room, containing four filthy beds and eight mean persons; the sheets stinking and dirty; scarcity of water is, I suppose, the cause. The beds lie on boards, not cords, and are so hard that I could not sleep. Three in one bed, all filth, no comfort, and yet this is an English tavern; no whiskey, no milk, and

[11] Illinois State Historical Society, *Transactions,* 1903, p. 156.

vile tea, in this land of prairies." [12] It is apparent that both of
these descriptions are colored by the personality and point of
view of the writers.

Closely connected with the subject of transportation was that
of postal service. Although the number of post offices in Illinois
was increased from 9 in 1814 to 16 in 1817 and new "post-roads"
were established at nearly every session of Congress, there was
constant demand for further expansion of the service. The same
session of Congress which passed the enabling act for Illinois
established, by act of April 20, 1818, what appears to have been
the first route across the territory—"from Belleville, by William
Padfield's and the seat of justice of Bond county [Perryville],
to Palmyra." The mail from the east destined for the settlements
on the west side of Illinois and in Missouri was still carried down
the Ohio and up the Mississippi to Kaskaskia, and thence via
Prairie du Rocher and Cahokia to St. Louis, although the Missouri legislature, as early as February 16, 1816, had petitioned
for direct service overland from Vincennes. Not until March 3,
1819, was a mail route established "from Vincennes, by Carlisle
and Belville, in Illinois, to St. Louis." The same act established
three other frontier postal routes: "From Edwardsville, by Alton,
to S. Charles, in the Missouri territory, and from Edwardsville,
by Ripley, to Perrysville. . . . From Vincennes by Palestine, to
York, in Illinois." [13]

The difficulties experienced by new settlements in the interior
with reference to postal facilities are indicated by a petition
drawn up in the English settlement probably soon after the
establishment of Wanborough in August, 1818. After stating
that "our correspondence is extensive and constant," the petitioners declared "that more than usual difficulties exist in the
communication with our present Office of deposit at Princeton
[Indiana], which is nearly forty miles from us, often consum-

[12] Thwaites, *Early Western Travels*, 11:252.

[13] Seybert, *Statistical Annals*, 379; *Table of Post-Offices in the United
States*; *Statutes at Large*, 2:584; 3:132, 222, 337, 457, 507; House Files, February 16, 1816; see also *Intelligencer*, December 11, 1818, January 22, November 6, 1817, and at dates indicated in the text.

ing as much time in the transmission thence as from the Eastern States." They asked, therefore, for the establishment of a post office in the settlement "to communicate with a route now existing between Vincennes and Shawnee Town, on the Western side of the Wabash," and Congress in the following year deflected this route to "pass by the English Prairie."

During the later years of the territorial period the mail was supposed to be carried once a week on the main routes and once in two weeks in the interior. It was a very frequent occurrence, however, for the newspapers to announce "No eastern mail this week," the principal cause of delays being floods on the Ohio River. In its issue of November 20, 1817, for example, the *Intelligencer* expressed "regret that our readers are again compelled to take hold of a barren paper, but the floods which have been so unseasonably and unexpectedly poured upon us of late, have prevented the usual arrivals of the eastern mails; three weeks have now expired since we have had a mail." There was also complaint of "unpardonable neglect of post masters to forward papers by the first opportunity." From Kaskaskia the mail was forwarded to points north and west; consequently the weekly mail to that place was particularly heavy; its volume appears to have been so great that at times "a large portion of the letters and papers intended for that quarter is necessarily delayed, or probably entirely thrown out at Shawnoetown, and either does not come on at all, or comes on after the information contained is stale and no longer useful." In consequence of this situation John Scott, the delegate from Missouri Territory, appealed to the postmaster general in December, 1816, for a semi-weekly service to Kaskaskia, St. Louis, and other points in Missouri. It was not until April 22, 1818, however, that the *Intelligencer* was able to announce that "a contract has been entered into for the conveyance of the mail twice a week from Shawnoetown to this place, and on to Saint Louis, which goes into operation on the first of May next. We therefore expect that all communications by mail may with some certainty be relied on. It is also designed that the eastern mail shall arrive at Shawnoetown twice in each week."

It appears to have been in connection with the transportation of the mail that the first stage service in Illinois began. No record has been found of stage lines in operation during the territorial period and it is probable that the mail was usually carried on horseback. The advertisement of the General Post Office for proposals for carrying the mail over the new routes established in Illinois in 1818 announces that "where the proposer intends to convey the mail in the body of a stage carriage, he is desired to state it in his proposals." A few months later, January 20, 1819, James Watson informed the public through the columns of the *Intelligencer* "that he can accommodate four stage passengers each trip he makes with the mail, to St. Louis. He starts from Kaskaskia every Sunday morning, and arrives at St. Louis the next day at 2 o'clock, p.m. Returning, he leaves St. Louis every Tuesday morning, and arrives at Kaskaskia the ensuing evening. Fare—$4 each passenger, payable in advance." This probably marks the beginning of regular stage service in Illinois. Before that time, travelers were obliged to make special arrangements or provide their own means of conveyance.

With such inadequate means of transportation by land it is small wonder that the farmers in Illinois in 1818 found it difficult to market their produce profitably. As an English observer wrote (November 4, 1819): "Mr. Nicholls, a cunning Caledonian, says, that farming, except near the rivers, cannot answer." [14] Certainly his remark was not intended as a reflection on the productivity of the soil, for from all accounts the land was extraordinarily fertile.

One visitor in Illinois in 1817 wrote home:

The common productions of the country are much the same as those of Kentucky, Indian corn, wheat, rye, oats, tobacco and hemp are raised with as much facility and ease as in the neighborhood of Lexington, where I was raised; and judging from information and appearances of the last crops I am persuaded that the productions in the American bottom in particular, are greater and reared with more ease than in the neighbourhood of my nativity—Such is its luxuriancy

[14] Thwaites, *Early Western Travels*, 11:218.

that one acre of land in that bottom has yielded its industrious cultivator 110 bushels of Indian corn in a season, but this is uncommon, the average is estimated at from 60 to 70.—A more congenial soil for general cultivation I believe no where exists, it may be called the Elysium of America.[15]

The "American bottom" to which the writer referred extended along the Mississippi from the Wood River to the Kaskaskia; it was about 80 or 90 miles in length and from 4 to 7 in width, with nearly equal portions of prairie and timbered land. The editors of the *Intelligencer* made the same claims for this country as the writer of the letter already quoted, but added: "The upper part of the territory, we learn is equally abundant in the productions of the soil."[16] A letter descriptive of the western country written early in 1818 and printed in the *Lynchburg Press* had the following to say:

The Illinois Territory, I have no doubt, furnishes greater inducements to emigration, than any other Territory belonging to the United States, to such men as are not holders of Slaves. I have no hesitation in saying, that one hand there can make as much annually, as any three in any other part with which I am acquainted. It is far the most fertile soil in the U. States; and quantity of prairie gives it advantages over and above what it would enjoy, from fertility alone. In the general, the farmer has nothing to do, but fence in his fields: plough his ground and plant his crop. He may then expect, from an acre, from 50 to 100 bushels [of] corn; and from 10 to 50 of wheat; the quality of both which articles is superior to that of any I ever saw. Moreover, much less labor than usual is requisite. A farm of any size may be gotten, free from grubs, stones, roots and every obstruction to the plough. In no instance is ploughing required more than twice and hoeing never: with these, the farmer keeps his fields cleaner, than they are where 4 or 5 ploughings, and 2 or 3 hoeings are customary. One man can cultivate 40 acres in corn; which quantity of ground, he can in the fall, sow in wheat.[17]

This writer's testimony regarding the ease with which the ground was worked is confirmed by a settler from Vermont. Under date of September 12, 1818, Gershom Flagg wrote from

[15] *Intelligencer*, May 14, 1817.
[16] *Intelligencer*, September 18, 1817.
[17] *Intelligencer*, March 25, 1818.

Edwardsville: "The method of Raising Corn here is to plough the ground once then furrow it both ways and plant the Corn 4 feet each way and plough between it 3 or 4 times in the Summer but never hoe it at all." [18] Yet the corn grew "from 12 to 15 feet high on an average."

Regarding the price paid for corn Flagg wrote: "The price of Corn last harvest was 33 1/3 cents in the spring 50 cents in the summer 75 cents." From the other side of the territory a young farmer wrote home: "Corn is worth in this settlement 75 cents in other places around us they have had the [conscience?] to take a dollar per bushel I do not think there is grain enough in the country to supply it oweing to the rapid settlement." [19] Yet this farmer was concerned not with raising for the market but only for his own use. "Our corn," he wrote, "we must not neglect under the penalty of starving." The attitude of this man seems to have been the prevalent one at that time; each and all raised produce not primarily to sell, but to save themselves from being obliged to buy. Accordingly the newcomers who reached Illinois too late in the season to plant found that the settlers took advantage of their extremity. An early settler in Jefferson County, according to the local historian, "long followed the business of going to Carmi, a distance of forty miles, with two or three pack-horses, and bringing back meal to sell to these 'movers.' This," comments the writer, "would seem a small business in this day of railroads, as he could only bring two or three sacks of meal at a time, but as he sold it at $2 a bushel, it was a lucrative business for that early day." [20] It is probable that the surplus meal for sale came almost entirely from the miller who received it in payment for grinding. The payment was regulated by law and was entirely in kind. By the law of 1819 the charge at a water mill for grinding wheat, rye, malt, or choppings was one-eighth of the whole, for corn, oats, barley, or buckwheat one-seventh. At a horse

[18] Illinois State Historical Society, *Transactions*, 1910, p. 162.
[19] G. Knight to C. Knight, Palmyra, June 21, 1818.
[20] Perrin, *History of Jefferson County*, 124. See also 127.

mill, the charge was doubled unless the farmer's horse furnished the motive power. Using the term "farmer" to include all those who raised only for their own consumption, there is probably no exaggeration in the statement made during the campaign of 1818 that 99 in 100 of the men in Illinois were farmers.

This meant that there was little division of labor. It meant also that though nearly every man farmed, he did not spend his whole time at it. The frontiersmen, who made up so large a part of the population, spent the remainder of their time in hunting or idleness. They felt no need for the things with which they could not furnish themselves by their own labor. Many detailed pictures of this pioneer life have been recorded; the following is an interesting example.

The pursuits of the people were agricultural. A very few merchants supplied them with the few necessaries which could not be produced or manufactured at home. The farmer raised his own provisions; tea and coffee were scarcely used, except on some grand occasions. The farmer's sheep furnished wool for his winter clothing; he raised cotton and flax for his summer clothing. His wife and daughters spun, wove, and made it into garments. A little copperas and indigo, with the bark of trees, furnished dye stuffs for coloring. The fur of the raccoon, made him a hat or cap. The skins of deer or of his cattle, tanned at a neighboring tan-yard, or dressed by himself, made him shoes or moccasins. Boots were rarely seen, even in the towns. And a log cabin, made entirely of wood, without glass, nails, hinges, or locks, furnished the residence of many a contented and happy family. The people were quick and ingenious to supply by invention, and with their own hands, the lack of mechanics and artificers. Each farmer, as a general thing, built his own house, made his own ploughs and harness, bedsteads, chairs, stools, cupboards, and tables. The carts and wagons for hauling, were generally made without iron, without tires, or boxes, and were run without tar, and might be heard creaking as they lumbered along the roads, for the distance of a mile or more.

As an example of the talents of this people to supply all deficiencies, and provide against accidents by a ready invention, the following anecdote is related of James Lemon, one of the old sort of Baptist preachers, formerly of Monroe county, but now deceased. Mr. Lemon was a farmer, and made all his own harness. The collars for his horses were made of straw or corn husks, plaited and sewed together by himself. Being engaged in breaking a piece of stubble ground, and having turned out for dinner, he left his harness on the beam of his plough.

His son, a wild youth, who was employed with a pitchfork to clear
the plough of the accumulating stubble, staid behind, and hid one
of the horse collars. This he did that he might rest whilst his father
made a new collar. But the old man, returning in the afternoon and
missing his collar, mused for a few minutes, and then, very much to
the disappointment of his truant son, he deliberately pulled off his
leather breeches, stuffed the legs of them with stubble, straddled them
across the neck of his horse for a collar, and ploughed the remainder of
the day, as bare-legged as he came into the world. In a more civilized
country, where the people are better acquainted with the great laws
which control the division of labor, a half day would have been lost in
providing for such a mishap.[21]

Under these economic conditions women had a heavy and
versatile role to play.

The wool, the flax and the cotton were raised on the farms by the
men, but this material passed in its raw state into the hands of the
women and came out cloth ready for the making, and the making was
done by the women, and in many instances, the clothing for an entire
family was made from the raw material, to its finishing stitch, by the
one woman, who was cook, laundress, nurse, and gardener, as well
as housekeeper and wife; and who made her own soap, or did without, and in the intervals of resting, knit all the hosiery for a large
family. . . . The old lady that picked up her knitting to do a few
rounds while the crowd gathered at her husband's funeral, may have
been an extreme type, but the anecdote illustrates the industry that
had become a fixed habit of their lives.[22]

Of ready money there was little, and little was needed.

Many a family lived a whole year without the possession or use of
fifty dollars in cash. Personal property, therefore, during many years,
consisted almost exclusively of the products of the farm and of articles
manufactured by the citizens at their own homes. The farms, in those
days, were worked chiefly by the use of oxen, horses being employed
mainly for riding, and for ploughing after the corn came up in the
spring. Even wagons and carts were generally drawn by oxen, not only
for the hauling of corn, hay, wood, rails, etc., but for church-going and
traveling. The productions of the farms were very few, such as a little
fall or spring wheat, oats, Indian corn, cotton, flax, in some cases castor-
beans, and as to fruits, scarcely anything but apples and some peaches.
But wild plums and grapes, of good quality, were produced in large

---

[21] Ford, *History of Illinois*, 41-42.
[22] Illinois State Historical Society, *Transactions*, 1904, pp. 509-510.

quantities in the timbered districts, especially at the edges of the prairies. There was no machinery used on the farms before 1835 or 1840. There were no corn-planters, no reaping or threshing machines, or fanning-mills. Corn was planted by hand, wheat, oats, and grass were cut with sickles or scythes by hand, cotton was gathered and picked by hand, flax was broken and scutched by hand, cotton and wool were carded into rolls by hand, and spinning and weaving were done by hand. Grain was trodden out by horses or beaten out with flails, and winnowed by the breezes or with sheets used like so many great fans. The only articles employed by the farmers that could properly be called machines, were flax-breaks, hackles, looms, hand-mills, and possibly an occasional cider-mill. There were, however, at intervals of ten or twenty miles, water-mills and horse-mills for grinding corn, wheat, rye, and barley; and from the earliest settlement of the country there were not wanting distilleries for the manufacture of whiskey, to minister to the cravings of the thirsty people, who claimed that they could not keep warm in winter or cool in summer, or perform their hard work without fainting, unless they could be assisted by the free use of the "good creature." But there were no breweries to be found, unless among the few Germans.

The clothing of the people, especially in the first settlement of the country, consisted almost wholly of materials prepared by the several families for themselves. The most frequent exception to this remark was found in the leather used for shoes, which was often tanned and dressed by some one man in a neighborhood, who gave a part of his time to a small tannery, of which he was the proprietor. But many were at once tanners, shoe-makers, and farmers; and their wives and daughters manufactured the flax and cotton, raised by them, into garments for the family. For during the first quarter of the century, cotton as well as flax was produced on many farms, and spinning-wheels were manufactured in almost every neighborhood for the use of the families, which were purchased from the makers by an exchange of various productions from the farms around. As lately as eleven or twelve years ago [about 1868], I found, on visiting Bond County, an old wheelwright still devoted to his former work, making spinning-wheels, both large and small, not to sell as curiosities, but to supply an actual demand from families that yet preferred to manufacture their own clothing as in former times. Not only were the materials and the cloth prepared, but the dyeing was done in the family; the bark of trees, especially of the butter-nut, and indigo raised on the farm, being used for this purpose. And then the mother made up the clothing for the household. In many cases, deer-skins were dressed by the men, and made into hunting-shirts, pantaloons, and moccasons [sic] by the women, all in the same family. The hunting-shirts were frequently ornamented with a fringe on the lower edge of the cape and at the bottom of the garment, which presented a not unpleasing appearance. Shoes were often confined, except in cold weather, to the adult females; the men and children going barefoot in spring, summer, and fall, unless they had occasion to appear in a public assembly. I have many a time seen even young women carry their shoes in their hands until they came near to church, and then put them on before coming to the door and entering. The men's hats for the summer were commonly made of wheat straw, rudely platted and sewed together by the women. Winter hats, usually of wool, were, of necessity, purchased from a manufacturer, who could almost always be found in some village not far distant. The clothes of the women, like those of the men, were almost entirely of home manufacture, except in the older villages. Their bonnets were occasionally purchased from the stores, but more commonly they were of the simple Virginia style, made of domestic materials, and kept in place either by pasteboard or wooden ribs.[23]

When the English farmers came to Illinois they expected, with plenty of land and capital, to be able to carry on farming on a large scale. They soon found to their surprise that their plans were impracticable owing to the difficulty of securing laborers. Accustomed as they were to a social system in which there was a numerous class of laborers who accepted their humble position as a matter of course and seldom aspired to raise themselves above it, these Englishmen had great difficulty in adjusting themselves to a society in which there was no definite and permanent servant class. "No white man or woman," wrote one of the Englishmen, "will bear being called a servant, but they will gladly do your work. Your hirelings must be spoken to with Civility and cheerfulness." Then, in a tone which suggests that he expected incredulity from his English readers, the writer added: "Respectable families from Kentucky . . . do all their domestic work, except washing, with their own hands." The reason for this absence of a laboring class was not hard to find. To quote from the same writer:

A man used to work will earn in one day what will suffice for the simple wants of a Backwoodsman a whole week. If he be sober and industrious, in two years he can enter a quarter section of land, buy a horse, a plough,

[23] Patterson, "Early Society in Southern Illinois," in *Fergus Historical Series,* no. 14:109-111.

and tools. The lowest price for labour now is 13$ per month with board
and lodging. I will give two years net proceeds in figures.

	$
12 months at 13$.................	156$
12 months at 13	156
	$312

	$
Clothing for two years—say............	100
One quarter of land...................	80
One horse and harness and plough......	100
Axe grubbing hoe &c...................	10
Gun and powder &c.....................	15
	$305

After putting in his crop of maize, he can supply himself with meat
and some money by hunting, or he can earn $1 per day in splitting rails
for his neighbors. Many men begin as independent farmers with half the
above mentioned sum, but they are thorough Backwoodsmen.

Now, is it not evident that while land can be bought, no matter how
far from navigable rivers, at $2 per acre, and when there are tracts they
may "squat" upon for nothing, that labour will be for many years
limited in price only by the ability of those who want it, to pay for it.
It is indeed the only expence; but is so overwhelming that I would
rather farm in old England with a capital of 2 or 3000£ than on the
North West of the Ohio. If we consider the immense territory to the
North West of us, and the roving spirit of the Americans, we may
wonder that any work can be hired. The truth is, none are to be hired
but Emigrants from the Eastern States, who intend to be land owners in
one, two, or three years. And these are few in number: for the steady
and prudent earn the money at home and bring it with them.[24]

For the English, the first solution of the difficulty was to import
labor. While still at Princeton, Indiana, Birkbeck wrote to a
prospective settler: "A single settler may get his labour done by
the piece on moderate terms, not higher than in some parts of
England; but if many families settle together, all requiring this
article, and none supplying it, they must obtain it from elsewhere. Let them import English labourers, or make advantageous proposals to such as are continually arriving at the eastern ports." Flower's scheme was to import those being paid poor

[24] Ogg, *Fordham's Personal Narrative*, 124-125, 210-211.

rates in England; and he offered to pay to the parishes half the expense of getting them to Illinois.[25] But importation was soon found to be only a very temporary solution of the problem. As early as June, 1818, Fordham wrote of Birkbeck's colony: "His English labourers have already caught the desire to be land owners."[26]

Before many months the English were forced to the conclusion that Illinois was a good location only for the small farmer who was willing to work his land without hired labor. There was only one alternative: that was to use slaves. Fordham shows by what process of reasoning an Englishman could reach this conclusion. In June, 1818, he wrote: "I would not have upon my conscience the moral guilt of extending Slavery over countries now free from it, for the whole North Western Territory. But, if it should take place, I do not see why I should not make use of it. If I do not have servants I cannot farm; and there are *no* free labourers here, except a few so worthless, and yet so haughty, that an English Gentleman can do nothing with them." Two months later he wrote at even greater length:

I cannot think that any elderly man, especially if he have a family delicately brought up, would live comfortably in a free state. In a slave State, if he have wealth, say, 5000£ and upwards, he may raise upon his own farm all the food and raiment, the latter manufactured at home, necessary to supply the wants of his own family.

This has been, till lately, the universal economy of the first Kentucky families. Thus, without living more expensively than in a free state, a family may have the comforts of domestic services, and yet find plenty of employment within doors; not sordid slavery that wears out the health, and depresses the spirits of Ohio, but useful yet light labours, that may be remitted and resumed at pleasure.

There is more difference between the manners of the female sex on the East and West sides of the Ohio River than on the East and West shores of the Atlantic Ocean. Servitude in any form is an evil, but the structure of civilized society is raised upon it. If the minds of women are left *unimproved*, their *morals* will be at the mercy of any

[25] Fearon, *Sketches of America*, 335; Thwaites, *Early Western Travels*, 11:279.

[26] Ogg, *Fordham's Personal Narrative*, 212.

man. It is much worse where there is no superior rank to influence
them by example, or to awe them by disapprobation. I am conscious
that I repeat again and again the same arguments—or rather I state
similar facts; but it is an important subject.

Society may suffer more by the abjectness of Slaves than by the
want of servants, and a father of a family would prefer to live where
there are good free servants as in Europe, or where slaves have more
liberty of action than servants, as in Kentucky. The question in these
wildernesses is this: Shall we have civilization and refinement, or
sordid manners and semi-barbarism, till time shall produce so much in-
equality of condition that the poor man must serve the rich man for
his daily bread? [27]

Not having the Englishman's prejudices to overcome, many
Americans had arrived much more readily at the same conclusion. The result was that the provision of the Northwest Ordinance prohibiting slavery was in practice continually evaded
under cloak of the indenture law, which made it possible to
indenture negroes under conditions amounting to slavery. In
1818 the indentured servants in the territory amounted to one-
fortieth of the population: a large proportion when one consid-
ers the extreme poverty of most of the settlers. That the indenture system was virtually identical with slavery is readily seen
in the form of indenture drawn up when a negro was transferred from one master to another. One is headed: "General
Indenture concerning sale of negro girl." Another, more detailed, reads as follows:

THIS INDENTURE made this twenty second day of June in the year
of our Lord, one thousand Eight hundred and fifteen, between Silvey
a Negroe Woman about the age of twenty four years, last out of the
State of Kaintuck and Livingston County, of the one part, and John
Morris of the Illinois Territory and Gallaton County of the other part,
WITNESSETH, that the said Silvey for and in consideration of the sum
of four hundred Dollars, to me paid in hand courant Money of the
United States, at or before the signing and delivery of these presents,
the Receipt whereof She doth hereby acknoledge, and in conformity
to a law of the said Teritory respecting the Introduction of Negroes
and Melattoes into the saim, hath put placed and bind himself to the
said Morris, to serve him from the date hereof, during the Term and

[27] Ogg, *Fordham's Personal Narrative*, 210, 228-229.

in full of forty years next enshuing, or in other words from the date hereoff untill the twenty second day of June, in the year of our Lord one thousand eight hundred and fifty five, during all which Term, the said Silvey, the said John Morris shall well and truly serve, and all his lawfull commands every whair obey, and that She shall not embezzel or waiste her said Masters Goods nor lend them to any person without her said Masters consent, or leave. Nor shall She at any time absent herself from her said Masters Service, or leave, but as a good and faithfull servant, shall and will at all times demean herself towards her said Master, during the Term aforesaid. And the said John Morrice convenants and agrees too and with the said Silvey, that he will furnish her with good and suficient Meat, Drink, lodging and apparell, together with all other needful conveniences fit for such a Servant, during the said Term. And for the true performance of each of the above and aforementioned, Convenants, and Agreements, each of the above and aformentioned parties, bind themselves each to the other, firmly by these presents.

In testimony whereof the aforementioned parties, have hereunto set their hands and Seals the date first above written. Silvey her mark

Executed and acknoledged in presence of Samuel Omelveny Deputy Clerk, for Joseph M. Street, Clerk of the Court, of Common pleas for Gallatin County—)   John Morris (S)

June 25th 1816. Attest Johna Scott Recorder of Pope County. Accompanying the above Indenture, is the following Bond, To wit,

United States Illinois Territory, Gallatin County, 'Know all men by these presents, that we John Morris and Isom Harrison of the Illinois Teritory and County of Gallaton, are held and firmly bound, unto Ninian Edwards Governor of the Illinois Teritory, and his Successors in Office, in the sum of four hundred Dollars, lawfull Money of the United States, to the payment of the sum aforesaid, to be well and truly made and dun we bind ourselves our heirs Executors and Administrators and Assigns, Jointly and severally, by these presents Given under our hands and Seals this 22nd day of June 1815.

The Condition of the above obligation is such, whereas on this day an Indenture was made and entered into by and between, John Morrice and silvey a Negroe Woman aged about twenty four years, and the above named, John Morrice, by which the said Indenture, the said Silvey agrees, to serve the said John Morrice the Term of forty years, pursuant to a law of the Teritory, respecting the Introduction of Negroes and Melatoes into the saim, at the expiration of the said Term the said Silvey will exceed the age of forty years. Now if the said John Morrice doth not suffer or permit the said Silvey to become a County charge, after the expiration of the said Sum, then this obligation to be voide, otherwise to remain in full force and virtue in law. Given under our hands and Seals, this 22ⁿᵈ of June 1815.

John Morris   (Seal)

I. Harrison   (Seal)

Executed in presence of Samuel Omelveny)

Deputy Clark for Joseph M. Street Clark) [28]

Indenture seems to have been recorded June 25, 1816.

From this it is seen that the price paid for the negro was equal to that paid at an out-and-out sale, the period of the indenture was made to cover the lifetime of the slave, the conditions under which the indentured servant was obliged to work and live did not differ from the conditions of bondage south of the Ohio River. Although the indenture law made it possible for slave owners to settle in Illinois, many hesitated to do so for fear conditions would be changed when Illinois became a state, as it was bound soon to do. For that reason they preferred to cross Illinois and locate in Missouri, which was free from the restriction contained in the Northwest Ordinance. Between 1810 and 1820, according to the United States census, the slave population of Missouri increased from 3,011 to 10,222; and many settlers in Illinois regarded with jealous eyes the great economic advantage which Missouri was gaining over their state.

In 1818, then, Illinois was suffering economically from two handicaps: the lack of adequate transportation facilities and the lack of a laboring class. To the greater part of the population, however, these handicaps were of no serious concern. The frontiersman was economically independent; he might exchange with his neighbors in a spirit of friendliness, but he did not buy or sell commodities or labor. The effort to raise Illinois to a higher economic plane was made by only a small class—those whom Fordham called the "enterprising men." "This class," he states, "consists of Young Doctors, Lawyers, Storekeepers, farmers, mechanics, &c., who found towns, trade, speculate in land, and begin the fabric of Society." [29] The work of this class merits consideration.

[28] Deed record, A, pp. 2-3, in Pope County.

[29] Ogg, *Fordham's Personal Narrative*, 126.

The farmer who wished to do more than produce for his own consumption turned to stock raising. It involved very little additional labor, and the only expense was the initial cost. "Cows," states one writer, "are generally suffered to run in the woods, and return to their calves mornings and evenings." "Hogs," wrote another settler, "will live & get fat in the Woods and Prairies. I have seen some as fat upon Hickorynuts, Acorns, Pecons & Walnuts, as ever I did those that were fat[t]ed upon Corn." [30] According to the same writer, horses and cattle could live all winter along the rivers without feeding. Even where this was not possible, the wild grass could be gathered as hay. "The grass on the Prairies," wrote one farmer, "is now [June 21] about waist high and looks beautiful we shall cut what hay we shall want whenever we get through with our corn." Of the quality of this hay Faux says: "What is gathered, is green and fragrant, but not so sweet as fine English hay. It is hard, harsh, and dry." Yet another maintained that the cattle came out in the spring "as fat as sheep from coleseed." [31]

The profits to be made were temptingly large, considering the purchasing power of money at the time. Richard Flower, for instance, writes of buying bullocks at $16 or $17 and selling them the next year, at the Albion market, for $28 to $31 each. The profits had to be large, however, in order to cover the heavy risks incurred in raising livestock in such a wild country. Many animals strayed away into the woods, or were shot, accidentally or maliciously, by hunters. Wolves were a constant menace, particularly to sheep and hogs. On one occasion they killed 50 of Flower's sheep in one raid, in spite of all the shepherd could do. Of conditions in Madison County Gershom Flagg wrote: "All that prevents this country being as full of Wild hogs as of Deer is the Wolves which kill the pigs when the sows are not shut up til the pigs are a few weeks old." [32] Flies were more than merely

[30] Thwaites, *Early Western Travels*, 10:281; Illinois State Historical Society, *Transactions*, 1910, p. 158.

[31] G. Knight to C. Knight, June 21, 1818; Thwaites, *Early Western Travels*, 10:122-123; 11:258.

[32] Illinois State Historical Society, *Transactions*, 1910, p. 158.

a nuisance. To quote from the preceding writer: "Cattle & horses do very well in this Country they get very fat by the middle of June. They do not gain much after this being so harrassed by swarms of flies which prevent their feeding any in the heat of the day. They were so bad upon horses that it is almost impossible to travel from the 15 June til the 1st Sept unles [*sic*] a horse is covered with blankets. Where ever a fly lights upon a horse a drop of blood starts. I have seen white horses red with blood that these flies had drawn out of him. As the Country becomes settled these flies disappear."

Even these disadvantages, however, were not severe enough to counterbalance the advantage of the slight expense; another advantage of weight was the sureness of the market. In 1818 the farmers were beginning "to raise stock for exportation . . . money flowed into the country . . . to repay many fold the farmer. . . . The Ohio drovers expended considerable money in the country for cattle." [33] Taking into consideration the labor conditions in Illinois it is easy to understand why the "enterprising" farmers put their capital into livestock and why Birkbeck wrote: "It is on the boundless scope for rearing and fattening hogs and cattle, that the farmers place their chief reliance." [34]

A second class that Fordham included among the enterprising men were the mechanics. There seems to have been a great scarcity of skilled laborers, and many towns made strenuous efforts to attract them. In most advertisements of town lots, for instance, lower rates were offered to "skilled mechanics." During the early part of 1818, the following advertisement appeared repeatedly in the *Intelligencer*:

Notice

TO MECHANICS & FARMERS

Mechanics of every description are much wanted at Edwardsville: more particularly the following, *a Taylor, Shoemaker, Waggon Maker, Hatter, Saddler, Tanner and Currier.* From *four* to *six Carpenters*

---

[33] Reynolds, *My Own Times*, 176.
[34] Birkbeck, *Letters from Illinois*, 68.

and *Joiners,* and from *four* to *six ax-men,* and from *six* to *eight farming labourers,* will find immediate employment and good wages; for further particulars enquire of col. Benjamin Stephenson and Doctor Jos. Bowers, at Edwardsville, or James Mason at St. Louis.

Edwardsville is the seat of justice for Madison county, Illinois territory, and has the land-office established there for the district of Edwardsville; and is surrounded on three sides by the Goshen settlement, which is one of the best settlements in the territory; besides the adjacent country in every direction, is equal in point of fertility of soil, to any other in the western region.

March 8 [35]

On April 22 appeared for the first time a notice to bridge builders which reads as follows:

To Bridge Builders

A Man is wanted to build a bridge over the Little Wabash river, at Carmi, Illinois territory. The river, when low, is about 130 feet wide, one foot deep, bottom smooth rock-banks about 35 feet high, The water rises to the depth of 32 feet   The above mentioned bridge will be let or contracted for on the first Monday in May next.—As a good bridge is more our object than a cheap one, a skilful bridge builder will meet with liberal encouragement.

Leonard White,)
Benja White,)
Will. M'Henry,)   Commissioners.
W. Hargrave,)
Lowry Hay,)
James Casey,)

Carmi, April 2

But, as has already been pointed out, few towns had actually reached a stage of development that would attract specialized labor. Fordham advised mechanics to locate "always in the most settled parts of the Western Country, and generally in the Slave States."

However it may have been with mechanics, there can be no doubt that the towns were beginning in 1818 to attract merchants. The character of the stores can easily be judged from the advertisements. The following from the *Intelligencer* of January 1 is characteristic:

---

[35] *Intelligencer,* March 18, 1818.

NEW GOODS

The Subscriber has just received from New York and Philadelphia
A LARGE AND HANDSOME ASSORTMENT OF GOODS,

CONSISTING OF

Superfine, Fine and	*Cambrics*
Coarse Broad	*Fancy Muslins, lace*
Cloths, Casimeres,	*British Cottons,*
Coatings, Flannels,	*Linens, Domestic,*
Hosings,	*Stripes, Plaids and*
Silk Shawls,	*Plains, Saddles,*
Cotton do.	*Bridles, Hats and*
Handerkerchiefs,	

A Large Assortment of Ladies and Gentlemen's
SHOES.

ALSO, A GENERAL ASSORTMENT OF
Hardware,

Which, with his former stock he offers low for *Cash,* or on a short
and approved credit.

He continues to receive in exchange for Goods,
Wheat, Pork, Butter, Furs, Peltries, &c. &c.

EDWARD COWLES.

Kaskaskia, Nov. 5

Six of the stores which advertised in the *Intelligencer* were
located in Kaskaskia; one of them, Thomas Cox's, had goods
"lately imported from Europe" besides those of domestic manufacture. Benjamin Stephenson of Edwardsville and the Reynolds brothers of Goshen advertised their wares in the *Intelligencer*; Missouri merchants also thought it worth while to
advertise in the Kaskaskia paper. From both St. Louis and St.
Genevieve the merchants were bidding for Illinois trade. For
the eastern side of the country the advertisements appeared in
the *Illinois Emigrant* of Shawneetown. The following is the
list of goods that John Grant of Carmi, White County, presented
for sale at either wholesale or retail.

NEW STORE,
Carmi, White County, Illinois.

The subscriber has opened a choice assortment of the following
Goods, which he has selected with care and attention in Philadelphia
and Pittsburgh, and which he will sell on reasonable terms, wholesale
and retail:

Domestick & imported superfine Cloths and Cassimeres,
Sattinets, Cassinets, and Kerseys,
Pelisse Cloths, Lion Skins and Coatings,
Velveteens and vestings,
Printed Calicoes,
Furniture ditto.
Domestick and imported Ginghams and Chambrays—plain and twilled,
Bombazets,
White and coloured Flannels,
Rose and point Blankets,
Steam-loom and domestick Shirtings,
Sheeting Muslins and Bedticks,
Men's and women's worsted and cotton Hose,
Men's and women's Gloves,
Waterloo Shawls and silk Handkerchiefs,
Cambrick, Jaconet and book Muslins,
Insertion Trimmings and Ribbons,
Scots Thread and cotton Balls—white and coloured,
Mantuas and Sevantines,
India Muslins,
Men's, women's and children's Boots and Shoes,
Looking-Glasses and Jap'd. Trays,
Tortoise, ivory and common Combs,
Hand Vices,
Millsaw and handsaw Files,
Pitt and cross-cut Saws,
German steel Handsaws,
Thumb Latches, Hinges and Locks,
Spades, Shovels, Hoes, Axes, Frying-pans, Pots, Teakettles, Dutch Ovens, Smoothing-irons, with a great variety of Cutlery, Cast, & Hollow Ware,
GROCERIES—HOLLOW GLASS WARE, of Bakewell's manufacture—Window Glass,
School Books and Stationary,
English Crowley Mellinton Steel,
Juniatta Bar-iron,
Sieves and Riddles,
Grind Stones of the best quality.

JOHN GRANT.

Carmi, Dec. 31, 1818
N. B. A liberal allowance shall be made to Storekeepers.

J.G. [36]

[36] *Illinois Emigrant*, January 23, 1819.

From the wording of the advertisements, it is evident that the merchants were trying to entice the farmers into town to exchange their produce for store goods. A Shawneetown merchant even offered to give the highest price in cash for any quantity of the following articles:

TALLOW,	POTATOES,
CANDLE COTTON,	TURNIPS,
or SOFT FLAX, for	ONIONS,
WICKS,	PARSNIPS,
VENISON HAMS,	CARROTS,
BUTTER,	HOPPS,
CHEESE,	SAGE,
EGGS,	TWILLED BAGS.[37]

There could be no trade until the people were roused from their contentment with goods of home manufacture; an effort in this direction was the attempt to bring the market nearer to the farmer. Augusta held out this lure to merchants to influence their choice of location.

THIS town is situate on the east side of Silver creek, Illinois territory, where the great roads cross leading from Vincennes and Shawnoetown to St. Louis, Edwardsville & Boon's lick. It is an interior central point, distant from St. Louis, 22 miles, from Edwardsville, 12, from Belleville, 20, from Perryville 40, from Ripley, 25, and from Covington, 30, surrounded by a fertile country, surpassed by none in the west, and calculated to support a crowded agricultural population.

It is most probably at this time the best populated section of country in the territory, and will shortly be almost wholly under the finest state of cultivation. The distance from market, the strength and wealth of the population, the fertility of the soil, and the great mass of surplus produce of the farmer, strongly require the establishment of a place for the transaction of business, where the industrious husbandman can make sale of the rich harvest of his farm, and carry home to his family the reward of his labor without having to consume the whole of his profits in transporting to remote markets. This place then holds out strong inducements to the mechanic, the merchant, the professional gentleman, and all the necessary branches of a well organised society.[38]

It is fair to say that 1818 marks the beginnings of trade in Illinois. Reynolds is authority for the statement that "the factory

[37] *Illinois Emigrant*, January 9, 1819.
[38] *Intelligencer*, May 20, 1818.

goods, from New England and Kentucky, reached Illinois about 1818, and then looms, cotton &c., disappeared—spinning also ceased then." [39] There can be no doubt that this change was the result of the great influx of population at that time; among the new population were many who were accustomed to buying what they needed, and furthermore, they brought with them the money necessary for trade. The change that was brought about has been depicted by Ford as follows:

Upon the conclusion of the war of 1812 the people from the old States began to come in, and settle in the country. They brought some money and property with them, and introduced some changes in the customs and modes of living. Before the war, such a thing as money was scarcely ever seen in the country, the skins of the deer and raccoon supplying the place of a circulating medium. The money which was now brought in, and which had before been paid by the United States to the militia during the war, turned the heads of all the people, and gave them new ideas and aspirations; so that by 1819 the whole country was in a rage for speculating in lands and town lots. The States of Ohio and Kentucky, a little before, had each incorporated a batch of about forty independent banks. The Illinois territory had incorporated two at home, one at Edwardsville and the other at Shawneetown; and the territory of Missouri added two more, at St. Louis. These banks made money very plenty; emigrants brought it to the State in great abundance. The owners of it had to use it in some way; and as it could not be used in legitimate commerce in a State where the material for commerce did not exist, the most of it was used to build houses in towns which the limited business of the country did not require, and to purchase land which the labor of the country was not sufficient to cultivate. This was called "developing the infant resources of a new country." [40]

The law establishing the Shawneetown bank was approved December 26, 1816, that for the one at Edwardsville a year later. Each was to have a capital stock of $300,000, one-third subscribed by the legislature, the rest by individuals. A share in the Shawneetown bank was put at $100, in the Edwardsville at $50. Of the $30,000 subscribed to the Edwardsville bank as the first installment, $22,625 came from Kentucky, $10,000 was given by one man, $1,800 came from St. Louis, $100 from New

[39] Reynolds, *My Own Times*, 71.
[40] Ford, *History of Illinois*, 43.

York. Only the remaining $5,475 came from within Illinois. The subscribers there were confined to Madison and St. Clair counties; few contributed more than $50. The bank opened for business when the first installment of one-tenth had been paid in.[41] The following editorial in the *Intelligencer* for January 1, 1817, reflects the general enthusiasm over the new enterprise.

ILLINOIS BANK.

The bill establishing a Bank at Shawnoetown has at length received the approbation and signature of the governor, and has consequently became a law. Whatever may be our opinion as to the ultimate effects that are likely to result from the extensive banking system adopted in the United States, we are inclined to think, that much advantage will result from this particular institution to our infant territory. The great scarcity of the precious metals that prevails, has rendered it necessary that some substituted circulating medium should be furnished; and bank paper is certainly the most convenient. But the remoteness of our situation, from the banks in the respective states has hither to rendered its circulation in many instances tardy and doubtful—and indeed the many frauds, and deceptions, that have been practiced in the country, by the circulation of spurious paper, purporting to be on banks at a distance, has very justly awakened the suspicion of those, to whom such paper was offered, and consequently cramped its circulation. But to the circulation of our own, there will not be the same objection—the people in general will soon become acquainted with it, and any attempts at fraud or imposition, will be much sooner detected. But at Shawnoetown, a place of growing prospects characterized by its commercial activity, & the eligibility of its situation, more essentially required a bank, than we ourselves, as well as many others, at first supposed. The fertility of the neighboring country on both sides of the Ohio river, and on the Wabash, gives rise to a great redundancy of produce of every description, and Shawnoetown is the only place of deposit for a considerable distance around. It is from that place that such produce must embark, for home as well as foreign markets. And it is there where the industrious farmer, will in future receive the price of his produce. Those engaged in commercial employments will meet at that place, the rich crops of the yeomanry of the country, ready to be wafted to the best markets, and the facilities of the bank, will enable them to procure on reasonable terms, the means of paying

[41] *Intelligencer*, January 15, 1817; *House Journal*, 1 General Assembly, 2 Session, 105, 106.

for their cargos in advance. And thus the farmer, as well as the merchant, will experience at once the benefits of the bank.

But the advantages of the bank will be more happily felt at the present time by those who are purchasing lands from the United States; many forfeitures of instalments already paid will no doubt be saved by the means derivable from the banks of securing the funds necessary to prevent such forfeitures. And if even forfeitures should not be prevented, it will be the means of preventing great individual sacrifices, such as would result from a necessity of selling lands already entered to secure payment. And this advantage need not be confirmed to the neighborhood of Shawnoetown, but may be co-extensive with the territory. There is also an extensive and fertile country in Kentucky, that is contigious [*sic*] to Shawnoetown—and from it we may expect to derive a neighborly advantage—it will be the means of drawing its produce in a great degree to that place as the point of delivery; indeed, as is the case in every new country where the resources of the country are not developed, new advantages will be hourly unfolding themselves. New inducements to industry will be furnished and individual wealth which always forms public wealth, will characterize the whole neighboring country. The salt trade will also be an additional source of wealth to the stockholders; many thousand bushels of salt are annually taken from the neighboring salines. And the bank will be rendered an easy means of facilitating that commerce. The local situation of the bank being thus eligible, and the prospects of its utility being thus flattering, we have no doubt but the whole of the stock subject to individual subscription, will be immediately taken; and as the territory will not likely in any short time be in a situation to subscribe, neither for the whole nor any part of the shares reserved to itself—if the commercial growth of that place, and the demands of the country should justify it, we see no reason why the legislature might not pass some act to authorize appropriations of the public shares, by individuals until the territory can raise the stock for its own use.

The craze for wildcat banking did not come until after Illinois became a state. Into a consideration of the conditions in Illinois attending that catastrophe it is scarcely necessary to enter. But the discussion over the establishment of a state bank at the second session of the first legislature produced an editorial bearing so directly on the economic conditions as to merit insertion here. After announcing the passage of the bill by both houses, the editor of the *Illinois Emigrant* clipped from the *Illinois In-*

telligencer the following words of conditional approbation and then added his own scathing comment.

An act incorporating A STATE BANK, so much desired by the people, has been passed by both branches of the General Assembly upon the principles heretofore published in a former number, except the duration of the charter—which is reduced from fifty to twenty-five years. If a board of directors, *known* to be friendly to the institution shall be elected, we again say, as we have before said, that we believe much publick good will result from it. We believe the people will have great reason (should that be the case) to congratulate themselves on the occasion, and to welcome home their representatives with smiles of approbation. But should the management of the institution be confided to a directory unfriendly to its prosperity, the salutary exertions of the Legislature will have been of no avail. *It will indeed be creating a light, and then putting it under a bushel.* (*ib.* [*Illinois Intelligencer*])

Thus we see, that while the legislatures of almost every other state in the Union are taking measures to repress that species of *swindling*, known by the term *banking*, the general assembly of Illinois, (we dare say from the most *considerate*, *pure* and *patriotick motives*) are creating a state Bank, with ten branches and a capital of *three millions* of dollars! It would be curious to know, what part of this stock is to be subscribed by the state, and out of what other bank it intends to *borrow* money to make the instalments? For is it not known that our treasury is bankrupt, and that, as a state, we have not the fee-simple of one inch of territory upon the globe—that our population (including men, women and children) does not exceed, by an unit, 40,000 souls—that perhaps one seventh part of this population may be men, above 21 years of age—and that, probably, one fourth part of this small number, may have paid for their possessions, and are able to purchase stock, tho' not to a great amount! What business, then, have we, (who, in addition to all, are not a commercial people, and whose great commercial towns, Cairo and America, to use a quaint phrase, cannot be seen for the trees) with banks? Because the constitution has given the legislature power to create a state bank, does it follow that it must be done *now*? that no regard should be paid to the expediency of the thing?—"*So much desired by the people!*" 'Tis false! the people never desired it—it is a gross insult to the good sense of the community—the people know that some citizens of Kaskaskia, and none else, desired it—and that there was not virtue enough in their representatives to preserve the state from disgrace, and themselves from the imputation of trifling with their powers and the wishes of the people. But, it is asked will the governour and counsel give their sanction to this bill? For our parts, we think they will not—we cannot believe that Mr. Bond will so far forget the sacred duty he owes the good people of this state, as to assign them over to the management of a set of bank directors; as in fact he will, if this bank go into operation with this consent—So fraught is banking with every evil consequence—so truly is it "the offspring of ignorance, chicanery, and a spirit of speculation." [42]

"The spirit of speculation" was pushing Illinois beyond the point of discretion, not only in its banking ventures, but more particularly in its attempts to stimulate the growth of towns. Speculation in land was the only outlet for any considerable amount of capital. But it was more than that—it was practically the only activity in which men could give free scope to their business ability, could take the chances of success or failure which make the game worth playing. The limitations in farming and trade have been pointed out. The development of the lead mines in the north had not begun. The manufacture of salt, which was conducted on a larger scale than any other industry in the territory, was owned by the United States. Milling was necessarily on a small scale, for grain was not raised for export. There was very little manufacturing outside the homes.[43] No one's business was on a large enough scale to occupy his whole time, and consequently land speculation was universally indulged in.

Among the leaders in land speculation in Illinois were to be found all the principal politicians. In a previous chapter attention was called to Governor Ninian Edwards' activities at Edwardsville. According to an early settler at Upper Alton, he held land there also. There was scarcely an issue of the *Intelligencer* which did not contain an advertisement signed by him. Under date of January 13, 1818, he ran the following notice:

[42] *Illinois Emigrant*, March 20, 1819.

[43] In November, 1817, Birkbeck wrote to Fearon: "The *manufactures* you mention may hereafter be eligible; cotton, woollen, linen, stockings, &c., Certainly not at present." *Letters from Illinois*, 32. In 1818, Jesse B. Thomas advertised that by June he would have in operation two carding machines; this was the first establishment of its kind in Illinois. *Intelligencer*, January 1, June 3, 1818.

NOTICE

I SHALL continue to sell LOTS in Belville (the seat of justice for St. Clair county) at $60 a lot, until the 1st January next, after which time, I do not intend to take less than $100 for any lot, unless it should be to accommodate some respectable mechan[i]ck who may be desirous of settling in that village.

NINIAN EDWARDS.

Kaskaskia, Dec. 8, 1127, [*sic*]

A little later this notice appeared:

Notice.

I WILL sell upon liberal terms, *ONE HUNDRED ACRES OF LAND*, including a very valuable mill seat on Mary's river, ten miles below this place and about three miles from the Mississippi.

The proximity of this situation to a great extent of fertile country, already, much improved, and rapidly improving its being surrounded with a great abundance of poplar and other timber suitable for making plank, the facility of transporting grain and timber to it—and a practicable and safe navigation to and from it—all combine to render it a most eligible seat for water works of any kind. A complete dam has been recently erected that has withstood all the late floods, and a very inconsiderable sum would be sufficient to put a saw mill into operation within a short time, that would most probably yield a profit of two thousand dollars a year.

If I should not sell shortly, I shall wish to employ workmen to build me both a sawmill and merchant mill.

I have also for sale, several *HORSES* and *MULES.*

NINIAN EDWARDS.

Kaskaskia, Dec. 20.

While this notice was still running, Edwards began to advertise an addition to Kaskaskia as follows:

Notice.

IS hereby given, that I shall make application to the circuit court for Randolph county, at its next August term, for an order to add to the village of Kaskaskia, a tract of land adjoining said villiage [*sic*], containing thirty four acres and three quarters; which was conveyed by John Edgar to Benjamin Stephenson, and by said Stephenson to myself, as by reference to both deeds now on record, will more fully appear.

Ninian Edwards.

March 30, 1818

That he had land in the northern settlements as well is shown from this advertisement:

I HAVE for Sale several valuable Tracts of Land near Belleville, and in other parts of Saint Clair county—Two quarter sections on Cahokia creek, in the vicinity of Edwardsville—and three quarter sections on Shoal creek, near Mr. Swearingen's; all of which, Mr. Thomas Estes of St. Louis, is fully empowered to sell.

Ninian Edwards.[44]

March 30, 1818

Not far behind Edwards in land speculation were his political co-workers Stephenson and Cook. The former has already been spoken of; his interest centered in Edwardsville, where he was receiver of the land office as well as merchant and president of the bank. Cook advertised land in localities as far apart as Madison and Edwards counties. To him, as to most other lawyers, land speculation held out peculiar charms. Most of the average lawyer's work was in connection with disputed claims to land; it was an easy and natural step for the lawyer who had capital to buy up claims which came under his notice and advance them for himself instead of for a client. The following letter from John Reynolds to Ninian Edwards gives a good picture of a lawyer's interest in land claims.

Cahokia 4th Decemb 1818

Dear Sir

Permit me to trouble you on my private business; and the greatest excuse I have to say in my favor is: that my claims of Government are just, and of course, should you befriend me therein; you will have the sensations of a person who knows he has done right.

In the first place; Mr Pope concluded the affair of the Piasa Land. I have executed to him an equal fifth of the claim; and has made the same contract in writing to you. Mr. Pope is to endeavor to send the Patent Certificate to the Commissioner of the General Land office but of this, no doubt, he will let you know in a more ample manner than I can do: so you can nourish the Claim in the hands of Mr. Meigs. as to the value of the Land it is immense. Major Hunter of St. Louis (so reports say) gave Meachan $10.000 for half of one quarter sec. of the

---

[44] *Intelligencer*, January 1, April 15, April 29, 1818.

Denegan Entry; that Bates had. this is to shew, that this Piasa Claim will justify great industry to gain it. . . .

I have this day bo't a claim on the United States for 100 Acres of Land from a certain Jean Baptiste Laducier who was Subject to militia duty in the Illinois Country on the 1st Aug.t 1790 but neglected to claim and prove it before the board of Commissioners in proper time. he had it proved by Mr. Arundale and others to the satisfaction of the Kaskaskia Register and Receiver and they reported to the Congress at the last session to the same effect. there is no doubt; this man was and is entitled to a hundred Acres from the Act of Congress. The proof were so late giting [*sic*] before the Land Committee last term; that there was no report made. Joseph A. Baird and myself bo't and paid for three hundred Acres of Land in the same situation. When we bo't; we thought his Donation was confirmed to him; but on examination, it was not. this right was proved by the most of the old people of our Village. this went on with the Claim of Laducier—this person, whose name is Jacques Miotte, had a militia right of 100 Acres confirmed to him; there then remains to him 300 to make his Donation of 400. where the proof of these two Claims have lain since last Congress, I know not. and I suppose it requires some friendly hand to put it [into] operation again.— Some years past, there were given by Congress Claims to Land in the same situation reported favorably on by the Kaskaskia Register and Receiver. I see no reason, why Congress will not extend its favors in similar cases. they are just; If you see the host of testimony, you will say, they are just—even should "Doctor" "Doubty" himself be in Congress; he would not doubt. I bo't a soldier's right of 160 Acres of Land his name is Enoch Jones and got his discharge from Kennerly commanding there at "PASS CHRISTIONNE" below New Orleans. this Discharge was sent too late to Mr. Pope last year. I wrote Mr. Pope how I should git his old letters; one of which contained Jone's Discharge, and to let you know; I wrote our Representative McLean to manage this affair, If you or he could git the Discharge.—

I have with Major Whiteside a pre emption right on the Mississippi out of the tract reserved for preemptions. yet I believe the first act of congress meant to embrace all settlers in the Territory: but Col. Stephenson had instructions to the Contrary. there were but a few out of the survey, and in good conscience are as much entitled to this previliage [*sic*] as other settlers, when any of them first settled there were no surveys made. I will If you please send this Claim with the proof to support it by the next mail to you. It is of considerable magnitude to me. you can, If you please, as with the above Claims, present it before the proper tribunal for Justice. I want no more. I fear by this time you are much tired with me and my claims but treat them and me as your feelings and Judgement may dictate and I shall be satisfied. I will write the other members on the above. I was lately at Edwardsville when I understood your family were well. no news. Pope is Register.

> May God preserve you and
> family for ever and longer.
> John Reynolds.

The Honorable N. Edwards.) [45]

So generally was this combination of law and land speculation understood that from an Albany lawyer Kane received the following query: "Can an attorney expect to succeed [in Illinois] without Some capital to embark in Speculations, and what is the Smallest Sum which will be requisite? . . . I have . . . from 1 to 2000 dollars. Will such funds justify the adventure?" [46] It was inevitable that the widespread speculation in land should make itself felt in politics. The entrepreneurs who had placed the heaviest stakes in the new territory were naturally the most keenly interested in its political development; few of them had any scruples against using every political weapon available for the furtherance of their undertakings. The territorial laws on labor and on the opening up of the country bear unmistakable evidence of the work of interested individuals; the Cairo scheme is not an unfair example of the kind of legislation that was passed. Undoubtedly the legislature merited the caricature which appeared in the *Intelligencer* for September 9, 1818. The writer, "Nemo," tells of a marvelous vision.

After passing Cape *ne plus ultra,* on the east, I saw in lat. 39° N. and Long. 8° W. in the open Prairie, above the head of the Little Wabash in the Illinois territory, another GREAT SEA SERPENT. As these monsters are now filling the world with wonder, I was determined to ascertain the size, nature, and if possible, to what tribe of animals this monster belonged. I therefore, hauled to my ship for that purpose, and I found this serpent to be exactly two hundred and seventy-five poles in length; and in thickness, different, as seemed to be necessary for the ends of creating that animal. On one part of the back of this monster, there was a territorial legislature in full session—at a small distance from the legislature, there was for the governor an house made very strong with

[45] Reynolds to Edwards, December 4, 1818, in Chicago Historical Society Manuscripts, 50:294.

[46] January 11, 1819, in Chicago Historical Society Manuscripts, 52:179.

absolute *vetos*. This legislature then, was discussing, whether nature had designed such and such rivers to be navigable or not.

I saw another place of bustle and business on this sea serpent, bearing from the legislature N. E. about one hundred poles. I made easy sale [*sic*] towards this place, and discovered its inhabitants to be very short men, with knocked knees, and crossed-eyes, fabricating new cities. I could distinctly perceive the stocks, where were built the famous cities of "Cairo," city of "America," city of "Illinois," "Covington," "St. Mary," and many others; these creators of cities, were all stamped on the forehead with the word "moneyism."

On a sudden, I saw this huge being in a great agitation of body, and on sailing to the S. W. towards the head of this serpent, I could discover very plainly [*sic*], that this monster was swallowing, and thereby exterminating the several banks of the Illinois Territory. This appeared to be a fatal day on banks. The bank at EDWARDSVILLE, the Kaskaskia bank, and that of Cairo, and of the Little Wabash Company, were utterly annihilated with all the others of the above territory. This extermination of banks was not a difficult matter, as the people of the Illinois had learnt by experience, that banks without any capital, created for private speculation, were injurious to the public. After the serpent finished this necessary work, it changed its course to the S. E. and made great head away for the Floridas, to aid general Jackson in conquering those Spanish provinces in time of peace. This serpent had a head of a great size, and when its mouth was open, it appeared within a fiery furnace.   *NEMO.*

Dated on board the ship ⎱
Prairie, 28 Aug. 1818.   ⎰

Chapter 6

Social Conditions

On each of the successive American frontiers, pioneer life has advanced by the same stages—first a relapse to primitive conditions, followed by the gradual development of a more complex civilization. Illinois was no exception to the rule. Even the pioneer who came to the Illinois wilderness from a region only recently advanced out of the frontier stage encountered inconveniences and privations; the immigrant from New England or from across the water must have found this adjustment to the new conditions very difficult. Fortunately, however, a spirit of hospitality and neighborliness usually accompanied the early settlers and helped them to overcome the difficulties. "When a new-comer arrived in the country," wrote a man who came to Illinois in 1817,

the settlers, without distinction or ceremony, went at once to pay him a visit, whom they usually found in a tent or camp. The warmest sentiments of friendship and good-will were interchanged, the old settlers assuring their new neighbor, that every thing they possessed, in the way of tools, teams, wagons, provisions, and their own personal services, were entirely at his command. Hence, in a few days, all hands, as the phrase then was, turned out, and built the new-comer a house, cut and split his rails, hauled them out, put them up in fence around the land he wished to cultivate, and then his land was broken up for him ready for the seed. Thus, in the space of a few days, the new-comer was in a comfortable condition, well acquainted, and upon the best terms of friendship, with the whole neighborhood. And to conclude these friendly attentions to the new-comer, a most joyous and convivial occasion was enjoyed, when the younger portion of the company would trip the light, fantastic toe, over some rough puncheon floor. Thus would be formed the most warm and enduring friendships—such as no ordinary circumstances could disturb.[1]

The spirit of cooperation did not disappear once the new-

[1] *Wisconsin Historical Collections*, 2:327-328.

comer was established. Whenever a task was to be performed which required many hands, the neighbors would gather from all directions. Most of the social gatherings in the country had their origin in utility. Apple parings, quiltings, corn huskings and barn raisings, and often there was a combination of these entertainments, a barn raising, or a corn husking would be held, and at the same time and place there would be a quilting party, and the women guests would help to cook and serve the dinner for the men who were doing the rougher work; and at night the young people stayed to dance, the more opulent ladies going and coming on their own horses with habits and side saddles. The less fortunate (or were they less fortunate?) riding behind their husbands, brothers or sweet-hearts on the same horse. Even when neighbors went visiting they carried their knitting or sewing —"calling" in its present sense, there was not.[2]

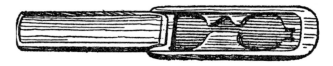

HANDMADE SPECTACLE CASE

But though the frontier men and women managed to combine some pleasure with their work, it was at best a hard life that they led. "There are in England," wrote Fordham, "comforts, nay, sources of happiness, which will for ages be denied to these half savage countries, good houses, good roads, a mild and healthy climate, healthy, because the country is old, society, the arts of life carried almost to perfection, and Laws well administered." There is abundant testimony to the prevalence of disease, especially among the newcomers, who had not become acclimated. In February, 1819, Gershom Flagg wrote from Edwardsville: "The principal objection I have to this Country is its unhealthiness the months of Aug. & Sept. are generally very Sickly. I was taken sick with the feever & ague the 15 Sept. which lasted me nearly two months. I shall try it one season more and if I do not have my health better than I have

[2] Illinois State Historical Society, *Transactions*, 1904, p. 510.

the season past I shall sell my property and leave the Country."[3]

Flower gives a more detailed description of his encounter with this disease:

The summer had been very hot and latterly wet. Thunder showers of daily occurrence sent mosquitoes in swarms. My cabin, recently built, of course, of green logs, unfurnished, with rank vegetation growing all around it and up to its very sides, was in its situation and in itself a sufficient cause of disease. My shepherd and his family came, bringing a few choice sheep and an English high-bred cow. His whole family, in a few days, all fell sick, lying in a small cabin just built about a hundred yards from my own. Mr. White, carpenter, from London, wife, and two children, occupied a two-horse wagon and a soldier's tent. There was no house for him; they all fell sick. My two sons were speedily taken with fever and ague, to us then a new disease. Miss Fordham, who shared our cabin, was attacked with the same disease. My constitution, strong

HANDMADE BABY CRADLE

and good, yielding from exposure to heat and rain, took another form of disease. Boils and irritable sores broke out on both my legs, from knee to ankle, incapacitating me, for a time, from walking. Thus we were situated for two or three weeks, without the slightest assistance from any source, or supplies other than from my own wagons, as they

[3] Ogg, *Fordham's Personal Narrative*, 227; Illinois State Historical Society, *Transactions*, 1910, pp. 163-164.

slowly arrived from Shawneetown, giving us sufficient bedding with flour and bacon. All the other merchandise and furniture did but add to our present embarrassment, in attempts to protect them from the weather, and in endeavoring to dry what was wet.

We were carried through this period of trial by the unremitting labor and self-sacrifice of my wife. She alone prepared all our food and bedding, and attended to the wants of the sick and the suffering by night and day. To all this was added a fatigue that a strong man might have shrunk from, in bringing water from that distant well. Sustained in her unremitting labors by unbounded devotion to her family, and a high sense of duty to all within her reach, her spirit and her power seemed to rise above the manifold trials by which she was surrounded. And thus we were saved from probable death or certain dispersion. The incessant labor of the mother told on the infant at the breast; it sickened and died. With returning health we worked our way unaided through our difficulties.

As Flower indicated, the principal cause of ill health was the stagnant water and decaying vegetation. In October, 1820, Flagg wrote: "Several towns in this state have been very sickly this season especially those situated contiguous to Rivers or mill-Ponds. The waters are very low and in many places covered with a green poison looking skum. The fogs arising from this [*sic*] stagnated waters makes the air very unwholesome." [4] As the country became more thickly settled, and more land was brought under cultivation, this condition was ameliorated. Apparently some of the more enterprising people were not content to leave the remedy to time, but proposed to take action themselves; for in November, 1819, Morris Birkbeck "returned from a tour through Illinois, by way of Kascasky, where he was chosen President of the agricultural society of Illinois, one grand object of which will be, to rid the state of stagnant waters." [5]

Various other factors doubtless contributed to the poor health of the people in the early days. Fordham reached the conclusion that

[4] Flower, *English Settlement*, 122-123; Illinois State Historical Society, *Transactions*, 1910, p. 166.

[5] Thwaites, *Early Western Travels*, 11:162.

there is, upon the whole, a superiority in the Climate of the western Country to that of England; though not so great as I at first imagined, or as you would expect from the latitude. Consumptions are almost unknown here. Bilious fevers are rather prevalent, but not dangerous when early attended to. Women have not such good health as the men have; but that is to be attributed to their mode of life,—being always in the house, usually without shoes and stockings, and roasting themselves over large fires.

People are not so long-lived here as in England, and they look old sooner. This I think may be justly attributed to

1st.   The universal use of spirituous liquors.

2dly.   The disregard of personal comfort and cleanliness, exposure to bad air near swamps &c, and want of good Clothing.

3dly.   The great stimulus and excitement of the mental passions, which adventurers and first settlers are, by their situation, subject to.

4thly.   (Perhaps) violent religious enthusiasm.

5thly.   In some instances, very early marriages.[6]

While the task of hewing out and developing a farm in the wilderness was undoubtedly an arduous one, many of the pioneers were quite willing to progress slowly. In a land where the soil was fertile and the woods full of game, it was not difficult to make a bare living; and for most of the settlers, this was enough. Gershom Flagg wrote in 1818: "The people of This Territory are from all parts of the United States & do the least work I believe of any people in the world."[7] This is corroborated by Daniel M. Parkinson. "The surrounding country, however," he wrote, with reference to Madison County in 1817, "was quite sparsely settled, and destitute of any energy or enterprise among the people; their labors and attention being chiefly confined to the hunting of game, which then abounded, and tilling a small patch of corn for bread, relying on game for the remaining supplies of the table. The inhabitants were of the most generous and hospitable character, and were principally from the southern States; harmony and the utmost good feeling prevailed throughout the country."[8]

[6] Ogg, *Fordham's Personal Narrative*, 200-201.

[7] Illinois State Historical Society, *Transactions*, 1910, p. 162.

[8] *Wisconsin Historical Collections*, 2:327.

Such descriptions apply particularly to the first comers; and
Flagg hastens to add that "these kind of People as soon as the
settlements become thick Clear out and go further into the new
Country." Even their successors, however, often took their
farming operations very casually, and found plenty of time to
devote to hunting and recreation of various sorts.

In the villages a favorite form of diversion was the celebration of anniversaries, participated in by the people of the surrounding country. Thus the Fourth of July, 1818, was marked
at Kaskaskia by a dinner to which all the people were invited
and which was followed by an oration by one of the local lawyers. At Edwardsville, a year later, the day was ushered in by
discharges of artillery, while "the American Flag waved trium-
phantly from the top of a lofty liberty pole." At noon a procession formed and marched through the main streets. After the
Declaration of Independence had been read on the public square,
dinner was served, followed by appropriate toasts. The Masonic
lodge at Kaskaskia was accustomed to celebrate the anniversaries
of St. John the Baptist in June and of St. John the Evangelist
in December, usually with a dinner and an oration. The annual inspection and review of militia and the occasional elections and court sessions at the county seats also furnished
occasions for amusements of various sorts. Horse racing, cock-
fighting, and gambling were favorite diversions, although attempts were made to suppress them by laws and ordinances.
Everybody played cards, and to play for money was both fashionable and honorable. Another and a somewhat more refined
form of recreation was the singing school. There was a singing
society in Edwardsville in 1819 which was called to meet at
the courthouse for the purpose of organizing a singing school
for the coming winter. Three dozen of the "most choice selection
of Music Books" had recently been received from Boston.[9]

Facilities for education were extremely limited in Illinois at
the close of the territorial period. A system of public schools
was scarcely dreamed of, and the few private schools in exist-

[9] *Spectator*, October 30, 1819; Reynolds, *My Own Times*, 82-86.

ence were very rudimentary in character. Although surveying
and bookkeeping were taught in a school near Belleville as early
as 1806 and a Mr. Sturgess in 1816 advertised a school at
Prairie du Rocher where grammer, geography, surveying, astronomy, Greek, and Latin would be taught, instruction was
generally confined to the "three R's." John Mason Peck, the
Baptist missionary, and one of the best-informed men on the
frontier in all that pertained to matters of culture, after a survey of educational conditions in the neighboring state of Missouri, where the frontier life was similar to that across the river,
reached the conclusion "that at least one-third of the schools
were really a public nuisance, and did the people more harm
than good; another third about balanced the account, by doing
about as much harm as good, and perhaps one-third were advantageous to the community in various degrees." [10]

The conditions in Illinois were thus described:

During the early history of Illinois, schools were almost unknown in
some neighborhoods, and in the most favored districts they were kept
up solely by subscription, and only in the winter season, each subscriber
agreeing to pay for one or more scholar, or stipulating to pay for his
children *pro rata* for the number of days they should be in attendance.
The teacher usually drew up articles of agreement, which stipulated
that the school should commence when a specified number of scholars
should be subscribed, at the rate of $2, $2.50, or $3 per scholar for the
quarter. In these written articles he bound himself to teach spelling,
reading, writing, and arithmetic, as far as the double rule of three. Occasionally a teacher would venture to include English grammar. But in
the earlier years of my youth, I knew of no teacher who attempted to
give instruction in grammar or geography. And such branches as history, natural philosophy, or astronomy, were not thought of. Many parents were unwilling that their children should study arithmetic, contend-
ing that it was quite unnecessary for farmers. And what was the use of
grammar to a person who could talk so as to be understood by everybody? I studied English grammar, and all the latter rules of arithmetic,
when about twelve years old, without the aid of a teacher, and geography at a later age, after I had begun to prepare for college.

The mode of conducting schools was peculiar. All the pupils studied
their lessons, by spelling or reading aloud simultaneously, while the

[10] Babcock, *Memoir of Peck*, 123; Ford, *History of Illinois*, 38; Reynolds,
My Own Times, 95; *Intelligencer*, September 5, 1816.

teacher usually heard each scholar recite alone; although, in the opening of the school, a chapter of the Bible was read by the older scholars by verses, in turn, and at the close in the evening, the whole school, except the beginners, stood up and spelled words in turn, as given out by the master.[11]

It would naturally be expected that schools of a somewhat better sort would be found in the capital of the territory, but such does not appear to have been the case. As late as November, 1816, the *Intelligencer* published a long editorial bewailing the lack of a school in Kaskaskia, "a place which must at some day be a towering city." About a year later one J. Cheek published a card *"To the Patrons of Literature"* in which he

INFORMS the friends and the guardians of erudition that he has opened a SCHOOL in the town of Kaskaskia, for the instruction of youth, in the different departments of *E*nglish literature.—He will extend the sphere of instruction, so as to include the following sciences, viz. *Reading, Writing, Orthography, Arithmetic, English Grammar, Geography, History, Rhetorick, Composition, Elocution,* ect. He flatters himself that from his attention of the morals and scientifick avocations of his pupils, he will share no inconsiderable portion of the patronage of a judicious and descerning people.[12]

A teacher who arrived in Kaskaskia in 1818 appears to have aspired to the role of public entertainer. The paper of December 2 published a notice in which "Mr. Cross respectfully informs his fellow citizens of Kaskaskia, that he will, this evening, ascend the Rostrum, in the Representatives' chamber, and exert his best efforts for their moral amusement." In the next issue of the paper,

MR. CROSS respectfully informs the citizens of Kaskaskia, and its vicinage, that he intends, should sufficient patronage be afforded, to open a *SCHOOL* in this town, for the instruction of youth, in *Orthography, Orthoepy, Reading, Writing, English Grammar, Arithmetic,* and *Elocution.*

Scholars who shall have graduated in these branches of tuition, will be instructed in the rudiments of *History, Geography, Natural Philosophy,* and *Mathematics.*

[11] Patterson, "Early Society in Southern Illinois," in *Fergus Historical Series,* no. 14:121-122.

[12] *Intelligencer,* January 1, 1818.

Mr. C. will endeavor to instill into the minds of his scholars, the vital importance of sound moral principle, and correct manners, which he will elucidate, by a regular course of lectures, every Saturday. As soon as he can procure the necessary appendages his school will be Lancasterian. No advance payment will be required, but a punctual compliance with the terms of subscription, at the expiration of each quarter, is confidently calculated upon.

Mr. C. will, this evening, in the Representative chamber, give various specimens of Elocution, Instructive and amusing, original and selected. Tickets to be had at Burr and Christy's Hotel, and at this office.[13]

An entertaining side light on the character of the man who thus proposed to instruct the children of the community and to furnish "moral amusement" for his fellow citizens may be learned from the opening paragraphs of a "Masonic Oration" which he delivered a few weeks later and which, printed in full at the request of the committee, filled nine columns of the paper.

THAT the rostrum has been assigned to me on this august festival, excites feelings which language faulters to impart, and I address you with sensations too strong for entire suppression. Oh permit me, your homeless, healthless brother, an exile from domestic enjoyment, to claim all the indulgence which our sacred relationship affords.

With a resolution and perseverance which I hope will win for the meridian of my life, the esteem and respect of society, and in obedience to my duty as a Mason, I have, under the blessing of the Great Architect, regained the narrow, but Heavenward path of temperance. No longer succumbing to the pressure of misfortune and far superior to the blandishments of indolence and dissipation with which the profession of arms and my sanguine nature have seduced me, I returned towards Missouri, of which I am a citizen, in the hope & belief that domestic happiness would reward my self-conquest, and that a friendship, which had proved as sincere and magnanimous as my delight in looking at the bright side of human nature induced me to believe it would have honored the Grecian Pythyas, awaited my embrace. You know, brethren, how my dearest earthly hopes have been blasted, and how little my heart deserved the remediless infliction.

I stand before you with a lacerated bosom, endeavoring to act with that fortitude and resignation which the principles of our order enjoins [*sic*]. Believe me, therefore, that I acknowledge with gratitude the influence of the oil and wine which, with the brethren of Columbia, Vir-

[13] *Intelligencer*, December 9, 1818.

ginia, Kentucky, Ohio, Indiana, Tennessee and Illinois, you have poured into my wounds; and, though you have much over-rated my talents by this honorable distinction, gratitude to the fraternity, and my ardent love of the soul-redeeming science of Masonry, must, at least for this day, absorb my individual sufferings.[14]

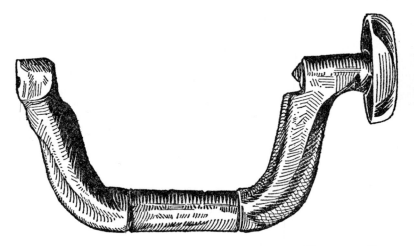

HANDMADE BRACE
Used in a machine shop in St. Clair County in 1818.

These rudimentary attempts at academic instruction were not supplemented to any considerable extent by reading. There were few books among the people of the frontier. A dozen years before Illinois became a state, according to Reynolds, "not a man in the country, professional, or otherwise, had any collection of books, that could acquire the name of library. There were some books scattered through the country, but they were not plenty. Although my father was a reading man, and possessed a strong mind, yet as far as I recollect, he brought to the country with him no books, except the Bible. Many of the immigrants acted in the same manner as to books." [15]

By 1818, some of the lawyers possessed fair collections of

[14] *Intelligencer*, January 6, 1819.
[15] Reynolds, *My Own Times*, 93.

books. In that year, one of the rooms of the market house erected in the English settlement of Albion "was fitted up for the reception of books, that were given by individuals in England, as a nucleus for a public-library, and was used for public-meetings, and public-worship." The credit for the establishment of this institution is due to Richard Flower, and something of its development and of the attitude of the American frontiersmen toward books may be seen in an extract from a letter which Flower wrote in January, 1820, to friends in England.

You would have been much amused if you had been with us a few weeks since, when I had a visit from Captain Burke, a sensible and intelligent backwoodsman. He paid me a short visit, put off his business that he might fetch his wife, which he did; we thought we saw through the plan; he returned with her the next day, and we felt disposed to gratify their curiosity. "There wife," said he, "did you ever see such fixings?" He felt the paper, looked in a mirror over our chimney-piece which reflected the cattle grazing in the field before the house, and gazed with amazement. But turning from these sights to the library,—"Now," said he to my wife, "does your old gentleman" (for that is my title here) "read those books?" "Yes," said she, "he has read most of them." —"Why if I was to read half of them, I should drive all the little sense in my head out of it." I replied that we read to increase our sense and our knowledge; but this untutored son of nature could not conceive of this till I took down a volume of Shaw's Zoology. "You, Mr. Burke, are an old hunter, and have met with many snakes in your time. I never saw above one in my life; now if I can tell you about your snakes and deer, and bears and wolves, as much or more than you know, you will see the use of books." I read to him a description of the rattle-snake, and then showed him the plate, and so on. His attention was arrested, and his thirst for knowledge fast increasing. "I never saw an Indian in my life, and yet," said I, "I can tell you all about them." I read again and shewed him a coloured plate. "There," said he, "wife, is it not wonderful, that this gentleman, coming so many miles, should know these things from books only? See ye," said he, pointing to the Indian, "got him to a turn." In short, I never felt more interested for an hour or two, to see how this man's mind thirsted after knowledge; and though he dreaded the appearance of so many books, he seemed, before he left us, as if he could spend his life amongst them.

Our library is now consolidated; and that the kind intentions of yourself and others may not be lost, and that your names may live in our memories and be perpetuated to future generations, I have conveyed all the books presented to us, in trust to the proprietors of the town, for the use of the Albion Library; writing the names of the donors in them; and in my next letter I shall, *pro forma*, be able to convey to you our united thanks for the books presented. Our little library is the admiration of travellers, and Americans say we have accomplished more in one year, than many new settlements have effected in fifty—a well supplied market, a neat place of worship, and a good library.[16]

This first public library in Illinois owed its existence to the unusual character of the the founders of Albion and cannot be considered as typical of frontier Illinois. Less than a year after it was founded, however, a subscription library was organized in Edwardsville, though the funds for it evidently were collected with some difficulty. On August 7, 1819, the "Director" gave notice through the *Spectator* that the books ordered from Boston had arrived, and urged those who were in arrears to pay their subscription, so that they might entitle "themselves and families to the use of one of the best collections of books in the country." Fortunately a catalog of the books in this library in November, 1819, has been preserved; it is worthy of reproduction in full as evidence of the books which were available for reading in this pioneer American community.

American State Papers, in 12 Volumes; Adams' Defense; Burns' Poems; Blair's Lectures; Brydon's Tour; Butler's Hudibras; Beauties of History; Bartram's Travels; Belknap's American Biography; Coeleb's in Search of a Wife; Cowper's Homer, 4 volumes; Campaign in Russia; Carvel's Travels; Camilla, or a Picture of Youth; Clarke's Travels; Christian Researches in Asia; Clarkson's History; Clark's Naval History; Depom's Voyage; Domestic Encyclopedia; Ely's Journal; Elements of Criticism; Ferguson's Roman Republic; The Federalist; Guy Mannering; Gibbon's Rome, 4 volumes; Goldsmith's Works, 6 volumes; Grand Pre's Voyage; Gil Blas, 4 volumes; History of Carraccas; History of Chili; History of Greece; History of Charles Fifth; History of England; Hawkworth's Voyages; Humboldt's New Spain; Jefferson's Notes; Letters of Junius; Marshall's Life of Washington; McFingal, a Modern Epic Poem; Mayo's Ancient Geography and History; Modern Europe; McLeod on the Revelation; McKenzie's Voyage; Moore's Poems; McNevins' Switzerland; Ossian's Poems; Practical Education; Plutarch's Lives; Porter's Travels; Ramsay's Washington; Rob Roy; Rollin's Ancient History, with atlas, 8 vol-

[16] Flower, *English Settlement*, 133; Thwaites, *Early Western Travels*, 10:126-128; Illinois State Historical Society, *Journal*, 6:248.

umes; Rumford's Essays; Robertson's America; Scottish Chiefs; Sterne's Works, 5 volumes; Scott's Works, 4 volumes; Salmagundi, 2 volumes; Shakespeare's Plays, 6 volumes; Spectator, 10 volumes; Tales of My Landlord; Telemachus; Warsaw; Travels of Anacharsis; Thompson's Seasons; Turnbull's Voyages; Universal Gazetteer; Vicissitudes Abroad, 6 volumes; Volney's America; Virginia Debates; Vicar of Wakefield; Views of Louisiana; Wirt's Life of Patrick Henry; Watt's Logic; Wealth of Nations; Young's Night Thoughts; Zimmerman on National Pride.[17]

A century ago, a considerable part of the reading of the people was furnished by newspapers, just as it is now. Besides outside publications, which were probably taken in considerable number, two weekly papers printed in Illinois at the time it became a state were available. The older of these was established at Kaskaskia in 1814 by Matthew Duncan, with the name of *Illinois Herald*. Its publication was made possible by both federal and territorial patronage, for it was paid liberally for printing the United States laws and proclamations, and had in addition a monopoly of the public printing for the territory. In 1816, probably in April, the paper was sold to "Daniel P. Cook and Co." and the name was changed to *Western Intelligencer*. Late in May the firm name was changed to "Cook and Blackwell," in September it became "Berry and Cook," and in October it changed once more, this time to "Berry and Blackwell." With the issue of May 27, 1818, the title was changed to *Illinois Intelligencer*.[18]

Under a United States law of November 21, 1814, the Secretary of State was "authorized to cause the laws of the United States, passed, or to be passed, during the present or any future session of congress, to be published in two of the public newspapers within each and every territory of the United States; *Provided,* In his opinion, it shall become necessary and expedient." [19] With only one paper printed in the territory it would seem that an opportunity was being missed, and this probably

[17] Illinois State Historical Society, *Journal,* 6:246-247.
[18] Scott, *Newspapers and Periodicals,* 28, 211-212; *Intelligencer, passim.*
[19] *Statutes at Large,* 3:145.

explains the establishment of the second paper in Illinois in the summer of 1818. The promoters of the enterprise were Henry Eddy, a young lawyer, and Peter Kimmel and his sons, printers, all of Pittsburgh. With the aid of Nathaniel Pope, the territorial

WOOL CARDER

delegate in Congress, they secured before leaving Pittsburgh authorization for printing the United States laws. Loading a press on a flatboat, they floated down the Ohio to Shawneetown, set up their establishment, and began to publish the *Illinois Emigrant*. The firm name was Eddy and Kimmel, and it is probable that the editorial work was done by Eddy while the Kimmels, who were somewhat illiterate, ran the printing establishment.[20]

The weekly issues of both papers consisted of four small pages of four columns each. Rarely were more than two columns devoted to local news and editorial comment. Often a full page or more was required for the printing of national or territorial laws, and further space was occupied by official notices and proclamations. When Congress was in session its proceedings and debates, copied from a Washington paper, were printed at great length, while the proceedings of the territorial legislature and the convention, reported briefly in the *Intelligencer,* were copied in the *Emigrant*. The remaining space was filled with foreign news and literary productions in both prose and poetry reprinted from other publications. As a rule about one-fourth of each issue was occupied with advertisements of various sorts. Local merchants called attention to their wares in notices which ran for months without the change of a word; lawyers and physicians published their cards; and those who wanted to buy feather beds, provisions, law books, or servants were told to "enquire of the printer." During a political campaign and occasionally at other times much space was given over to lengthy communications. Often these were published in series and sometimes they took the form of a debate which would drag on and on until the issue under discussion would become almost wholly obscured by personalities.[21]

The spiritual welfare of the Illinois pioneers was not neglected. The religious observances, with the exception of those of the

[20] Kimmel to Pope, December 22, 1817, Pope to Adams, January 22, 1818, Adams to Pope, January 23, 1818, in United States State Department, Bureau of Indexes and Archives, Miscellaneous Letters; Scott, *Newspapers and Periodicals*, xxix, 314. The *Shawnee Chief* listed by Scott is a myth. The paper was called the *Illinois Emigrant* from the beginning. There appears to be no evidence that the two papers were the organs of rival parties in 1818.

[21] For examples of the above see chs. 5, 8, 9.

French Catholics, were of the familiar frontier type. The principal Protestant denominations at the close of the territorial period were the Methodists and the Baptists, the latter classified as "regular," or "hardshell," and separating. Presbyterianism was just beginning to get a foothold. The ministers were of two types—the circuit rider, who covered wide stretches of country and devoted all his time to religious work, and the occasional preacher, who supplemented his meager income from the church by farming or some other occupation. Governor Ford has left an account of the unlearned but zealous frontier preachers, of their sermons, and of the results of their work, which cannot easily be improved upon.

Preachers of the gospel frequently sprung up from the body of the people at home, without previous training, except in religious exercises and in the study of the Holy Scriptures. In those primitive times it was not thought to be necessary that a teacher of religion should be a scholar. It was thought to be his business to preach from a knowledge of the Scriptures alone, to make appeals warm from the heart, to paint heaven and hell to the imagination of the sinner, to terrify him with the one, and to promise the other as a reward for a life of righteousness. However ignorant these first preachers may have been, they could be at no loss to find congregations still more ignorant, so that they were still capable of instructing some one. Many of them added to their knowledge of the Bible, a diligent perusal of Young's Night Thoughts, Watts' hymns, Milton's Paradise Lost, and Hervey's Meditations, a knowledge of which gave more compass to their thoughts, to be expressed in a profuse, flowery language, and raised their feelings to the utmost height of poetical enthusiasm.

Sometimes their sermons turned upon matters of controversy; unlearned arguments on the subject of free grace, baptism, free will, election, faith, good works, justification, sanctification, and the final perseverance of the saints. But that in which they excelled, was the earnestness of their words and manner, leaving no doubt of the strongest conviction in their own minds, and in the vividness of the pictures which they drew of the ineffable blessedness of heaven, and the awful torments of the wicked in the fire and brimstone appointed for eternal punishment. These, with the love of God to sinful men, the sufferings of the Saviour, the dangerous apathy of sinners, and exhortations to repentance, furnished themes for the most vehement and passionate declamations. But above all, they continually inculcated the great principles of justice and sound morality.

As many of these preachers were nearly destitute of learning and knowledge, they made up in loud hallooing and violent action what they lacked in information. And it was a matter of astonishment to what length they could spin out a sermon embracing only a few ideas. The merit of a sermon was measured somewhat by the length of it, by the flowery language of the speaker, and by his vociferation and violent gestures. Nevertheless, these first preachers were of incalculable benefit to the country. They inculcated justice and morality, and to the sanction of the highest human motives to regard them, added those which arise from a belief of the greatest conceivable amount of future rewards and punishments. They were truly patriotic also; for at a time when the country was so poor that no other kind of ministry could have been maintained in it, they preached without charge to the people, working week days to aid the scanty charities of their flocks, in furnishing themselves with a scantier living. They believed with a positive certainty that they saw the souls of men rushing to perdition; and they stepped forward to warn and to save, with all the enthusiasm and self-devotion of a generous man who risks his own life to save his neighbor from drowning. And to them are we indebted for the first Christian character of the Protestant portion of this people.[22]

The Methodist church was very active during the later territorial period, under the leadership of such vigorous characters as Jesse Walker and Peter Cartwright. In 1818 there were five circuits in the Illinois district, one with three preachers, four with one preacher each. In addition there was a presiding elder for the district. A contemporary account of one of the rounds of Jesse Walker and John Scripps, as written by the latter, will serve to illustrate the character of the work and the difficulties encountered.

He commenced this round at Goshen meeting-house, near the site of the present town of Edwardsville, Illinois, on Friday, the 1st of April. Closing his meeting on Monday, the 4th, he traveled a zigzag route, filling daily and nightly appointments in different neighborhoods in the Illinois Circuit, till he arrived at the Big Spring meeting-house on Friday, the 8th, where, in a protracted meeting, he labored till Monday, the 11th. A second week of similar services, through otherwise destitute settlements, brought him to Davis's school-house, below the confluence of the Big Muddy River with the Mississippi, probably one hundred miles south of his starting-point. I found him here on Saturday, the

[22] Ford, *History of Illinois*, 38-40.

16th, accompanied by Jacob Whitesides (then just putting on the itinerant harness). At this place there were some conversions, and a class
of sixteen persons was formed. Jacob Whitesides was sent back to labor
in the field of the last week's operations, with directions to form a new
circuit, which was eventually effected, and it was denominated the Okaw
Circuit.

On Monday, the 18th, Jesse Walker, J. Patterson, and myself set out
for the Massac camp-meeting, to be held at the Rock and Cave, on the
Ohio River. We traveled this day in an easterly direction, through a
generally uninhabited country and almost pathless woods, thirty-two
miles, to Thomas Standard's, where a congregation, previously notified
by Brother Patterson, awaited our arrival. The exercises of the evening
were thrillingly interesting, and continued till midnight. About noon the
next day we separated, still tending onward in devious paths to hold
night-meetings six or eight miles apart, to meet again the next day,
probably again to part for the night, to hold as many meetings as our
numbers and the localities of the neighborhood would admit of. On
Friday, the 22d, we arrived at the camp-ground. Services commenced
immediately upon our arrival, and during the entire progress of the
meeting we had precious seasons of refreshing from the presence of the
Lord, several conversions, and many accessions to the Church. Brother
J. Johnson was with us one of the nights, and preached for us. This
meeting broke on Monday. Brother Walker closed the services with an
interesting discourse; but Monday night found him several miles on
his way to his next appointment, again holding forth to a large congregation in Proctor's meeting-house. But to particularize his labors would
swell this account to too great an extent. Suffice it to say that, crossing
the Big Wabash near its mouth, we ascended that river in the then
Territory of Indiana, crossed the Black River, Patoka and White
Rivers, to Brother Johnson's, about twelve miles from Vincennes. By
the next Friday, April 29th, the quarterly-meeting for Vincennes Circuit was held. It was a time of power, and closed Monday morning. We
made a short travel that day of six or eight miles, and held a night-
meeting at Dr. Messick's; the next day, noon, at Harrington's Tavern;
at night at Anthony Griffin's, on Black River. We recrossed the Wabash,
and commenced the Wabash Quarterly-meeting, Friday, May 6th, at
Brother Hannah's, in a block-house, from which our next appointment
was one hundred and seventy or eighty miles south-west across the
Mississippi, to New Madrid Circuit, Missouri Territory, commencing
Friday, the 13th; thence sixty miles north to Cape Girardeau Circuit,
May 20th. At both these appointments, and all subsequent to them
through the Summer, camp-meetings were held, the necessity for which
grew out of the fact that no one-room, or even two-room, log-cabin (and
we had no other sort of houses) was capable of entertaining one-half
or even one-fourth of Jesse Walker's quarterly-meetings; for his regu-

lar Sabbath congregations collected, far and near, from ten, twenty, or thirty miles around, to these attractive centers of religious services. From Cape Girardeau Brother Walker proceeded, by himself, to hold a camp and quarterly meeting on Saline Circuit, commencing Friday, 27th; on the Maramec Circuit, June 3d; Cold Water, 10th; and Missouri Circuit, June 17th; to which appointment, following the circuitous route he had to travel, it was upwards of two hundred miles north; and here, on Monday, the 20th of June, he concluded his second round of meetings, about eighty miles north-west of home, and sixty from Goshen, the commencement of this round, where he again preached in returning to his family, there to enjoy a few day's respite, to repair his itinerant gear, and prepare for the still more extensive operations of the Summer campaign, under the more favorable auspices of shallow streams, better roads, longer days, and the sweltering fervor of a July sun.

Such labors as I have recounted would, in these times of good roads, bridged waters, wealthy friends, comfortable accommodations, and table luxuries, be deemed great; but the circumstances under which Jesse Walker performed them were characterized by difficulties, dangers, privations, and sufferings almost inconceivable in the present improved state of things. Our roads were narrow, winding horse-paths, sometimes scarcely perceptible, and frequently for miles no path at all, amid tangled brushwood, over fallen timber, rocky glens, mountainous precipices; through swamps and low grounds, overflowed or saturated with water for miles together, and consequently muddy, which the breaking up of the Winter and the continued rains gave a continued supply of; the streams some of them large and rapid, swollen to over-flowing, we had to swim on our horses, carrying our saddle-bags on our shoulders. It was a common occurrence, in our journeying, to close our day's ride drenched to the skin by continually descending rains, for which that Spring was remarkable. Our nights were spent, not in two but in one room log-cabins, each generally constituting our evening meeting-house, kitchen, nursery, parlor, dining and bed room,—all within the dimensions of sixteen feet square, and not unfrequently a loom occupying one-fourth of it, together with spinning-wheels and other apparatus for manufacturing their apparel—our congregations requiring our services till ten or twelve o'clock; our supper after dismission, not of select, but of just such aliment as our hospitable entertainers could provide (for hospitable, in the highest sense of the word, they were); corn-cakes, fried bacon, sometimes butter, with milk or herb-tea, or some substitute for coffee. At the Rock and Cave camp-meeting, the measles being very prevalent in the congregation, I took them. Very high fevers were the first symptom; but, unconscious of the cause and nature of my affliction, I continued traveling through all weathers for upwards of two weeks, before the complaint developed its character. My stomach became very delicate, and through a populous part of our journey I in-

quired for coffee at every house we passed, and was invariably directed
to Mr. L.'s, several miles ahead, as the only probable place for the pro-
curement of the grateful beverage. On making known my wants to
Mrs. L., she searched and found a few scattered grains at the bottom
of a chest, of which she made us two cupfuls.

We have sometimes sat in the large fire-place, occupying the entire
end of a log cabin, and plucked from out the smoke of the chimney
above us pieces of dried and smoked venison, or jerk, the only provision
the place could afford us, and the only food the inmates had to sustain
themselves, till they could obtain it by the cultivation of the soil. Our
horses fared worse, in muddy pens, or tied up to saplings or corners
of the cabin, regaled with the refuse of the Winter's fodder, sometimes (when we could not restrain over-liberality) with seed-corn, purchased in Kentucky at a dollar per bushel, and brought in small quantities, according to the circumstances of the purchaser, one hundred
miles or more at some expense and trouble. This, when they had it, our
remonstrances to the contrary could not prevent being pounded in
mortars to make us bread. Our lodgings were on beds of various qualities, generally feather-beds, but not unfrequently fodder, chaff, shucks,
straw, and sometimes only deer-skins, but always the best the house
afforded, either spread on the rough puncheon floor before the fire
(from which we must rise early to make room for breakfast operations),
or on a patched-up platform attached to the wall, which not unfrequently would fall down, sometimes in the night, with its triplicate burden
of three in a bed. Such incidents would occasion a little mirth among
us, but we would soon fix up and be asleep again. Now, I would here
remark, that many of these privations could have been avoided by
keeping a more direct course from one quarterly-meeting to another,
and selecting, with a view to comfort, our lodging-places. But Brother
Walker sought not personal comfort so much as the good of souls, and
he sought the most destitute, in their most retired recesses, and in their
earliest settlements.[23]

In spite of the tremendous exertions of the pioneer preachers,
many of the remote settlements must have been practically
devoid of religious observances, and even in the older settlements the influence of occasional visitations, however inspiring
they might be, was often lacking in permanence. "The American inhabitants in the Vil[l]ages," wrote John Messinger in
1815, "appear to have very little reverence for christianity or
serious things in any point of view." [24] Reynolds is authority for

[23] Leaton, *Methodism in Illinois*, 110-115, 151.
[24] Messinger to Lee, June 30, 1815, Messinger Manuscripts.

the statement that "in early times, in many settlements of Illinois, Sunday was observed by the Americans only as a day of rest from work. They generally were employed in hunting, fishing, getting up their stock, hunting bees, breaking young horses, shooting at marks, horse and foot racing and the like. When the Americans were to make an important journey they generally started on Sunday and never on Friday—they often said 'The better the day the better the deed.' " [25]

In view of the inadequate facilities for educational and religious developments, the mental quality of the Illinois pioneers was surprisingly high, according to the recollections of Robert W. Patterson. "But in spite of the prejudices and illiteracy of many of our early citizens," he states,

they were by no means an unthinking people, their minds were stimulated by the necessity of invention imposed upon them by their peculiar circumstances; by the political discussions in which they became interested from one election to another; by the moral questions that were debated among them; and, above all, by the religious discourses to which they often listened, and the controversies between the adherents of different sects, in which almost everybody sympathized with one party or another. It was surprising to find men and women of little or no reading, ready to defend their opinions on almost every subject, with plausible, and sometimes exceedingly forcible, reasons. Women, especially, were even more accustomed then than now to discuss grave questions which required thought and provoked earnest reflection. Often a woman of unpromising appearance and manners would prove more than a match for a well-educated man in a religious dispute. In one sense the people were intelligent, while they had little of such knowledge as readers usually derive from books. Their intelligence consisted mainly in the results of reflection, and conversations one with another, and in varied information derived from their ancestors by tradition. In respect to knowledge of human nature and judgments upon the characters of men, they were far in advance of many who were learned in literature, science, art, and history; and, accordingly, many men of inferior education in those days competed successfully with rivals who had enjoyed the best early advantages. This was often witnessed in the political conflicts of the times, and in the ministerial, legal, and medical profession.[26]

[25] Reynolds, *My Own Times*, 80.

[26] Patterson, "Early Society in Southern Illinois," in *Fergus Historical Series*, no. 14:124-125.

✠ *Chapter 7*

The Political Situation

At the beginning of 1818 the region now included in the state
of Illinois together with the extensive area to the northward
stretching to the international boundary comprised the territory
of Illinois. After the occupation of the French villages in the
Illinois country by Virginia troops under George Rogers Clark,
the region was organized as a county of Virginia,[1] but in 1784
Virginia ceded her claims to the federal government. The act
by which this cession was accomplished contained one clause of
great importance for the future of the Illinois country. This
provided "that the French and Canadian inhabitants, and other
settlers of the Kaskaskies, Saint Vincents, and the neighboring
villages, who have professed themselves citizens of Virginia,
shall have their possessions and titles confirmed to them, and
be protected in the enjoyment of their rights and liberties."[2] At
the moment this provision confirmed to the inhabitants their
titles to a few negro slaves; in future years it was to be invoked
as a guarantee of the institution of slavery in the state.

The claims of other states to jurisdiction over the northwest
also having been surrendered to the federal government, the congress of the confederation, as one of its last acts, passed the
Ordinance of 1787, by which was organized the "territory of the
United States northwest of the river Ohio."[3] This ordinance
laid the foundation of the American colonial or territorial system; and the political and governmental conditions in Illinois
Territory cannot be understood without a consideration of its
essential provisions. The government of the territory was vested
for the time being in a governor, a secretary, and three judges,

[1] Alvord, *Cahokia Records,* lii.
[2] Thorpe, *Constitutions,* 2:956.
[3] Thorpe, *Constitutions,* 2:957-962.

to be appointed by Congress.[4] The governor and judges sitting as a legislature were authorized to adopt such laws of the original states as might be necessary; the governor singly was given the power to appoint all local magistrates and other civil officers and also all militia officers below the rank of general officers, the last being appointed by Congress. It will thus be seen that the people of the territory were given no voice whatever in their government, either general or local. This was only a temporary arrangement; whenever there should "be five thousand free male inhabitants, of full age, in the district" a legislature was to be established consisting of the governor, representatives elected by the freeholders, and a council of five members selected by Congress from ten nominated by the territorial house of representatives. This legislature was to have authority to make laws not repugnant to the ordinance; but to the governor was given the power to convene, prorogue, and dissolve the legislature, as well as an absolute veto over all its acts. The legislature, by joint ballot, was to elect a delegate to Congress, who should have the right to speak but not to vote. Among the qualifications required of members of the legislature was the possession of a freehold of 200 acres of land for a representative and 500 for a councilor.

The last section of the ordinance consisted of six "articles of compact, between the original States and the people and States in the said territory" which were forever to "remain unalterable, unless by common consent." It should be noted, however, that this was a one-sided compact, as the consent of the people residing in the district was never asked or secured. Two of these articles are of special significance in connection with a study of Illinois in 1818. One of these, the fifth, provided that "there shall be formed in the said territory not less than three, nor more than five States." The boundary between the two western states was to be the Wabash as far north as "Post Vincents"

---

[4] When the new government under the Constitution was established, it was provided that the appointments should be made by the President instead of by Congress. Thorpe, *Constitutions*, 2:963-964.

and thence a direct line drawn from the Wabash and "Post Vincents," due north, to the territorial line between the United States and Canada. Should the establishment of more than three states seem expedient, Congress was to "have authority to form one or two States in that part of the said territory which lies north of an east and west line drawn through the southerly bend or extreme of Lake Michigan." Each of these states was to be admitted into the Union whenever there should be 60,000 free inhabitants within its limits.

The most famous feature of the ordinance was that contained in the sixth of the articles of compact, which provided that "there shall be neither slavery nor involuntary servitude in the said territory, otherwise than in punishment of crimes, whereof the party shall have been duly convicted." This would seem to be a positive prohibition of the continuance of slavery northwest of the Ohio; but, in view of the guarantee in the Virginia act of cession, it was interpreted from the beginning as applying only to the future introduction of slavery; and slaves continued to be held in the region for half a century.

The government provided for by the ordinance was established at Marietta in 1788 and two years later it was extended to the Illinois country, which was organized at St. Clair County. Knox County, formed the same year with its seat at Vincennes, included the eastern half of what is now the state of Illinois.[5] In 1795 Randolph County was established from the southern part of St. Clair. In accordance with the provisions of the ordinance, all the officials in these counties were appointed by the governor. After ten years of rule by the governor and judges, the territory passed to the second grade; and the first legislature met in Cincinnati in 1799. St. Clair and Randolph counties were represented in the house by Shadrach Bond and John Edgar respectively. William Henry Harrison, recently appointed secretary of the territory, was elected by this legislature

[5] In 1801 the boundaries of St. Clair and Randolph counties were extended nearly to the Wabash, and the remainder of Knox County in what became Illinois was incorporated with them when the division took place in 1809. *Illinois Blue Book*, 1905, p. 376.

as the delegate to Congress, and there in 1800 secured the passage of an act dividing the Northwest Territory and establishing the western part as Indiana Territory. He also secured his own appointment as governor of the new territory. The provisions for the government of Indiana Territory were practically identical with those contained in the Ordinance of 1787, with the exception that it might pass to the second grade whenever the governor should be convinced that the majority of the people desired the change.

During the period from 1800 to 1809, when Illinois was a part of Indiana Territory, the principal issues of a political character were the passage to the second grade and the division of the territory; and inextricably bound up with these was the question of the admission of slavery. There is no evidence that national politics affected to any appreciable extent the politics of the territory during this period, but the people and their political leaders divided on the above issues and also to some extent into personal factions. The more influential of the new settlers in the Illinois country as well as the old French inhabitants were strongly in favor of the repeal or at least the suspension of the slavery article in the ordinance, probably because they believed it hampered the development of the territory. As early as 1796 a petition was sent to Congress praying for the repeal of the article, signed by John Edgar, William Morrison, William St. Clair, and John Dumoulin, leading men in St. Clair and Randolph counties. These men professed to sign "for and on behalf of the inhabitants" of the counties and there is little doubt that they expressed the sentiments of a large majority of those inhabitants; but they presented no evidence to that effect and the petition was rejected.[6]

When Indiana Territory was established it is probable that

[6] The best account of the politics of Indiana Territory from 1800 to 1809 is in Dunn, *Indiana*, chs. 8-10. The originals of the petitions and memorials referred to below are in House and Senate Files. Some of them have been printed in Indiana Historical Society, *Publications*, 2:447-529. See also Woollen, *Biographical and Historical Sketches of Early Indiana*, 4-5; *American State Papers, Miscellaneous*, 1:450, 467, 477, 484-485, 922, 945.

a majority of its inhabitants were in favor of a change in the slavery article. The Illinois people at once prepared another petition to Congress praying for such a change and for the extinction of the Indian title in southern Illinois. This document, dated October 1, 1800, bears 270 signatures, mostly French, but including the names of such leading Americans as John Edgar, John Rice Jones, William Morrison, Robert Morrison, and Shadrach Bond. The fact that Congress ignored the petition was probably a factor in inducing the Illinois leaders the following year to agitate for advance to the second grade, in order that the territory might have a delegate to urge the desired measure

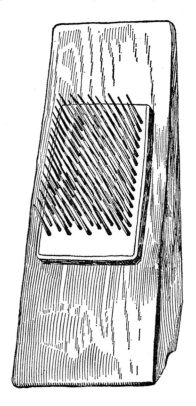

FLAX HACKLE

in Congress. In this action, however, they met with the opposition of Governor Harrison, who had no desire to give up so soon a part of his extensive power. The governor had a numerous coterie of followers in Knox County and by means of the patronage exerted a powerful influence throughout the territory. He had little difficulty, therefore, in suppressing the movement by issuing a letter in which attention was called to the increased expenses which would be involved.

Harrison and his party differed with what may for convenience be called the Edgar and Morrison party as to methods rather than ends, for both factions were in favor of the introduction of more slaves. The method selected by the governor was the calling of an extralegal convention which met in Vincennes in 1802 and petitioned Congress for a suspension of the slavery article for a term of ten years. Neither Edgar nor William Morrison were among the six Illinois men in this convention although Robert Morrison, a brother of William, was one of them. In the national House of Representatives this petition was referred to a committee, which through its chairman, John Randolph, presented an adverse report. In later sessions other committees reported in favor of suspension, but no action was ever taken.

Having failed in this direction the governor and judges proceeded in 1803 to pass "A Law Concerning Servants" which provided that a person coming into the territory "under contract to serve another in any trade or occupation shall be compelled to perform such contract specifically during the term thereof." The purpose of this act was to introduce a form of slavery in the guise of indentured servitude, but the legislative powers of the governor and judges were so limited that the Harrison faction executed an about-face on the question of advancing to the second grade; for it was believed that an unrestricted legislature could pass a more satisfactory indenture law. On August 4, 1804, therefore, the governor issued a proclamation for an election to be held September 11 to determine the wishes of the people on the subject.

Meanwhile the members of the Edgar and Morrison faction in Illinois, probably because of dissatisfaction with the distribution of the patronage, were becoming more and more hostile to the governor and his supporters, and in 1803 they grasped at what appeared to be an opportunity at once of escaping from his control and of securing the coveted admission of slavery. Learning of the purchase of Louisiana, they prepared petitions asking Congress to join the Illinois country to the new territory to be formed west of the River. Congress instead placed the new district of Louisiana temporarily under the governor and judges of Indiana Territory but not as a part of that territory.

In spite of the advantages for the proslavery advocates which the advance to the second grade offered, the Edgar and Morrison faction reversed their former position and opposed the change, apparently for no other reason than their hostility to the governor and his faction. They were able to carry St. Clair County against the measure, the vote being 22 to 59, but Harrison's friends and appointees in Randolph, led by Dr. George Fisher and Pierre Menard, carried that county by a vote of 40 to 21. Knox County voted overwhelmingly for the change, but the attitude of Dearborn County in eastern Indiana, where all the 26 votes were cast against the measure, indicates the appearance of a new faction in Indiana politics, a faction strongly opposed to the introduction of slavery. The totals were 269 to 131, making a majority on the face of the returns of 138 in favor of the change. No election was held in Wayne County (Detroit), however, and the light vote cast would indicate that there was some truth in the charge that the whole affair was a snap election.

Governor Harrison at once issued a proclamation for an election of nine representatives; these assembled in Vincennes in 1805 and proceeded to nominate councilors to the President. The representatives from the Illinois counties were Shadrach Bond and William Biggs of St. Clair and Dr. George Fisher of Randolph, while Jesse B. Thomas, later of Illinois, represented Dearborn County. Of the five councilors selected by Harrison from the ten nominated by the house—for the President secretly delegated his power of choice to the governor—two, Pierre Menard and John Hay, were from the Illinois country. The legislature selected Benjamin Parke of Vincennes, a personal and political friend of the governor, as delegate to Congress, and then proceeded to the passage of an indenture law. This act of 1805, which was revised and re-enacted in 1807, provided that a slave over 15 years of age might be brought into the territory and within 30 days enter into a formal agreement to serve as an indentured servant for a certain number of years. The agreement was to be made a matter of record, and should the slave refuse to bind himself, the master was allowed 60 days in which to remove him from the territory. Children born of indentured servants were to serve the master of the mother, males to the age of 30, and females, of 28. Slaves under 15 might be brought in and simply registered to serve, males until 35 and females until 32 years of age.

It is useless at this date to raise the question as to whether the indentured servitude established by this act was or was not "slavery or involuntary servitude" and thus in violation of the ordinance. Certain it is that the ends sought by the act were approved by a majority of the people in Illinois and in the western part of what came to be the state of Indiana. Only in Dearborn and Clark counties of Indiana was there any considerable opposition to it.

During the summer of 1805 the anti-Harrison faction in Illinois circulated a petition for the division of Indiana Territory. In this they were probably actuated principally by the belief that such a division would improve their political fortunes and would be distasteful to their opponents, the Harrison faction; but they may have been influenced also by a feeling that a separate Illinois might secure complete and unrestricted slavery and also by a fear that the growing antislavery population of eastern Indiana would put in jeopardy the indenture system. Besides praying for division they asked that the slavery article might be repealed or modified so far as it affected the proposed new territory. Among the grievances alleged by the petitioners was their "having been unwarrantably precipitated into the second grade of territorial government," and the story of that transaction was recounted at some length.

Knowing that such a petition was in circulation, the supporters of Harrison introduced in the legislative session of 1805 a memorial to Congress, praying among other things for the introduction of slavery and protesting against the proposed division of the territory. A proposition was also embodied in this memorial for the admission of the territory as a state before division, together with a suggestion that division when it should come might well be by an east and west instead of a north and south line. Obviously such a division would be greatly to the advantage of Vincennes. The memorial was not adopted by the legislature but was sent to Congress as a "Petition of the subscribers, members of the Legislative Council and House of Representatives of the Indiana Territory, and constituting a majority of the two Houses, respectively." The five members whose names do not appear on the petition were the councilors and representatives from St. Clair and Clark counties. Councilor Menard and Representative Fisher of Randolph, both followers of Harrison, signed, as did also Representative Jesse B. Thomas of Dearborn. The name of another Dearborn man, Benjamin Chambers, president of the council, appears; but he afterwards denied that he signed the petition. Both Thomas and Chambers, if Chambers signed, probably misrepresented their constituents. The people of Dearborn County the same year prepared a petition to Congress complaining of the advance to second grade, protesting against the indenture law, and praying that they might be joined to the state of Ohio.[7]

These three documents emanating from three distinct factions and representing the views of three distinct sections of the territory reached Congress in December, 1805, and on the eight-

---

[7] Indiana Historical Society, *Publications*, 2:476-483, 492-494; *American State Papers, Miscellaneous*, 1:485; Dunn, *Indiana*, 336-341, 345.

eenth were referred to a select committee, of which the delegate from Indiana Territory was a member. A month later a number of additional documents from the Illinois counties were referred to the same committee. They consisted of a memorial prepared by "a Committee from the Several Townships in the Counties" and the minutes of the committee, including a series of resolutions. It would seem that the anti-Harrison faction felt some further action to be necessary to counteract the effect of the legislative petition. The resolutions, after calling for a division of the territory, express the respect of the people for the ordinance and call attention to "the Violation thereof By the late act of the Legislature of this Territory Authorizing the importation of Slaves, and involuntary servitude for a term of years." From this it might be inferred that the committee was hostile to the introduction of slaves, but the succeeding sentences show that this was for political effect entirely. "And altho' this Committee entertain no doubt but that the Act in Question will render service, by adding a Spring to the Growth of this Country, They express the disapprobation of a people, who never will Consent to a Violation of that ordinance, for *this* privilege of slavery. When Congress should deem a Change of the Ordinance expedient, they will Cheerfully agree to the measure." The memorial itself sets forth many reasons for desiring a division of the territory, condemns the petition of the members of the legislature, and asks for the permission to hold slaves as "promotive of the prosperity of this Country." No mention is made of the indenture law in the memorial, but other acts of the legislature are denounced because they increased the power of the governor. Accompanying the memorial and the minutes was a census estimate by Robert Morrison, who had taken a census in 1801; he reckoned the population of St. Clair and Randolph counties at 4,311.

The special committee, in its report of February 14, 1806, to the House of Representatives, opposed the admission of the territory as a state before the division and also the proposals for immediate division, but favored the suspension of the slavery article for ten years. No action was ever taken on the report, but it was clear that Congress would never authorize the admission of the territory as a single state. The result was a momentary truce between the two proslavery factions in the legislative session of November, 1806, and the adoption by unanimous vote of a series of resolutions asking for a suspension of the "sixth article." Benjamin Parke, the delegate from Indiana, was chairman of the committee of the House of Representatives to which these resolutions were referred; and on February 12, 1807, he presented a report favoring suspension of the slavery article. This report was referred to the Committee of the Whole House but was never considered.

Meanwhile the advocates of division in Illinois were continuing their campaign and on February 20, 1807, another memorial from their committee was referred to the same committee of the House of Representatives which had reported on the legislative resolutions. At the same time a counter-petition from Randolph County was received which denied the representative character of the Illinois committee and opposed division. This petition bears 102 signatures, but nearly all the names are French and 42 are signed with a mark. Among recognized supporters of Harrison who signed were Dr. George Fisher, James Gilbreath, and two of the Menards. Six days after receiving these petitions the committee reported to the House a resolution declaring the expediency of division. This resolution was adopted, but no further action followed.

The election of the second house of representatives of the Indiana territorial legislature in February, 1807, showed an increase in the strength of the factions opposed to Harrison, but all three of the Illinois representatives were re-elected. At the first session of the legislature, in August, 1807, the principal matters of interest were the re-election of Parke to Congress and the adoption of another memorial asking for the suspension of the slavery article. Between the first and second sessions of the second territorial legislature the political situation changed materially. John Rice Jones, member of the council from Knox County, broke with Harrison, probably on a matter of patronage, and joined the opposition. Menard and Hay resigned from the council, and Fisher and Bond [8] were promoted to their places, thus necessitating the election of a representative in each of the Illinois counties. These elections resulted, after a bitter contest between the factions, in victories for the anti-Harrison party in both cases, the successful candidates being Rice Jones, a son of the councilor, in Randolph, and John Messinger, the first "Yankee" in Illinois politics, in St. Clair. As a result of these changes the anti-Harrison factions had a majority in the legislative session of 1808 and were able to effect a combination on the question of division. This was possible in spite of their radical differences on the slavery issue because the elimination of the Illinois counties would in all probability give the antislavery forces a majority in Indiana proper. Early in the session resolutions in favor of division were adopted and forwarded to Congress, but it took several weeks for the two factions to agree on a delegate to take the place of Parke, who had resigned. The man finally selected was Jesse B. Thomas, of Dearborn County, who pledged himself to work for division. The Harrison men supported Michael Jones, register of the land office at Kaskaskia, possibly with the object of inducing the Illinois representatives to support an Illinois man, but Jones received only three of the ten votes.

Sometime in the spring of 1808 the Illinois advocates of division had prepared three petitions to Congress which on April 16 were referred to a committee of the House of Representatives of which Parke was a member. The first of these petitions points out the weakness of the counter-petition presented in 1807, as signed by so large a proportion of illiterate Frenchmen, and asserts that the committee which signed the memorials of 1806 and 1807 was truly representative of the sentiment of the counties; the second contains an elaborate series of charges against Governor Harrison including among them his sanctioning of the indenture law "which may properly be entitled 'A Law for the

[8] This Bond was the nephew of the Shadrach Bond who served in the legislature of the Northwest Territory. He was sometimes known as Shadrach Bond, Jr.

Establishment of disguised slavery in opposition to the National Will' ''; while the third was merely a brief request for division. Inasmuch as the names of John Edgar and William Morrison appear at the head of the signatures to the second petition it is clear that the reference to the indenture law was not an indication of antislavery sentiment.

Parke failed to secure a favorable report on these petitions, although he had agreed to support the division movement, and in December, 1808, they were referred to a new committee appointed to inquire into the expediency of dividing Indiana Territory and headed by Jesse B. Thomas. This committee had various other documents before it—the legislative resolution already mentioned, a petition from the grand jury of St. Clair County praying for division, presented December 2, depositions denying their signatures from men whose names appeared on the petition containing the attack on Harrison, and a petition from Harrison's followers in Knox County, including Benjamin Parke, opposing division. Thomas appears to have had little difficulty in securing a report favorable to division, and the passage of an act, approved February 9, 1809, for the establishment of the territory of Illinois.

From the foregoing account of politics in Indiana Territory it is evident that there were in Illinois in 1809 two parties or factions which had been working at cross-purposes for a number of years. These may be classified as the Harrison and anti-Harrison parties, the former comprising most of the holders of office and the latter headed by a number of men of considerable wealth and influence. It is doubtful if the great majority of the people owned affiliations with either of the factions, and on the rare occasions when elections were held the voters were doubtless influenced as much by the personality of the candidates as by their party alignments or their positions on the issues of the day. In the struggle over division, the anti-Harrison party had been victorious, but that struggle was only an incident in the hostility between the two groups, which persisted for a number of years and exerted an appreciable influence upon the politics of Illinois Territory.

The Ordinance of 1787 again formed the basis of the constitu·

ent act of the new territory and for the third time the people of Illinois found themselves under the rule of a governor and judges.[9] The faction which had favored division apparently expected to secure the offices, and Jesse B. Thomas, who as delegate had brought about the separation, did succeed in securing one of the judgeships for himself. For governor, however, the President selected Ninian Edwards, chief justice of the court of appeals of Kentucky, who endeavored to hold himself aloof from both of the factions. Both of the other judges were from outside the territory, while the secretary was Nathaniel Pope, also of Kentucky, and a personal and political friend of the governor. Around these two men there gradually grew up a new party composed largely of importations but receiving, on the whole, more supporters from the ranks of the old anti-Harrison faction than from those of their opponents.

Had Edwards accepted the suggestions made to him that none but advocates of division should be appointed to office, he would doubtless have received the complete support of the anti-Harrison men, and the old factions would have been continued as the "ins" and the "outs." With reference to the patronage, however, the governor adopted the policy of refusing to remove men who were giving satisfactory service and of following the wishes of the people concerned, so far as they could be ascertained, in such appointments as were made. Thus the militia companies were allowed to select their own officers, and civil appointments were frequently based on recommendations or petitions from the township or county. Occasionally, however, personal factions played a part; as when Benjamin Stephenson, a newcomer from Kentucky, was appointed sheriff of Randolph County in 1809.[10] Stephenson was soon recognized as one of the leaders of the Edwards party and in 1814 was sent as delegate to Congress, a position which enabled him to secure an appointment as receiver of the new land office at Edwardsville.

[9] Thorpe, *Constitutions*, 2:966.
[10] Edwards, *History of Illinois*, 28-41; Washburne, *Edwards Papers*, 42-46, 76; James, *Territorial Records*, 8.

For the first three years of the territory the attorney general-
ship was the chief piece of territorial patronage at the governor's
disposal, but after the passage to second grade he had the appointment of a territorial treasurer and an auditor of public accounts as well. In 1816 Edwards appointed to the latter office
Daniel Pope Cook of Kentucky, a young nephew of Nathaniel
Pope, the secretary.[11] At the close of the territorial period Cook
was a close personal and political friend of the governor and later
became his son-in-law.

The principal local officers in 1809, all of whom were appointed
by the governor, were three judges and a clerk of the court of
commons pleas, sheriff, coroner, surveyor, treasurer, recorder, and
as many justices of the peace as might be needed in each of the
counties. By the Indiana law in force at the time of the division,
the court of common pleas conducted the administrative business
of the county, heard appeals from justices' courts, and had original jurisdiction in civil and criminal cases, with appeal to the
general court of the territory. These courts of common pleas were
notoriously inefficient so far as their judicial functions were concerned, for the compensation was too low to induce men trained
in the law to serve as judges; and by a series of laws adopted by
the governor and judges in June and July, 1809, the systems of
judicature and local administration were reorganized. The courts
of common pleas were abolished. Their administrative functions
were transferred to courts made up of the justices of the peace
of the county, which were also empowered to hear appeals from
decisions of individual justices of the peace in cases of judgments
not exceeding $20. All other jurisdiction of the courts of common
pleas, both civil and criminal, was transferred to the "general
court," composed of the United States judges, which was required
to hold two terms annually in each of the two counties. This
simple system was doubtless satisfactory to all parties concerned,
so long as the amount of litigation was small and there were only

[11] James, *Territorial Records,* 40

two counties. In January, 1811, however, possibly in anticipation of the increase in the number of counties which came the following year, the governor and judges passed an act restoring the courts of common pleas in the place of the county courts made up of justices, but from the phraseology of the act it would appear that the jurisdiction over civil and criminal cases transferred to the general court in 1809 was not at this time restored to the courts of common pleas.[12]

The advance of Illinois to the second grade of territorial government took place in 1812, apparently without any opposition. As had been the case with Indiana Territory the governor was authorized to make the change whenever convinced that a majority of the freeholders desired it. On March 14 he issued a proclamation calling for a vote on the question on the second Monday in April. The result of the election was favorable, and in the normal course of events a restricted form of popular government would have been established in Illinois similar to that set up in the Northwest Territory in 1798 and in Indiana in 1805. A strong sentiment had been developing, however, especially in the west, in favor of greater participation by the people in their governments. Several of the state constitutions recently adopted had dropped all property qualifications for suffrage; and Congress, by an act of 1809, had liberalized the government of Indiana Territory to the extent of providing for the election of the delegate and the councilors by the people, although the suffrage qualification remained unchanged.

In Illinois the restriction of suffrage and officeholding to freeholders would have been especially objectionable in 1812, for there were no sales of land until 1814 and the great majority of the inhabitants were squatters waiting patiently for the opportunity to purchase the land on which they had located. On the very day on which he issued the proclamation for the election, Governor Edwards wrote a long letter to Colonel Richard M. Johnson, congressman from Kentucky, explaining the situation

[12] Alvord, *Laws of the Territory*, 2-6, 28.

and asking for his assistance in securing an act removing the property qualification for suffrage and providing for the election of the delegate by popular vote. Should the provisions of the ordinance remain in force, he claimed, a majority of the present freeholders, who constituted less than one-tenth of the male population of voting age, would be able to control the government for at least five years. The establishment of new counties, moreover, would be hampered by the impossibility of finding men with requisite qualifications to represent them in the legislature.

Two weeks later, March 30, Edwards transmitted to the speaker of the House of Representatives two petitions numerously signed, praying for the extension of the suffrage and the privilege of electing the delegate by popular vote.[13] One of these petitions, from "Inhabitants of the Land district East of Kaskaskia," in which the squatters comprised practically the whole population, rehearsed the arguments presented in Edwards' letter to Johnson. The other, from "citizens of the Territory," was signed by many of the leading residents of Kaskaskia. Colonel Johnson secured prompt action by Congress, and on May 20 the President approved a law which enabled the people of Illinois to establish the most democratic form of territorial government to be found in the United States at that time. By the terms of this act suffrage was granted to all free white males, 21 years of age, who had paid a county or territorial tax, no matter how small, and had resided in the territory one year. It was further provided that the five councilors should be elected in five districts to be designated by the governor, and finally the delegate to Congress was to be elected by the people instead of by the legislature.

On September 14, 1812, Governor Edwards issued two important proclamations. The first of these established three new counties, Madison, Gallatin, and Johnson, making five in all, to serve as the districts for the five members of the council. The second

[13] Edwards, *History of Illinois*, 306-309. The original of this letter and the petitions noted in the following paragraph are in House Files.

proclamation made provision for an election to be held October 8-10, for delegate, members of the council, and representatives. Two representatives each were assigned to St. Clair and Gallatin counties and one each to the other three. The returns of this election are not known to be in existence, but Shadrach Bond, who had been both representative and councilor in the Indiana territorial legislature before the division, with leanings toward the Harrison party, was elected delegate to Congress. Apparently there was some opposition to his election, for on November 11 a petition from Benjamin M. Piatt, attorney general of the territory and an appointee of Governor Edwards, was presented to Congress "complaining of the undue election" of Bond and praying for an investigation. No investigation appears to have followed and Bond took his seat on December 3, 1812.

Aside from the patronage the only political issue of a general nature during the existence of Illinois Territory had to do with the judiciary system. As has already been seen, several changes were made in this system during the period when the governor and judges had complete control. With the assembling of the first territorial legislature on November 25, 1812, the question came before the representatives of the people. The establishment of the three new counties made some readjustment necessary, and the outcome was the complete restoration to the courts of common pleas of the jurisdiction which they had exercised under the laws of Indiana Territory. This of course relieved the general court of the local work which had been imposed upon it in 1809 and in fact left it with very little to do, a situation which appears to have been quite satisfactory to the judges. All of them were absent from the territory for long periods of time, much to the dissatisfaction of the people. "The grand jury of St. Clair and Randolph counties," wrote Bond to Edwards, August 17, 1813, "presented all our judges for non-residence and non-attendance, but before they [the presentments] arrived judge Stuart resigned." This resignation did not, however, improve conditions, for William Sprigg, who was appointed to take the place of Stuart, absolutely refused to recognize the right of the legislature to regulate the court. On February 23, 1814, Bond wrote that he was "trying to get a law passed to compel our judges to perform such duties as our Legislature have required of them." [14]

Two years' experience with the courts of common pleas apparently convinced the people of the necessity of having trained judges, and in December, 1814, the legislature reversed its action of 1812. The court of common pleas was again abolished and its administrative functions transferred to a county court of three men, while the United States judges were organized as a supreme court and directed to hold two courts annually in each county and a court of appeals at the capital. Upon the former devolved the judicial functions formerly exercised by the courts of common pleas. It was expected that the judges would divide up the counties into circuits and hold the local courts individually, but these were to be termed sessions of the supreme court in order to avoid objections which the judges had raised to any breaking up of the unity of their court. There was nothing in the act to prevent all or several of the judges from holding court jointly in each county if they so desired, as had been done when there were only two counties. Judges Thomas and Sprigg, however, at once addressed a letter to the legislature protesting against the change and denying the authority of the legislature over them. They took the position that the supreme court established by the act was a new court to which "the court established by the ordinance" was to be subjected, and asserted that "an appeal from the same court to the same is a solecism."

The legislature forwarded the letter to Governor Edwards and requested of him an opinion upon the subject, which he furnished at great length in a communication of December 12, 1814. The governor explained that the words of the ordinance "are that 'there shall be appointed a court, to consist of three judges, who shall have a common law jurisdiction,' but how, when or where

[14] House Files, March 14, 30, 1812; *Laws of Illinois Territory*, 1812, pp. 15-16, 46-48; *Pope's Digest*, 2:311-312; Washburne, *Edwards Papers*, 103, 110.

that jurisdiction is to be exercised is not pointed out, and therefore it is subjected to the modification and direction of the Territorial Legislature." [15] The judges still refused to acknowledge the validity of the law, and on December 21 the legislature forwarded all the documents to Congress together with a memorial praying for relief. One sentence of this memorial reads: "There being no intermixture of party spirit or individual hostility with this proceeding, the objections of the Judges to executing the law doubtless arise, more from a conviction in their own minds of the want of Power in the Legislature to pass it, than from any indisposition on their part to perform the duties therein assigned to them." This was probably a bit of subtle sarcasm, for the judges were certainly not anxious to assume any additional burdens and the politicians were certainly grouping themselves into supporters and opponents of Governor Edwards, of whom the former upheld the judiciary law and the latter supported the judges. Together with these documents in the House files is a long letter from Edwards, dated January 2, 1815, recounting the arguments in favor of the validity of the law.

The result of this appeal to Congress was the passage of an act "regulating and defining the duties of the United States Judges for the territory of Illinois" which required them to hold circuit courts in each county. That this victory of the Edwards party was not won without opposition is evident from Benjamin Stephenson's review of his work as a delegate in Congress, in which he says: "With regard to our judiciary system, I should at all times, have been happy to see such a one established, as would, if possible, have been agreeable to the judges, and convenient to the people. But I felt it my duty to oppose, and I did oppose with success, the attempt that was made when this subject was before the last Congress, to destroy the circuit system, and to have a general court to sit in two or three places only." [16]

[15] *A Law Establishing a Supreme Court and Documents;* Edwards, *History of Illinois,* 86-92.

[16] *Statutes at Large,* 3:237-239; *Intelligencer,* June 19, 1816.

Just at this point in the fight, Griswold, the one judge who had not actively opposed the territorial law, died; and the efforts of the two factions to get their respective candidates appointed throw light on the alignment of men in 1815, particularly in Gallatin County. Griswold died in Shawneetown on August 21; and four days later a meeting was held there at which a petition was circulated in favor of Thomas Towles of Kentucky as his successor. The men present at this meeting were Towles himself, Leonard White, Benjamin Talbott, Thomas Sloo, and John Caldwell. The opposition at once put up Jeptha Hardin, a Kentuckian, who had been practicing law in Gallatin County since 1813 and a man who, according to John Reynolds, "possessed a strong original mind, and seemed to disdain scholastic education." Hardin's chief support came from Judge Thomas; and his political manager in the campaign appears to have been Joseph M. Street, clerk of both the county and circuit courts of Gallatin County. Towles, however, secured the appointment.

The victorious faction at Shawneetown in this contest was composed largely of men connected with the United States saline, and in that way closely associated with Edwards, who had been appointed superintendent of the saline in 1809. Leonard White was United States agent at the saline, while Sloo and Caldwell were register and receiver of the Shawneetown land office and thus concerned with the reservation. Towles himself, according to information given to Hardin by Caldwell, "was at the lick" with White and Talbott when Griswold died, and may have been connected with the saline in a private capacity. The men opposed to Towles were also opposed to the management of the saline, and in 1816 they sent two petitions to Congress against the renewal of the lease of John Bate. Street's name is first on one of these and Hardin's on the other. It would seem probable, therefore, that the saline was a considerable factor in Illinois politics. It added a business interest to the struggles over the patronage.

Among the members of the anti-Edwards faction at this time was Elias Kent Kane of Kaskaskia, one of the most promising

of the younger lawyers, and a "keen, shrewd, talented politician."
Born in New York and educated at Yale, he began practice in
Illinois in 1814 when only 20 years of age. From the first he seems
to have been on terms of intimacy with Judges Thomas and
Sprigg, and Street considered him a person of influence in 1815.
Another member of this faction and an intimate friend of Kane
was John McLean, a young Kentuckian, who came to Shawneetown in 1815 and was admitted to the bar the following year.
Mention should also be made of Thomas C. Browne, another
lawyer from Kentucky, who located in Shawneetown in 1812
and who threw in his lot with the Edwards men. In 1815 Browne
was one of the leaders in an attempt to deprive Street of his
position as clerk of the circuit court.

The usual alignment of party leaders during the territorial
period runs Edwards, Pope, Cook, White, and Browne on one
side and Bond, Thomas, Michael Jones, Kane, and McLean on
the other. This is derived from a statement of John Reynolds,
who began to take an interest in politics about 1818, and it is in
the main correct.[17] The Michael Jones referred to may have
been the young lawyer who was located in Shawneetown as early
as 1812 and who played a prominent part in politics after the
admission of the state. He was a half brother of Jesse B. Thomas
and a brother-in-law of Hardin so that his family affiliations
were with the anti-Edwards party. There was another Michael
Jones, however, a native of Pennsylvania, who came to Kaskaskia in 1804 as register of the land office, and held his position
there throughout the territorial period. He had been the candidate of the Harrison faction against Thomas for delegate from
Indiana Territory in 1808 and served for a time as lieutenant
colonel of the militia, from which position Edwards removed him
in 1811. There was bitter feeling between him and the governor
over the settlement of land claims also, and he could doubtless be

[17] Street to Kane, March 26, 1815, and Hardin to Kane, September 29,
1815, in Chicago Historical Society Manuscripts; Lippincott, "Early Days
in Madison County," no. 13; Reynolds, *Pioneer History*, 330; Reynolds,
My Own Times, 210.

included as a member of the faction opposed to the governor.[18]

The placing of Bond's name first in Reynolds' list has led many local historians to speak of the opposition to Edwards as the Bond party. The real leaders of this faction, however, at the close of the territorial period were Thomas and Kane; and there is no strictly contemporary evidence to indicate that Bond was counted as a member of the party until, as first governor of the state, he fell under the influence of Kane, the secretary of state. Bond had been considered a member of the Harrison faction in the Indiana territorial legislature, and in 1809 he objected strenuously to Edwards' proposition that he go into an election with William B. Whiteside for the position of colonel of the militia, then held by Bond. Whiteside received the appointment. In 1812, however, as has been seen, Bond was elected delegate to Congress, and his letters to the governor during his term indicate that at that time they were working in perfect harmony. Bond came back from Washington in 1814 with an appointment as receiver of the land office at Kaskaskia. Two years later when Nathaniel Pope resigned the secretaryship to run for the position of delegate to Congress, Bond secured Pope's support for the position of secretary and wrote confidentially to the governor: "I now ask, and flatter myself, that you will support my view." [19] The appointment went to Captain Joseph B. Phillips of Tennessee, who was the first chief justice of the supreme court of

[18] *Illinois Gazette,* August 5, 1826; James, *Territorial Records,* 18, 28; Washburne, *Edwards Papers,* 71-78; Reynolds, *Pioneer History,* 351.

The secondary writers have all treated these two men as one, the usual statement being that he moved from Kaskaskia to Shawneetown in 1814. The conclusion that there were two men of this name was first based on a comparison of signatures and on a cumulation of circumstantial evidence. Finally, however, positive proof was found in a letter from Edward Humphreys, receiver of the land office at Kaskaskia, to the commissioner of the General Land Office, dated November 30, 1822, which announces the death of "Col. Mich. Jones Regr. of the Land Office at this place" on the twenty-sixth. Land records, auditor's office, Springfield.

[19] Lippincott, "Early Days in Madison County," no. 13; Washburne, *Edwards Papers,* 42-46, 93-98, 101-117, 126, 150.

the state and the candidate of the Thomas and Kane party for governor in 1822, but there is no evidence that Edwards was in any way responsible.

The truth seems to be that Bond and many of the other men, such as Pierre Menard and Dr. George Fisher, who had been prominent in politics during the period when Illinois was a part of Indiana Territory, held aloof from both of the new factions and relied upon their popularity with the voters for political preferment. Menard represented Randolph County in all three sessions of the legislature of Illinois Territory, serving as president of the council, while Fisher was the representative from the same county and speaker of the house in the first and third legislatures. In 1816 these two men had only to announce their candidacy in order to assure their elections, and the same appears to have been true of Bond whenever he aspired to an elective office.

On the whole, it would appear that the political factions during the last years of Illinois Territory may be characterized as combinations of men for the purpose of holding or seeking appointive offices, either local or territorial. The people as a whole played little part in politics, for the only elections were those for delegate and members of the legislature every two years. It is doubtful if any considerable number of voters considered themselves as members of either of the political parties, and in the elections they were concerned less with questions of policy regarding the territory as a whole than with what the representatives whom they sent to the legislature could procure for their particular county. This local interest was often a desire for a dam, a ferry, a road, or some other public improvement; and in 1818 the legislature was satirized as "discussing, whether nature had designed such and such rivers to be navigable or not." In 1816 the important issue of the judiciary system was pending, but the fight in St. Clair County centered around the purely local issue of the division of the county, and the candidates pledged themselves to give primary consideration to local interests. In Randolph, as has been noted, the popular candidates had little opposition, regardless of their stand on territorial issues, and such seems to have been the situation wherever no local issue was at stake.[20]

The action of the third territorial legislature on the judiciary question illustrates the lack of political convictions on the part of the members and the absence of strict party affiliation.[21] The United States law of 1815 having proved unsatisfactory in some of its details, the legislature of 1816 asked Congress to make certain changes and also to give to the legislature the power to make such changes as might be required in the future. This request was granted by a law of April 29, 1816, but unfortunately the phraseology of the act was such that the judges could claim that it would be of no effect after the close of the following session of the legislature, although the obvious intent of Congress was merely to limit those parts of the law making specific provisions for the time being and to leave the legislature absolutely free to regulate the judicial system of the territory in the future. The interpretation of the judges, if accepted, would have had the effect of throwing the question back into the same situation as before the passage of the United States law of 1815, with only the brief and doubtful language of the Ordinance of 1787 to fall back upon.

At the first session of the third territorial legislature, a committee of the house on the "state of the Judiciary" reported a bill "to establish circuit courts of their own creation; to give a salary of about $800—to have two judges; and to hold three

[20] *Intelligencer*, September 9, 1818; July 9, 24, 1816.

[21] The list of representatives in this legislature in the *Illinois Blue Book*, 1913-14, p. 133, is inaccurate and incomplete. It is supplemented in the following list from a vote reported in the *Intelligencer* of December 25, 1817. All of these men were elected in 1816 and all were present at the second session. Davenport may not have attended the first session but there is evidence that all the others were present, in the issues of the *Intelligencer* for December 4, 11, 18, 25, 1816, and January 22, 1817. George Fisher (speaker), Randolph; C. R. Matheny, St. Clair; William H. Bradsby, St. Clair; Nathan Davis, Jackson; M. S. Davenport, Gallatin; Joseph Palmer, Johnson; Seth Gard, Edwards; Samuel Omelveny, Pope; Willis Hargrave, White; John Mordock, Monroe; —— Gilham, Madison; Edward N. Cullom, Crawford.

courts in each county." This bill, if enacted, would have relieved
the United States judges of circuit work entirely, but the members of the legislature felt that the people of the territory should
not be called upon to pay for service which they had a right to
demand of the United States judges. Another bill was substituted, therefore, which practically continued the system then in
force under the United States statute, and this was enacted into
a law. Judges Thomas and Towles held courts in their circuits
in accordance with this act although the former expressed doubts
of its validity, but Judge Sprigg absolutely refused to recognize
the act on the ground that the United States law had expired
and that the territorial act was a violation of the ordinance. In
March, when he should have been making his first round of
counties, he was on his way to Maryland. He returned to the
territory in October and shortly afterward announced his refusal to obey the law. As a result the people of the circuit assigned to him were deprived of facilities for the determination
of lawsuits, and criminals went untried.[22]

When the same legislature met for its second session in December, 1817, it was obvious that something must be done to
relieve the situation. Representatives Bradsby and Matheny of
St. Clair opposed any concession to the judges and advocated
"an appeal to that tribunal which is competent for that purpose."
This would have meant more delay, however, and the majority
of the legislature appears to have been governed by expediency.
The first bill considered would have re-established the old courts
of common pleas but this was killed in committee of the whole
house and a measure was adopted similar to the one which failed
to pass in the first session. This provided for two circuit judges
appointed by the governor, with salaries of $1,000 a year. The
United States judges were relieved of all circuit duty and required to hold or y four general courts a year, two at Kaskaskia
and two at Shawneetown. "The object of this act," commented

[22] Street to Kane, March 31, 1817, in Chicago Historical Society Manuscripts, 52:167; *Intelligencer*, December 4, 11, 18, 1816; October 23, November 6, 1817.

the editors of the *Intelligencer*, "is to remove the inconveniences under which the people labor, in consequence of the refusal of one of the U. States Judges to act, and because it is believed to be a better system than to allow the same Judges to hold courts of original jurisdiction, and of appellate jurisdiction also." [23] That the legislature was not entirely subservient to the judges is indicated by the fact that it adopted resolutions requesting the delegate in Congress to lay before the House of Representatives charges against Judge Sprigg for his refusal to hold courts as required by the territorial law and for absenting himself from the territory "for an unreasonable time." [24]

When in November, 1817, the question of advance to statehood was suddenly thrust before the people of Illinois, the political situation may be summed up as follows: two coteries of politicians, the one led by Edwards and the other by Thomas and Kane, were opposing each other in a contest of several years' standing over the patronage and the judiciary; Menard, Bond, and others of the old established politicians, relying on their personal popularity, refused to align themselves with either of the factions; while the people, a simple people concerned principally with local interests and the advancement of material prosperity, readily gave their votes to any man who had won their personal liking. Besides these there was a small band of antislavery men watching and waiting for the opportune moment in which to free Illinois from any semblance of slavery.

[23] *Intelligencer*, January 13, 1818. See also *ibid.*, December 25, 1817; *Laws of Illinois Territory*, 1817-18, pp. 90-98. This act also restored the "Justices' Courts," composed of all the justices of the peace in each of the counties, such as had existed from 1809 to 1811.

[24] *Intelligencer*, January 13, 1818. According to Edwards, *History of Illinois*, 28, Richard Graham was appointed judge on April 20, 1818. If this is correct Sprigg must either have resigned or have been removed. At the first session of the first general assembly of the state in October, 1818, he failed in an attempt to secure a nomination for the office of United States district judge for Illinois. *House Journal*, 1 General Assembly, 1 Session, 28.

Chapter 8

The Movement for Admission

The undemocratic features of the American territorial system have frequently proved unpalatable to the people of the territories. Thus the house of representatives of Indiana Territory on October 11, 1808, adopted resolutions requesting Congress to permit the delegate and members of the council to be elected by the people and to repeal "that part of the Ordinance which vests in the Governor of this Territory an absolute negative on all acts; and also that part which confers on him the power of proroguing and dissolving the General Assembly."[1] As has been already noted Congress passed an act in 1809 granting the first plea of the petitioners, but leaving the powers of the governor unchanged.

The still more democratic form of government allowed to Illinois Territory by the act of 1812 was unsatisfactory to the members of the legislature, and in 1814 a memorial was drawn up praying for the repeal of the clause in the ordinance which gave the governor an absolute veto. "To freemen," it reads, "this clause wears the aspect of slavery—vesting our Executive with a Despotism that can frustrate the most deliberate and well digested measures of our Council and House of Representatives. . . . The good people of this Territory have the privilege, the trouble and the vast expense of electing and sending Representatives in a Legislative Capacity to convene and to consult together for the public good but by their mutual and most elaborate exertions they become not law-makers but only recommenders of laws."[2] Two years later, January 13, 1816, another memorial, much more moderate in tone but to the same effect, was sent to Congress. This asked not only that the executive veto be abolished, but also that the legislature might have a part

---

[1] House Files, October 19, 1808.

[2] Miscellaneous Assembly Papers, December 19, 1814, secretary of state's office.

in the appointive power. Congress denied the request, and the issue reappeared in the campaign of the following summer. A writer in the *Intelligencer*, who signed himself "Aristides," deplored "the colonial and degraded state of this country, under the government of the Ordinance, that accursed badge of despotism, which withholds from the people, the only true source of all power, a participation in those rights guaranteed by the constitutions of every state in the union." The voters of the territory were urged to see to it that the delegate to be elected should "advocate a redress of colonial grievances, and honestly exert his influence to obtain that change (so long withholden) which will place us on that proud eminence of freemen." [3]

Apparently "Aristides" had in mind merely a modification of the territorial government for the time being; but he went on to state that "the present rapid influx of population, that growing and prosperous state of the country, justifies the belief that it will not be more than 3 or 4 years before we will burst the chains of despotism, by which we are now bound, and stand a sovereign and independent state." The people were urged, therefore, "to begin to think and talk about that form of state government that so soon must take place.'

The editors of the *Intelligencer* apparently considered that "a redress of colonial grievances" could come only with transition to statehood, for in their comment on the communication they declared that they considered "the question not very important at present, as the population of the territory will not in all probability, within the time for which the present delegate is to be elected, entitle us to the redress alluded to. So soon as the population is sufficient we hope that those evils will be obviated by a state government." [4] There is, however, no evidence that the question of statehood was an issue in the election of this year, when Nathaniel Pope was selected to represent the territory in Congress.

About a year and a half later, in November, 1817, a movement

[3] *Intelligencer,* August 21, 1816.
[4] *Intelligencer,* August 21, 1816.

for immediate transition to statehood was suddenly inaugurated, and the man who was responsible was Daniel Pope Cook. Cook, who at this time was only 20 years old, had been appointed auditor of public accounts by the governor in January, 1816. About the same time he had purchased from Matthew Duncan the only newspaper then published in the territory, *The Illinois Herald*, and changed its name to *The Western Intelligencer*. Nominally he had continued as one of the editors of the paper until October, 1817, when it appeared under the names of Berry and Blackwell, each of whom in turn had been associated with Cook in its management.[5] In February, 1817, Cook had gone to Washington, expecting to return in April, but while there he was offered an appointment to carry dispatches to John Quincy Adams in London and had accepted in the hopes that a sea voyage would improve his health.[6] Returning to the United States in September, he had remained in Washington a few weeks on the lookout for a political opening. On September 25, he wrote to Governor Edwards: "As yet I do not know what I am to engage in. I can get a clerkship in the State department with a good salary, but I won't go into it; it is too confining. I shall know in a few days whether I go as Secretary of Alabama Territory or not. The President, it is feared, has made up his mind; if so, I shall fail; there is no situation vacant at present for me but that." Then in a postscript he added: "I am not yet well. May it not be better for me to return to Kaskaskia and wait for prospects in that country if I don't go to Alabama?"[7]

Failing to get the appointment desired, Cook returned to Illinois, arriving in Kaskaskia on November 18, 1817. There, instead of waiting for "prospects," he proceeded to make them.

[5] James, *Territorial Records*, 40; Scott, *Newspapers and Periodicals*, 211-212; *Intelligencer*, October 23, 1817.

[6] Washburne, *Edwards Papers*, 128; Cook to Edwards, March 6, 1817, in Chicago Historical Society Manuscripts, 49:303. On April 5, Cook's partner, Robert Blackwell, was appointed auditor in his place. James, *Territorial Records*, 47.

[7] Washburne, *Edwards Papers*, 135-141.

Two days after his arrival the following editorial appeared in the
Intelligencer:

While we are laboring under so many of the grievances of a territorial,
or semi-monarchial government, might not our claims to a state government be justly urged? That part of our territory which must ultimately form a state, will no doubt be willing to take the burthen of a
state government upon themselves at this time, rather than submit
any longer to those degredations [*sic*], which they have so long been
compelled to put up with. We hope in our next to present to our
readers, such a view of the subject as will induce our fellow citizens, as
well as the legislature, to take such measures as will bring it before
the national legislature, at their approaching season. We invite a discussion of the measure by such gentlemen as have, or will reflect on the
subject.

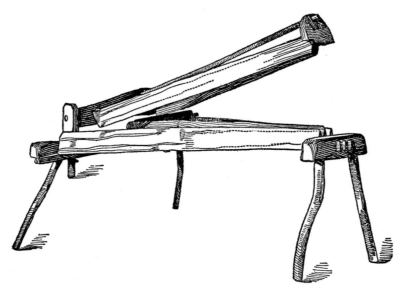

FLAX BRAKE

This utterance, whether inspired by Cook or not, was the prelude to a discussion of the subject in which he took the leading
part. In the next issue of the paper there appeared the expected

"view of the subject," written by Cook over the signature "A republican." [8] Asserting that the population of the territory had "increased to a sufficient number to enable us to take into our own hands the reins of self-government," he proceeded "to enquire into the policy of our doing so, as well as the practicability of obtaining the sanction of the general government, to such a measure." Possible objections were first considered, one of which was the additional expense to the people which statehood would involve. The national government was paying salaries for Illinois Territory to the amount of $6,200, a sum which in that day of small things was worthy of serious consideration. Cook could only hold out the forlorn hope that under state government, officials might be prevailed upon to accept smaller salaries at first. Another objection considered was the ignorance of the population, which, he maintained, was based on the assumption that a large proportion of the people were French. This assumption he controverted by the claim that nine-tenths of the voters were Americans who, previous to coming to Illinois, had taken part in state government.

Turning from negative to positive arguments, the writer dwelt upon the advantages of state government. Not only would the legislature be freed from the absolute veto of the governor but it would become supreme in the internal affairs of the state. The reference here was to the inability of the territorial government to enforce the judicial act, the results of which were painted in lurid colors. "Crimes of the blackest dye, (even murder itself,) have defied its feeble powers and laughed in guilty triumph, at their suffering victims. Honest labor has had its bread taken out of its mouth, and injuries of all kinds have implored relief in vain." As Cook professed, in the following April, the demoralized condition of the judiciary "was alone a sufficient reason for wishing for a state government." [9]

As to "the practicability of obtaining the sanction of the gen-

[8] *Intelligencer*, November 27, 1817. For evidence of authorship see editorial in *ibid.*, April 15, 1818.

[9] *Intelligencer*, April 22, 1818.

eral government" for admission with a population less than the 60,000, which under the ordinance would have given a right to statehood to Illinois, Cook was very sanguine. Such admission would not, he maintained, "be inconsistent with the general interest of the confederacy." It would, moreover, have the positive advantage of relieving Congress of the burden of legislating for the local concerns of the territory, while "the strength and respectability of the nation would be greatly augmented" by the opening up of "a new field for the enlargement of the human understanding." This was merely an oratorical way of stating that the change would give an added impetus to immigration. This Cook believed to be true because "at present it is doubtful whether slavery will be tolerated when a state government is formed. And many on both sides of the question are remaining in the anxiety of suspense, to know how it will be settled. It is therefore desirable to settle the question at as early a period as possible, for the purpose of giving relief to those who are wanting to emigrate to the territory."

Three days after this communication appeared in the *Intelligencer*, the legislature assembled in Kaskaskia; and on the following day, December 2, 1817, Governor Edwards delivered his message to the two houses.[10] The members "and the citizens at large" were congratulated "upon the flattering prospects which our astonishingly rapid increase of population affords that our present temporary government must soon give place to one more congenial to the principles of natural liberty." The governor's recommendation "for the purpose of facilitating this desirable event, and as preparatory thereto" was "to provide by law for taking the census of all the inhabitants of this territory, so that it may be laid before the legislature at its next session."

This would have been the ordinary procedure, but it was altogether too leisurely for those who were eager for immediate statehood. Daniel Pope Cook, having been elected clerk of the house of representatives, was in a position to exert considerable influence; and on the same day upon which the governor's mes-

[10] *Intelligencer*, December 4, 1817.

sage was delivered, the house resolved, upon the motion of Bradsby of St. Clair, "that a committee be appointed to draft a memorial to Congress praying for this territory to be admitted into the union, with all the rights and privileges of a state government." Four days later, December 6, the memorial was adopted by the house, and on the tenth it received the approval of the council and was laid before the governor. The rapidity of its passage was possible only because of the lack of opposition, it being the "unanimous voice of our representatives from every part of the territory, that are desirous to enter into a state government." [11]

The memorial consists of two long paragraphs, of which the first has many points of similarity with the communication of "A republican" in the paper of November 27, and may well have been written by Cook. The territorial government is characterized as "a species of despotism in direct hostility with the principles of a republican government" which "ought to exist no longer than *absolute necessity* may require it." The population is estimated at "not less than forty thousand souls" and the fitness for self-government of the citizens of the territory "mostly composed of those who have im[m]igrated hither from the atlantic and western states" is pointed out. The second paragraph, probably the work of some mind more practical than Cook's, suggested a solution of the financial difficulty. Congress was asked

for a grant to the inhabitants of the state of the Lead Mines and Salt Springs; together with the lands adjoining, which have been reserved from sale within the limits of the state; also that section sixteen in each township reserved from sale, may be granted to the inhabitants of the township for the use of schools—also that a part of the net proceeds of the lands lying within the state, which may be sold by the authority of your honorable body may be appropriated to the laying out and making public roads; and finally for all such gifts and privileges as were made and given by the congress of the United States to the states of Ohio, Indiana and Mississippi, and upon the like conditions.

[11] *Intelligencer,* December 4, 11, 1817; manuscript journal of the legislative council, 1817-18, secretary of state's office.

Two points of special interest present themselves in connection with this memorial. Would Congress accept the unsupported statement that the territory had a population of 40,000 souls? Was the step contemplated really desired by the people of the territory? In answer to the first of these questions, Cook wrote in the *Intelligencer* of December 11: "The census not having been taken certainly can make no difference, when, the representatives of the people from each county agree that there are 40,000 inhabitants—their information is the best except that which would be derived from actual enumeration.—The willingness of the people, with this strong evidence of their numbers, ought to secure the privilege prayed for." This tone of confidence in the young man just from Washington and high in the esteem of officials there was probably an important factor in securing the immediate adoption of the memorial. On the second question, the memorial itself states that among the whole people "there is an unusual coincidence of sentiment as to the propriety of forming a state government," while the editors of the *Intelligencer* declared it to be "the first wish of the people." Yet the initiative certainly did not come from the people. The members of the legislature had all been elected in 1816, when the question of statehood was not an issue; and in 1817 the subject was not broached in time for any adequate public discussion. Three weeks from the time of Cook's return to Kaskaskia and the first intimation of the movement in the newspaper, the memorial was ready to be sent to Washington.

The usual procedure would have been for this legislature to have provided for a census to be laid before the next legislative session, as recommended by the governor. The question of statehood would then have been an issue in the election of 1818, and the members of the next legislature could have acted on the subject with adequate knowledge of the population of the territory and of the wishes of their constituents. Was there any reason for the haste with which the movement was put through other than the feverish energy of its youthful promoter and the desire for a "redress of colonial grievances"? The answer to this question may be sought in a study of the attempt made during this session to brand the system of indentured servitude in force in the territory as a violation of the Ordinance of 1787.

The indenture act of Indiana as revised in 1807 had continued in effect in Illinois by virtue of the resolution adopted by the governor and judges of Illinois Territory in 1809, that "the laws of Indiana Territory of a general nature . . . are still in force in this Territory." [12] Although in Indiana the act had been repealed shortly after the separation, no attempt seems to have been made to repeal it in Illinois prior to the legislative session of 1817-18. During the territorial period, however, especially as the northwestern counties filled up in the years after 1815, there was certainly a growing sentiment against the institution as it existed in the territory. [13]

To the men who represented that sentiment it may well have seemed in 1817 that the time had come to strike for freedom. A month or two before the inauguration of the movement for statehood in Illinois, petitions asking for admission to the Union began to be circulated in Missouri. There was every reason to believe that Missouri would come in as a slave state, and if that should happen before Illinois was admitted, the existence of slavery there would be the strongest argument for allowing it in Illinois also. The passage of the slaveholding immigrants across Illinois to locate in Missouri was always galling to the people of Illinois, anxious as they were for the rapid development of the country. The opponents of slavery maintained, however, that its exclusion did not retard the development of the state, and it is quite possible that they felt that if Illinois could achieve statehood before her rival across the river, it would strengthen their argument. It was important, therefore, from the point of view of the antislavery men, that Illinois should become a state with a free constitution as provided by the ordinance before the constitution of Missouri should become a subject for discussion.

But these men could not be content with merely the oppor-

[12] Alvord, *Laws of the Territory*, 1. See above, pp. 186-187.
[13] See appendix, pp. 317-318.

tunity for Illinois to frame a constitution in accord with the ordinance as it was then interpreted. That would permit the
continuance indefinitely of such slavery as existed prior to the
adoption of the ordinance and especially of the system of indentured servitude. This, it is believed, is the explanation of
the introduction in the house of representatives on December
10, the day before the final passage by the council of the memorial asking for statehood, of a bill, not only for the repeal of
the law establishing the indenture system, but containing also
a preamble declaring that law to be in contravention to the para-
mount law of the land. Apparently the intention was to establish the invalidity of the law in such a way and at such a time
as to make it impossible for the constitutional convention to
ignore the action. The bill, when introduced by Matheny, "gave
rise to some warmth and animation of argument on both sides."
Bradsby and Matheny, both of whom had been members of
the committee of four which framed the statehood memorial,
defended it, and Dr. Fisher, the speaker, opposed it.

Bradsby was careful to ask that the question be considered
as "envolving the enquiry, whether the legislature which passed
the law which it is the object of this bill to repeal, exercised its
legislative power within constitutional limits." The argument
was, of course, that the action of a slave in indenturing himself
to his master could not be considered as voluntary and consequently the whole system was "involuntary servitude" and a
violation of the ordinance. Emphasis was laid also upon the fact
that this provision of the ordinance was one of the articles of
compact "intended 'to fix and establish those principles as the
basis of all laws, constitutions, and governments which forever
hereafter shall be formed in this Territory.'" Fisher in reply
contended that it was outside the province of the legislature to
pass upon the constitutionality of a law. "If it be unconstitutional there is no necessity of our repealing it, it is of itself void,
and requires no annulling act of the legislature. . . . The law
was passed by a former legislature, and whether it is constitutional or not is for the judiciary to determine, and even if we
believe it so, it is no violation of our oaths, to leave it to a tri-

bunal having the power and authority to determine upon it. As it has stood so long I see no impropriety in leaving it to be settled by the convention who shall frame our constitution, which will not be long hence." Matheny in his reply to Fisher took the curious position that the bill if passed, although it declared the indenture act a violation of the ordinance, would "have no influence on contracts that have been heretofore made, if such were its intended operation, it would be an expost facto law, and therefore unconstitutional."

Unfortunately the vote by which this bill passed the house is not available. On December 13, the bill was sent to the council, where it was twice debated in committee of the whole; and, on the seventeenth that body concurred without amendment. Those voting in favor of the measure were Amos of St. Clair, Grammar of Johnson, and Lofton of Madison; against it were Browne of Gallatin and Menard of Randolph.[14]

Whatever may have been the attitude of Governor Edwards toward the institution of slavery, he was unwilling to approve the measure in the form which it had taken; and on January 1, 1818, he returned the bill to the house in which it had originated, accompanied by his objections:

passing over minor objections to the preamble of the bill, and considering that the law, which I suppose it was intended to repeal, was enacted first, by the legislature of the Indiana Territory—that it was subsequently modified by the Governor and Judges of this Territory—that being so modified, it was re-enacted unanimously, by our general assembly, at its first session and has been acquiesced in, and sanctioned at every subsequent session: I cannot think it either proper, or necessary, to impute to our predecessors, a total disregard of their oaths, and an intentional violation of their duty; which I think is done by the preamble in question, and which also implies a great reproach and censure upon ourselves for having neglected to act upon the subject at our last session; for if we *then* entertained such sentiments, how can we answer it to our country? to our consciences? to our God, before whom we solemnly swore to endeavor to fulfil our duties? for not having attempted *at least,* to arrest an evil, which under insidious "pre-

---

[14] This whole discussion may be followed in the *Intelligencer* for December, 1817, and January, 1818, and in the manuscript journal of the legislative council, 1817-18, secretary of state's office.

tences, it was intended," to fix upon our territory, to its great detriment, "contrary to the ordinance, and to the feelings and wishes of our fellow citizens."

After declaring that questions of the validity of laws "ought rather to be left to the decision of the judiciary, to whose province it more peculiarly belongs," he proceeded to a long disquisition intended to prove that the indenture law in question was not a violation of the ordinance. In conclusion he pointed out that his remarks were "intended to apply to the question of legislative power, and not to the propriety, or expediency of its exercise, in the particular instance alluded to"; and finally, he declared himself "no advocate for slavery, and if it depended upon my vote alone, it should never be admitted in any state or Territory, not already cursed with so great an evil. I have no objection to the repeal which I suppose was intended."

Two weeks later, in his speech proroguing the legislature, the governor felt it necessary, "for the purpose of preventing all possible misapprehension," to discuss the subject again. After stating that he had not desired to "defeat the measure, that was intended to be adopted," he pointed out that the "particular friends of the measure" might after his veto "have introduced and passed a bill less objectionable, and better calculated to effect the object that seemed to be so greatly desired." Or, he continued, "the object could have been completely effected by the passage of a bill to amend the law alluded to, by limiting the period of service to one year only." [15] Such a measure would have confirmed the validity of the indenture system, and the failure of the legislature to take any further action after the veto indicates clearly that it was the preamble of the bill, the very part to which the governor objected, that the antislavery men had at heart.

The result of this antislavery movement in the last territorial legislative session, and of its failure, was the establishment of slavery as the dominant issue in the forthcoming campaign for delegates to the constitutional convention. In this the

[15] *Intelligencer,* January 1, 13, 1818.

proslavery men had the advantage, for the extreme antislavery men, by declaring themselves so positively at the very beginning, left the whole of the middle ground to their opponents. They made it necessary for those who sought only to keep conditions as they were to work together with advocates of unrestricted slavery. The line of argument to be followed was already indicated by Fisher in his speech against the repeal of the indenture law. Referring to the constitutional convention, he said: "We then perhaps may do something which will lead to a gradual emancipation of slavery in a partial degree, and so ultimately benefit them [the slaves] in their condition. For although I am opposed to slavery upon principle, yet I think if we can better their condition and gradually emancipate them, by bringing them to our Territory, we are doing a laudable thing."[16]

Although the legislature had decided in favor of an appeal to Congress for admission to the Union without waiting for a census, some doubts were entertained apparently as to the willingness of Congress to allow the movement to proceed without positive evidence as to the population of the territory. Toward the close of the session a law was enacted providing for a census of all the inhabitants. The enumeration was to begin April 1 and the returns, instead of being laid before the next legislature, as the governor had suggested, were to be deposited in the office of the secretary on or before June 1. The commissioners were instructed "to take a list of all citizens, of all ages, sexes and colour, within their respective counties, particularly noting whether white or black, and also noting particularly free male inhabitants above the age of twenty-one years." [17]

Realizing apparently that its optimistic predictions as to population might not be fulfilled at so early a date as June 1, the legislature enacted a supplementary law, the preamble of which suggested that "a great increase of population may be expected between the first day of next June and December following."

[16] *Intelligencer,* December 18, 1817.
[17] *Laws of Illinois Territory,* 1817-18, pp. 42-44.

In accordance with this preamble the act directed the commissioners to "continue to take the census of all persons who may remove into their respective counties between the first day of June and the first day of December next, succeeding; of which additional returns shall be made to the secretary's office, within the first week in December next." In order to prevent unnecessary expenditure, a provision was added "that no such additional service shall be performed if congress should authorize the citizens of this territory to form a state government without it." [18]

One other action of this legislature is of interest in connection with the movement for statehood. Between 1812 and 1818, seven counties, Edwards, White, Jackson, Pope, Monroe, Crawford, and Bond had been added by the legislature to the five existing when the second stage of territorial government was adopted. By acts of January 2, 1818, three new counties, Washington, Franklin, and Union, were established, making a total of 15 counties in Illinois in the year of admission. The significance of the establishment of new counties in 1818 lies in its bearing on the question of apportionment of delegates to the convention, for the practice had grown up in Illinois Territory of ignoring population to a considerable extent in the apportionment of members of the legislature. About the same time that bills for the new counties were passed by the two houses, a joint resolution was adopted authorizing representatives to be apportioned for a convention to form a permanent constitution. No copy of this resolution has been found, but it is probable that the apportionment section of the enabling act embodied its provisions.

The legislative memorial praying for statehood was doubtless dispatched to Washington immediately after its adoption by the council on December 10, 1817. Once there, its fate depended upon the exertions of Nathaniel Pope, the delegate from the territory in the House of Representatives. Pope must have left Illinois

[18] *Laws of Illinois Territory,* 1817-18, pp. 44-45.

before the return of Cook to Kaskaskia,[19] and it is quite improbable, therefore, that he had any part in the inception of
the movement for statehood. During the campaign for the
election of members of the convention the editor of the *Intelligencer* said of Pope: "It is well known that he had no agency
in putting on foot the application to congress for a state government." [20] However that may have been, he must have been
in complete sympathy with it; and the rapidity with which matters were pushed along would indicate that he, too, realized the
importance of getting in ahead of Missouri.

The Illinois memorial was laid before the House by Pope on
January 16, 1818, and was immediately referred to a select
committee of which the Illinois delegate was chairman. Claiborne of Tennessee, Johnson of Kentucky, Spencer of New
York, and Whitman of Massachusetts were the other members
of the committee. Five days later Pope wrote a letter to the
editors of the *Intelligencer* which throws light on the attitude
of the committee: "The only difficulty I have to overcome is,
whether we have the population supposed by the Legislature;
no enumeration of the inhabitants having lately been taken. In
order to evade that objection the bill contains a *proviso*, that
the census shall be taken previously to the meeting of the Convention—I hope however to have that feature of the bill struck
out before its final passage, if it passes at all, of which I have
strong hopes. . . . If it were certain that we had even thirty-five
thousand inhabitants, no objection I think would be made to
our admission." [21] Thirty-five thousand inhabitants was the ratio
of congressional apportionment at that time, and it would appear that some member of the committee—possibly Spencer,
who made a similar point the following November—felt that

[19] He arrived in Washington on December 6; see *Intelligencer*, January
21, 1818. For action of the Illinois legislative council, see *Laws of Illinois
Territory*, 1817-18, pp. 11-17, 39-41; manuscript journal of the legislative
council, 1817-18, secretary of state's office.

[20] *Intelligencer*, June 24, 1818.

[21] *Intelligencer*, March 4, 1818.

positive evidence of at least that many should be insisted upon. Pope's letter of January 21, just referred to, states his intention of reporting the bill that day; but it was not brought in until the twenty-third, one week after the committee was appointed. For this bill "To enable the people of Illinois Territory, to form a Constitution and state government, and for the admission of such state into the union, on an equal footing with the original states," the Indiana enabling act of 1816 served as a model.[22] After authorizing the inhabitants of the territory "to form for themselves, a constitution and state government, and to assume such name as they shall deem proper," the boundaries of the proposed state were fixed as they are at present with the exception that the northern boundary was to be "an east and west line drawn through a point ten miles north of the southern extreme of Lake Michigan." This was not the line proposed by the Ordinance of 1787, but the same was true of Indiana's northern boundary, which had been fixed in the same way, the obvious purpose in both cases being to give the state an outlet on Lake Michigan. Possibly to obviate any difficulties over the validity of a change in the ordinance, the convention was required to "ratify the boundaries, aforesaid; otherwise they shall be, and remain as now prescribed, by the ordinance."

Section three of the bill authorized "all white male citizens of the U. States, who shall have arrived at the age of twenty-one years, and have resided in said territory, six months previous to the day of election, and all persons having in other respects the legal qualifications to vote for representatives in the general assembly of the said territory . . . to choose representatives to form a convention." This was a change from the Indiana act, which required a year's residence in the territory for voting at the election, and from the rule of Illinois Territory, in which a similar qualification for voters prevailed. The general sentiment in the west, however, was in favor of allowing immigrants to vote as soon as possible, and the six months' qualification

[22] The bill as introduced can be found in the *Intelligencer*, March 11, 1818. The act as finally passed is in Thorpe, *Constitutions*, 2:967-970. The Indiana enabling act is in *ibid.*, 1053-56.

was incorporated in the state constitution. In the enabling acts for Missouri and Alabama, the time was further reduced to three months. This section concluded with a list of the 12 counties formed before 1818, with blanks opposite each for the apportionment of delegates to the convention. In sending the bill to the *Intelligencer*, Pope wrote: "It will also be observed that I have provided for a representation but for twelve counties. The simple reason is this, I have not heard whether any other counties have been created by the legislature at the last session." [23]

The delegates thus to be elected were authorized by section four of the bill to convene on a date which was left to be filled in later. They were first to "determine by a majority of the whole number elected, whether it be, or be not expedient at that time to form a constitution and state government for the people within the said territory; and if it be expedient, the convention shall be, and hereby is authorized to form a constitution and state government." Should the convention prefer, however, it might adopt an ordinance providing for another convention to form the constitution and state government. This feature, which was common in enabling acts, appears to have been designed to enable the people through the first convention to determine the apportionment, manner of choice, and time of sitting of the constitutional convention; but the territories rarely, if ever, took advantage of it, and the possibility of following this alternative procedure does not appear to have been considered in Illinois.

To this section were added two important provisos: first, that the constitution, "whenever formed, shall be republican, and not repugnant to the ordinance" except as concerns boundaries; and second, "that it shall appear from the enumeration hereinafter directed to be made, that there are within the proposed state, not less than ————— thousand inhabitants." With this second proviso should be considered section twelve, which directed the United States marshal of the territory to take a census and make his returns to the convention. This was the feature of the bill that Pope hoped to have eliminated.

[23] *Intelligencer*, March 11, 1818.

Section five provided for one representative from the state in the lower house of Congress, and section six contained the usual set of propositions offered to the convention "for their free acceptance or rejection." These included section sixteen of each township of land for the use of schools; all salt springs and lead mines "and the land reserved for the use of the same"; "five per cent. of the net proceeds of the lands lying within the said territory" for roads; and "thirty-six sections or one entire township, which shall be designated by the President of the United States, together with the one heretofore reserved for that purpose," for "a seminary of learning." These grants were made on condition that all lands sold by the United States should remain exempt from taxation for six years after date of sale. They differed from the grants to Indiana only in the inclusion of lead mines, as requested by the Illinois memorial, and the exclusion of a grant of four sections of land "for the purpose of fixing their seat of government thereon." The failure to ask for land for a capital site was probably an oversight on the part of the men who drew up the memorial. Had it been included among the grants in the enabling act, the question of the location of the capital would doubtless have been an issue in the pre-convention campaign, as it was later in the convention itself.

This completes the enumeration of the provisions finally comprised in the enabling act. The remaining sections of the bill, numbered seven to eleven inclusive, provided for the establishment of a United States court for the Illinois district, with all its attendant officials. Nothing comparable to these sections is to be found in the enabling act of any other state, and they were dropped from the bill before it was passed. The objection to them doubtless was that they were out of place in the bill, for at the next session of Congress they were enacted word for word as "An Act to provide for the due execution of the laws of the United States within the state of Illinois." [24]

[24] *Statutes at Large*, 3:502. It might be noted in passing that Nathaniel Pope was the first United States judge appointed under this act.

This enabling bill, introduced by Pope for the committee on Friday, January 23, "was read twice, and committed to a Committee of the Whole, on Monday next." Not until April 4, however, was it taken up for consideration, "in consequence of the great number of bills which were introduced before and claimed a prior[i]ty."[25]

When the bill finally came up in the House, Pope at once introduced an amendment to fix the northern boundary on the line 42° 30″ north latitude—about 41 miles north of the line fixed in the bill and 51 miles north of the dividing line proposed in the ordinance. As early as January 27, four days after the bill was introduced, Pope had reached the conclusion that such a change was desirable, for in his letter of that date forwarding a copy of the bill to the *Intelligencer* he wrote: "You will remark that the northern line is ten miles north of the southernly extremity of Lake Michigan—Indiana goes as far north. When the bill is taken up, I will endeavour to procure twenty or thirty miles farther north, and make Lake Michigan a part of our eastern boundary. I shall not attempt to explain the importance of such an accession of territory; it is too obvious to every man who looks to the prospective weight and influence of the state of Illinois." In support of the amendment, Pope said that its object

was to gain, for the proposed State, a coast on Lake Michigan. This would afford additional security to the perpetuity of the Union, inasmuch as the State would thereby be connected with the States of Indiana, Ohio, Pennsylvania, and New York, through the Lakes. The facility of opening a canal between Lake Michigan and the Illinois river, said Mr. P., is acknowledged by every one who has visited the place. Giving to the proposed State the port of Chicago, (embraced in the proposed limits,) will draw its attention to the opening of the communication between the Illinois river and that place, and the improvement of that harbor.

Since the line proposed by the ordinance had not been adopted in the case of Indiana nor in the bill itself to which this amend-

[25] *Annals of Congress*, 15 Congress, 1 Session, 1:814; 2:1677; *Intelligencer*, April 15, 1818.

ment was proposed, it was difficult to object to the change on the grounds of a violation of that document, and the motion to amend "was agreed to without a division." [26]

The advantages of this change, from the point of view of those who desired that Illinois should ultimately be a free instead of a slave state, are obvious; and Pope's argument might be taken as an indication that he had those advantages in mind.[27] Whatever may have been the real motives back of the amendment, and however it may have originated, it appears to have aroused little interest in Illinois at the time. It was mentioned without comment in an article in the *Intelligencer* of April 29, based on a letter from Pope dated April 6; while an editorial on the enabling act as finally passed, in the issue of May 20, recounts many of its advantageous features and expresses deep appreciation of Pope's services but makes no mention of the change in boundary. The important consequences which have flowed from this change, not only for Illinois but for the country as a whole, have often been pointed out and need not be dwelt upon here.[28] It added to Illinois a region of over 8,000 square miles in which lie the greater part of 14 counties containing, with the city of Chicago, over half the population of the state.

A second amendment proposed by Pope on April 4 provided that 3 of the 5 per cent [29] of the proceeds of federal land sales in Illinois should be used not for roads and canals in the state as provided in the bill and in previous enabling acts, but "for the encouragement of learning, of which one[-sixth] part shall be exclusively bestowed on a college or university." In explain-

[26] *Intelligencer,* March 11, 1818; *Annals of Congress,* 15 Congress, 1 Session, 2:1677.

[27] See appendix, pp. 317-318.

[28] For a discussion of this subject and an account of the attempts made later in the region affected, and in Wisconsin to restore the ordinance boundary, see Moses, *Illinois,* 1:278-282.

[29] The other 2 per cent was to be used "under the direction of Congress, in making roads leading to the State."

ing this amendment Pope pointed out that the application of this fund to roads in the other states had "not been productive of the good anticipated; on the contrary, it had been exhausted on local and neighborhood objects, by its distribution among the counties." The statement that "nature had left little to be done in the proposed State of Illinois, in order to have the finest roads in the world" would hardly be concurred in by one familiar with the roads in the central part of the state nearly a century later; but no exception need be taken to the emphasis upon the "importance of education in a Republic." Moreover, "that no immediate aid could be derived in new count[r]ies from waste lands was not less obvious; and that no active fund would be provided in a new State, the history of the Western States too clearly proved." This amendment too was accepted without a division.

"Some further amendments" were then agreed to, including one moved by Taylor of New York adding a proviso "that the bounty-lands granted, or hereafter to be granted, for military services during the late war, shall, while they continue to be held by the patentees, or their heirs, remain exempt, as aforesaid, from all taxes, for the term of three years, from and after the date of the patents respectively; and that all the lands belonging to the citizens of the United States, residing without the said State, shall never be taxed higher than lands belonging to persons residing therein." [30] Pope does not appear to have opposed this amendment although it must have been unpalatable to him. Early in the session a resolution had been introduced to exempt the bounty lands from taxation for five years, a proposition which Pope believed "would enable speculators to hold up their lands from market, and prevent the territory from taxing three and a half millions of acres of land, and most of that belonging to individuals, who obtained it at less than fifty cents per acre." On January 21, he wrote that he had no fears that the measure

[30] *Annals of Congress*, 15 Congress, 1 Session, 2:1677; Thorpe, *Constitutions*, 2:969-970.

would succeed, "so that we may calculate upon a handsome revenue from that quarter." The provision introduced in the enabling act was less objectionable because it was restricted to three years and then applied only if the land was retained by the patentees or their heirs. "We shall not," the editors of the *Intelligencer* consoled the people, "lose much by that, because most of it will pass into the hands of others." [31]

It must have been at this time that the grant of lead mines was stricken out and the provision relative to the census changed. Pope did not succeed in getting the census feature eliminated from the bill; but section twelve, which provided that the count should be made by the marshal, was stricken out and section four modified to allow the convention to rely upon "the enumeration directed to be made by the legislature of the said Territory."

The blank for the population to be required was filled in as 40,000, the number claimed in the memorial from the legislature. The apportionment of delegates in the convention was set at three each to Madison, St. Clair, and Gallatin counties and two each to the others, including the three counties established in January, 1818. No statistics as to the population of the counties were at hand, of course, and it is probable that the legislative resolution on the subject was followed.[32] A fair apportionment of the same number of representatives—33—on the basis of the census of 1818 would have given five to Madison County; four to St. Clair; three each to Randolph, Gallatin, and White; two each to Washington, Union, Pope, Edwards, and Crawford; and one each to Bond, Monroe, Jackson, Johnson, and Franklin.

Some of the amendments were adopted in the House itself after the committee rose and reported the bill. It was then "ordered to be engrossed, as amended, and read a third time, *nemine contradicente.*" The third reading and final passage of the bill in the House took place on April 6, also, apparently,

[31] *Intelligencer,* January 21, March 4, April 29, 1818.
[32] Thorpe, *Constitutions,* 2:968. See also above, p. 220.

without opposition; and it was transmitted to the Senate the following day. There the bill was given its first and second readings at once and then referred to the Committee on Public Lands.

The Senate committee reported the bill with amendments the day after it was received, and on the thirteenth it was taken up in Committee of the Whole. Here the measure met with opposition from Tait of Georgia, who moved "to postpone the further consideration thereof until the fourth day of July next." His objection, he explained, was not due to any opposition to "the admission of this State into the Union, but on the ground that there was not sufficiently authentic information that its population was forty thousand, as stated from conjecture, or even that its population was sufficient to entitle it to a representative in Congress." Morrow of Ohio, Talbot of Kentucky, and Barbour of Virginia "replied, and opposed the postponement, believing the evidence on this head to be so strong as to admit of no doubt." This motion produced the only record vote on the bill in either house, but only four senators, Daggett of Connecticut, King and Sanford of New York, and Tait voted in favor of postponement.

According to Pope, "the application of the three per cent. to schools instead of roads, was violently opposed in the Senate, as being altogether for the benefit of the state, and not for that of the United States. That it gave to Illinois greater advantages than was ever allowed to any other state admitted into the union. It was urged that we had no claims to such preference, that that fund was granted to the other states with a view of raising the price of the public lands." These objections were answered by the Kentucky senators, Crittenden and Talbot, by Burrill of Rhode Island, and by Morrow, their arguments being along lines similar to those followed by Pope in his support of this feature in the House. The "one great objection to emigrating to new countries," they contended, "was the want of the means of education. Apply this money to schools and that objection will be removed, and then thousands will go who would otherwise stay. In this manner they proved that the United States would gain rather than lose." The provision in question, Pope wrote, "passed by a great majority, and has given a character to Illinois that nothing else could have effected. Almost every man agrees that it will greatly promote our prosperity." [33]

The question of the northern boundary was also raised in the Senate apparently, for Pope wrote that "some jealousy was felt against our gaining so much territory north, say sixty miles." This opposition could not have been very extensive, however, for there is no record of a vote on the question. Just which of the differences between the final act and the original bill were embodied in the Senate amendments cannot be determined, but Pope wrote that these amendments were unimportant. Possibly it was at this time that a section was added providing that the part of Illinois Territory not included in the boundaries of the proposed state should be attached to the territory of Michigan. At the close of the discussion the committee rose and reported the bill with the amendments, and on the following day, April 14, it was read the third time and passed without division. In the House, the Senate amendments were referred to a select committee headed by Pope which on the fifteenth "reported the agreement of the committee to the said amendments, and the amendments were then concurred in by the House." The bill then went to the President, who approved it on April 18, 1818.

If the hypothesis be correct that those behind the movement were trying to outrun Missouri in the race for statehood, they had won the first heat. The first petitions from Missouri asking for statehood were received in the House on January 8, eight days before Pope presented the Illinois memorial. These, with a petition presented February 2, were laid on the table; but when still more petitions were received on March 6, they were all referred to a select committee of which Scott, the Missouri delegate, was chairman. Not until April 3 did this committee

[33] *Intelligencer,* May 6, 1818.

report a bill for an enabling act and it was then too late to hope for its passage at that session. If the proponents of statehood in Illinois were to keep the lead, however, it was necessary that the census returns show a population of 40,000. Furthermore, if the antislavery men were to obtain a constitution such as they wished, they had next to secure a majority of delegates to the convention who would be favorable to their views. Illinois had a lively campaign in prospect.

✠ *Chapter 9*

The Convention Campaign

When the movement for admission to statehood was inaugurated in Illinois, in November, 1817, it was "at first little thought of" and Cook himself says that his early remarks on the subject "were thought to be the effusions of visionary hopes." It is quite possible that this attitude, together with the suddenness with which the proposition was sprung upon them, explains the unanimity of the members of the legislature in voting for the memorial. As time passed, however, and favorable news began to arrive from Washington, the movement attracted more attention and, as will be seen, more opposition as well.

At first the prospect of statehood evoked some pleasurable anticipations. At the Washington's birthday celebration in Bennett's tavern at Kaskaskia, February 22, 1818, one of the toasts was to *"The Territory of Illinois*—May she rise refulgent from the shackles of a colonial government, and shine in the Federal Union." The *Intelligencer*, which gave an account of this dinner, noted in the usual reprint of the proceedings of Congress that the Illinois bill had been introduced in the House of Representatives. Commenting on this measure "so important to the citizens of this territory," the editors declared that it "will in all probability finally pass." One week later, March 4, the *Intelligencer* published Pope's letter of January 21, expressing "strong hopes" of the passage of the bill. "A moment of enjoyment is grateful to an anxious people," said the editors. "Let us therefore enjoy the pleasing intelligence which Mr. Pope's letter communicates relative to our obtaining a state government. His hopes that the bill will pass, which we find has been read a second time, certainly is cheering to us all who are friendly to a free government." [1]

On March 11, the bill itself was published in the paper, with

[1] *Intelligencer*, February 25, March 4, April 22, 1818.

the comment that it "will pass, we have no doubt." Six weeks later, April 29, the readers were informed that the measure had passed the House and that the elections for representatives in the convention were fixed for the first Monday in July and the two following days, while the convention itself was to meet the first Monday in August. The next issue of the paper announced the passage of the bill in the Senate, and the act as finally approved by the President was published in full in the issue of May 20. Commenting upon the measure in one of his letters, Pope wrote: "Its success will have a great influence on the emigration to that country. I cannot describe the interest Illinois awakens in the minds of the Atlantic people. I have no hesitation in hazarding the opinion that next season will add greatly to our population." The act attracted attention in a neighboring state also. The *Kentucky Argus,* in announcing its passage, said: "The agricultural and mercantile advantages of this state will render it a star of the first magnitude in our constellation of free states. . . . *We hail thee, sister Illinois, and are ready to welcome thee into our happy Union."* The editors of the Kaskaskia paper celebrated the passage of the enabling act by changing its name from *The Western Intelligencer* to *The Illinois Intelligencer.* "We have made this change," they wrote, "believing it to be a more appropriate name, in as much as it is the same establishment from which the first paper eminated [*sic*] in the territory, and more particularly as we shall soon go into a state under the name of Illinois."[2]

The same issue of the paper which contained information on the passage of the enabling bill by the Senate announced the candidacy of Elias K. Kane "for the Convention from the county of Randolph" and that of Daniel P. Cook "for Congress to represent us in the Lower House." The convention campaign began at least two months earlier, however, for the *Intelligencer* of March 11, in which the bill was first printed, contained an editorial on the importance of the election of members of the convention:

---

[2] *Intelligencer,* April 22 to May 27, 1818.

In this election, party and private feeling should alike be suspended, and the public interest alone should be the polestar of every voter. . . . Let not a difference of opinion on one particular and unimportant point, influence you to reject men, whose reading, and whose experience, qualifies them for so arduous and important an undertaking; for although you may find men enough who will agree to support any measure to secure their election; yet it is not on any one measure alone, that the public interest will depend. No! it depend[s] on many. Then let us urge you to elect those men, who are best qualified to decide on all measures—and not suffer the ambitious, without merit, to use their flexibility, to the injury of intelligent men, and the public weal.[3]

The advice of the editors as to party feeling may have been heeded, for there is no evidence that the political factions played even as slight a part in this election as they had in the territorial elections; but the "one particular and unimportant point," which was doubtless the slavery question, was the only real issue of the campaign. Because of the existing situation, however, this was not the clear-cut issue as to whether Illinois should be a free or a slave state. It involved also the questions of what to do with existing slavery, of the validity of the indentures based on the territorial law, and of the continuance of the indenture system. Congress, moreover, in the enabling act, directed that the constitution of the new state should not be repugnant to the Ordinance of 1787, and this enabled some of the leaders, ignoring all questions of interpretation, to claim that the matter was settled. As a result, no simple classification can cover the situation with reference to the slavery question. There were some who favored unrestricted slavery for the new state, there were some who would at once wipe out every vestige of the institution, but most of the politicians and voters appear to have occupied a variety of positions between these two extremes.

The campaign of the extreme proslavery men was a quiet one and took the form of urging delay, doubtless with the expectation that Congress could be induced to remove the restriction. Some, however, feeling that they could not be bound by an ordinance in the making of which they had had no part, would have

[3] *Intelligencer*, May 6, March 11, 1818.

ignored the slavery article. "The United States," wrote an Englishman familiar with the eastern part of the territory, " . . . has forbidden Slavery, according to its Ordinance for the Government of the North Western Territory. But the people here are utterly regardless of ordinances, and will take the subject into their own hands, and say they will make a treaty with Congress as an independent State." [4] No communications openly advocating unrestricted slavery were published in the *Intelligencer* during the campaign, and arguments in favor of the institution put forth by this faction can only be inferred from the answers of those opposed to it.

The campaign over slavery really began, as has been seen, with the attempt to repeal the indenture law in the last session of the territorial legislature, but it was only as the passage of the enabling bill became a probability that the issue came to be connected with the selection of representatives to the convention. As early as April 1, Cook opened up the subject in the *Intelligencer* with a communication over the signature "A republican." "The certainty," he wrote,

of our obtaining leave to form a state government, in a **short** time, induces me to call the public attention to that question which some call the *"great desideratum"* with the people, I mean the question of *slavery.* This question, which is now convulsing the public mind, presents itself in different shapes, to different characters. . . . Our country is thinly settled, and the great desire is, to see it filled. The cry is, "admit slavery and the forests will immediately be converted into the cultivated habitations of men." The *beast* of prey will relinquish his abode to *that* of domestic utility. Such is the beguiling language of sophistry, and such the fanaticism of her followers. But where the calm voice of reason has reached the intellectual ear, sophistry has been invariably disarmed, and an opposition to slavery has been universally excited. And first, the assertion "that slavery would increase the tide of emigration," is flatly denied. We all know that the emigration from the Eastern and Northern states has been far greater to every part of the Western country, than from the Southern. We know that those states are possessed of a greater population, and will therefore admit of greater emigration; and our emigration has been mostly from the former. . . . Many are in favor of admitting slavery because it is already admitted in some of

[4] Ogg, *Fordham's Personal Narrative,* 221.

our sister states—they say that it will render them less dangerous if they are dispersed all over the nation. Such may be the fact for a moment.—But who can reason and deny that they will ultimately become more dangerous than if concentrated to narrow limits.

After presenting at some length the economic and social disadvantages of slavery, "for the purpose of attempting to prove the impolicy of wishing to have slavery in our state," the writer declared that

the friends of this measure must doubtless fail. By the compact between Virginia and Congress, it is provided expressly, that "there shall be neither slavery nor involuntary servitude in the territory," and this provision is made "unalterable," except with the consent, both of congress and the people and this state. . . . After the expression of the policy, both of Congress and Virginia, can we suppose that a change of that policy is likely to be affected? It seems improbable. Let us then drop the *hobby*—let us all unite in trying to obtain the best constitution we can, and put the question of slavery to rest.[5]

It is significant that the communication contains no reference to indentured servitude or to the slavery already existing in Illinois.

Commenting on this communication, the editors declared slavery to be

a subject which the people are greatly interested in—they should examine it deliberately and thoroughly before they form an opinion.— Some would oppose it from popular motives, and others, doubtless, from principle. And on the other hand, we believe that the most of the advocates for the admission of slavery in this territory, are candidly of the opinion that it would tend very much to draw the tide of emigration hither. Whatever the people shall dispassionately say on the subject, we will acquiesce in without a murmur, and for that purpose, we invite investigation. Our columns will be open as well to the friends of the measure, as the opponents.[6]

Two weeks later appeared a communication signed "Caution" and dated at "Silver creek, St. Clair county, March 29th, 1818," before the appearance of Cook's article. This writer, though opposed to slavery, apparently differed with the other antislav-

[5] Cook evidently confused the Ordinance of 1787 with the Virginia act of cession. See above, pp. 180, 182.

[6] *Intelligencer*, April 1, 1818.

ery leaders as to the expediency of bringing on the contest at that time. Besides expressing doubts as to the "sufficiency of men of talents and political experience to form a constitution" and as to the benefits of statehood in general under existing circumstances, he propounded the following query: "In equity ought not our constitution to be formed as well for the future emigrant, as for the present settler? And does not the influx begin to flow from a different channel than it did formerly? I mean from the northern states and of people opposed to a certain *toleration*, which will be the grand question at the election for members of the convention. . . . Whether would members chosen now, or members chosen in 1823 be most in favor of the toleration of slavery?" Answering his own question, he declared that:

Our future population will be principally from the northern states, and avowed enemies to slavery. The wealthy southern planter, will not part with the plantation Gods, which he worships, starves and whips, for the blessings of the western woods, while we are a territory, and doubtful as to the future toleration of slavery. To those that are uninterested, I need not say a word as to the horrors of slavery, and to those who are, they would be words thrown away. But I caution the enemies of this hellish system against the fascinating bate of *"state government"* at present, although, it might be doubtful if at this time a majority could be had in favor of the barter of human flesh, and placing a part of mankind on an equality with brutes; yet, a few years patience, in our present state, will certainly preponderate the scale in favor of humanity and freedom.[7]

The editors of the *Intelligencer* replied to "Caution" in the same number, and Cook answered in the issue of the following week. In both replies the advantages of statehood were set forth, stress being laid on the opportunity it offered for securing internal improvements and for putting an end to the judiciary troubles. Cook made no reference, however, to that part of the argument relating to slavery and the prospects of the increase of antislavery sentiment by immigration, while the editors merely said that, in spite of the disastrous results of the judiciary difficulties, "friend *Caution* would beseech us to wait five years, till

7 *Intelligencer,* April 15, 1818.

his brothers of the north could come in with their *notions* and make a constitution for us. We like the northern emigration, but we don't think it proper to wait for them exclusively to frame our constitution."

A statement made by Cook in his reply to "Caution" throws light on the form which the campaign was taking:

The opposition which some are making to our going into a state government, is as I understand it, for the purpose of preventing the election of men to the convention, who are in favor of our now framing a constitution, but to promote the election of men who will decide in favor of postponing that work to a future period. It is as I remarked in the commencement to oppose this idea that I venture before the public. If we should have it in our power to elect a convention, we should certainly know beforehand what the *elected* will do on this subject. If the advantages of a state government are worth struggling for, I should certainly recommend the election of men who will favor such a decision when in the convention. And if our bill do not pass, I should also recommend the election of a Delegate who will favor its passage at the next session of congress.

The advocates of delay whom Cook had in mind, as will appear later, were probably the proslavery rather than the antislavery men.

Another opponent of slavery from St. Clair County, writing under the signature of "Candor," in a communication dated April 25, took exception to Cook's theory that the slavery question was settled by the ordinance. This, he contended, would be a "sure plan to lull the people to sleep, and conteract the principle for which he [Cook] would seem to contend." "Candor's" position was that

the Ordinance of Congress and cession of Virginia could only govern us whilst a territory. . . . The principle was never doubted in forming the constitutions for the states of Ohio and Indiana, that they might either tolerate or prohibit slavery; and that if the matter were passed over in silence, slaves might then be imported with impunity; for the ordinance for the government of the north western territory would no longer be binding, but merely a dead letter, superceded by the constitution. In this manner it would be decided in a court of law or equity. The last named states made the exclusion of slaves, leading features of their constitutions: We doubt the framers of these were as wise and as capable of explaining our jurisprudence, as we could expect to find men in this territory. Yet here in this secluded corner, we find people start up and gravely tell us, that it would be unnecessary trouble; that these men did not understand the matter as well as they do.

A great majority of the people, he contended, were "opposed to the toleration of slavery; yet I fear this majority will be defeated, by the cunning of those who have a contrary interest; and where interest is opposed, the public good is too often forgotten. On people of this description, I would advise to be kept a scrutinizing eye." The writer was opposed, therefore, to dropping the hobby, for he considered it to be "the *hobby* by which we, and our posterity, are either to be happy or miserable. In electing men to form a constitution, we may find those as capable among the opposers, as among the friends of slavery." [8]

The best opportunity for those favorable to delay, whether for or against slavery, came in June, when the results of the census were made known. Governor Edwards appointed the first commissioners for the taking of the census on January 9, two days after the act was passed, and by the nineteenth they had been appointed in all but three counties. On March 11 and 13, appointments were made for Washington and Jackson, and on May 18 for Franklin, but the man selected for Franklin refused to serve, and the final appointment was not made until June 14, two weeks after the returns were due. The pay was small, and most of the men appointed were local politicians, men who had held nothing higher than county offices. The only one of greater prominence was Samuel Omelveny of Pope, a member of the house of representatives at the time of his appointment. Two were young men who had held no offices themselves but whose fathers were in politics—William Cullom of Crawford and William Moore of St. Clair. For them and a number of others the taking of the census was the beginning of a political career.

There were not enough returns in by June 10 for the *Intelligencer* to give an estimate of the territorial population. A week later, however, the paper published a statement supplied

[8] *Intelligencer,* April 22, May 6, 1818.

by the secretary, showing a total population, for all the counties except Franklin, of only 34,620. It was obvious that the returns from Franklin County would not bring the total up to 40,000. There was a chance, however, that the supplementary act might yet save the day, and the editors of the paper expressed the hope that "the honest vigilance of the Commissioners author-[i]sed to take the census will not be suffered to sleep so long as our population is found increasing." Four weeks later, July 15, the paper contained another communication from the secretary dated July 6, which indicates that the reliability of even these meager returns was open to question. "It appears," he wrote,

that we have not yet the population required to form a constitution and state government, which with the repeated reports of official abuse on the part of some of the commissioners employed in taking our territorial census, induces me to renew to them your just request, that they proceed in the discharge of their duties with honest vigilance, and make additional returns to my office on or before the first Monday in August next. We are told that some commissioners have neglected to take even the citizens of their respective counties; while others with a zeal unbecoming their situation, have taken some people two or three times, and have placed on their lists the mere passengers through their counties, and even the territory.

The secretary expressed disbelief in these reports, but a comparison of the returns with those of the United States census of 1820 bears out, to some extent, the charge of padding. The return for Gallatin County was 3,256, which is 101 more than the United States census figures for the same county. Undoubtedly the permanent population of the county increased during the two years, and, as Shawneetown was a port of entry for emigrants, it is probable that many were included in the census who were merely passing through. In Washington County also, a similar situation appears, the return of a population of 1,707 being 190 above the figures of the United States census of 1820. This county even more than Gallatin was attracting permanent settlers during the two years and there is ample reason for believing that many travelers along the Vincennes road, which passed through the county, were included in the census. The returns for Madison County were padded in a different way. To his regular report the commissioner added, by way of postscript, that "from good information" there were 680 souls at Fort Crawford, 70 at Fort Edwards, and 80 at Fort Clark, "making in the whole 5466 souls within the boundary of Madison County." Fort Crawford was located at the mouth of the Wisconsin River and thus north of the Illinois boundary.[9] The enabling act had stipulated that there should be 40,000 inhabitants "within the proposed state"; yet these figures were included in the secretary's statement.

Even before the returns were published, a correspondent who wrote over the signature of "Anticipator" sent a communication to the *Intelligencer* in which he maintained "that it is the spirit of the law for the members of the body, to be the judges of the fact—that if we have not the population called for, it will be in the power of the convention, not only to form an ordinance, but a constitution for the consideration of the people." In the same issue in which the statement of population was published, the editors announced that

the fact that our population will not amount to 40,000, having become generally known, we understand that some doubts are entertained as to the propriety of electing members of the Convention.—The diversity of opinions which prevailed on this subject, was such, as to induce us to enquire of Mr. Pope, upon his arrival, as to what were his views on the subject; and he gives it as his opinion, that it will be proper to elect a convention, and for them to meet. And if it should appear from the returns made, that we have not 40,000, then for the Convention to pass an Ordinance, authorising an election for members of convention after the last returns shall be made, which are to be in the first week of December next. And if we then have 40,000 souls, that such Convention will have the right to frame a Constitution.[10]

Pope's opinion was not allowed to pass unchallenged. The next issue of the *Intelligencer* contained a communication from "A friend to enquiry" which maintained not only that no special weight should be attached to that opinion but "that his [Pope's]

[9] The original schedules are found in the secretary of state's office, but see appendix, pp. 317, 319. See James, *Territorial Records*, 54-58.

[10] *Intelligencer*, June 10, June 17, 1818.

connexion with the law itself, however correct his opinions are in the general, would lead him more readily into false reasoning, than an individual less interested." The writer reached the conclusion, therefore, "that the people are in the present instance to enquire and judge for themselves in relation to their powers; and that their enquiries may enable them to know, and to act within the provisions of the law is my most earnest wish. For, I do consider it a matter of much doubt whether a constitution, not within the law established for our guide, would be anything more than a dead letter, though it should receive a subsequent ratification by congress." From the reply of the editors in the same issue and from a second communication from "A friend to enquiry," which was published after the elections had taken place, it appears that the points at issue in the controversy were: whether the enabling act required a population of 40,000 at the time of deciding the question of the expediency of forming a state government or merely when the constitution was framed; and whether or not any action contrary to the enabling act would be binding on the people of the state, even if accepted by Congress. A third article from the same correspondent, published on July 22, shows his opposition to the exclusion of slavery, which may explain his advocacy of delay.

Before taking up the arguments on slavery advanced by "A friend to enquiry" it will be well to consider those of another writer which appeared in the *Intelligencer* for June 17 and July 1. By far the ablest communications which appeared in this campaign were those sent in from Madison County under date of May, 1818, by a writer who signed himself "Agis." The author was evidently a man of culture and of wide experience, not only in different parts of the United States but in England as well, and his point of view was clearly that of an outsider. All this establishes the probability that the writer was none other than Edward Coles, destined to be the second governor of the state and a leader of the antislavery forces in the struggle of 1824. Coles was a Virginian, an owner of slaves by inheritance, and yet an abolitionist of the extreme type. From 1809 to 1815 he served as private secretary to President Madison; when he resigned in the latter year, he intended to take his slaves to the northwest and set them free. In the following spring, however, he was selected by the President for a special mission to Russia; later he traveled in Germany, France, and England. On April 13, 1818, he received from Madison a letter of introduction to Governor Edwards and probably he set out for Illinois at once. If so he could easily have been in Edwardsville, his future home, by the middle of May. It is certain that he visited Kaskaskia in July, during the session of the convention, and interested himself in the contest over slavery at that time.

The first of the communications of "Agis" begins as follows:

Fellow Citizens—As the period cannot now be very distant when you will be called upon to form, by your representatives, a constitution of government for yourselves and for your posterity, I trust you will not deem it premature or improper for one, whose interests are united with yours, and whose warmest wishes are for your welfare, to call your attention to a subject of the utmost importance to individual and national happiness—I mean the momentous question whether this shall be a free or a slave state. Already have the advocates of slavery taken the field; and one may frequently hear them descanting upon the advantages which would attend the admission of slavery, and murmuring because this territory is not permitted to enjoy this *inestimable blessing* as well as some other states and territories. "Were slavery admitted," say they, "the territory would be immediately settled; mills, manufactories and bridges, would be erected, and the whole country would wear a new appearance." [11]

Believing, however, that the question should be considered from the standpoint of right rather than from that of expediency, the writer maintains with cogent arguments the injustice of slavery. Moreover he declares himself to be "one of those who consider the present [l]aws of this territory, admitting slavery under certain restrictions & regulations, as not only unjust, but as plainly inconsistent with the law of Congress which declares that there shall be 'neither slavery nor involuntary servitude' in this territory." The arguments of Governor Edwards in favor of the

---

[11] *Intelligencer*, June 17, 1818. See also Washburne, *Edward Coles*, 13-45; extract from a letter from Coles to Lippincott about 1860, copied as a manuscript note in the latter's set of clippings of his "Conflict of the Century."

validity of the indenture law are ably refuted. "It must be a subject of regret to every lover of liberty," the writer concludes, "that although our last legislature passed an act to repeal the odious law for the admission of slavery, yet the repealing act has been defeated by the *veto* of his excellency the governor. Let us hail the approach of that period when we shall be delivered from the trammels and shackles of territorial bondage—when it shall not be in the power of an individual, in whose appointment we have no voice, to set aside the will of the people, as expressed by their representatives."

In his second number, printed five days before the beginning of the election,[12] "Agis" proceeded "to show that no solid reason can be produced in favor of the expediency of slavery." His principal points were: the danger of insurrection, the corruption of public and private morals, and the discouragement of free labor.

But were slavery admitted, many emigrants, who now pass through our territory, on their way to Boon's lick, and other parts of the Missouri territory, followed by a long concourse of slaves, might settle in Illinois. Perhaps they might; and this is the most plausible argument which has been adduced in favor of the admission of slavery. Yet for my own part, I would rather see our rich meadows and fertile woodlands inhabited alone by the wild beasts and birds of the air, than that they should ever echo the sound of the slave driver's scourge, or resound with the cries of the oppressed African. I would rather that our citizens should live fearlessly and contentedly in their peaceful and modest cabins, than that, surrounded by a host of slaves, and inhabiting splendid palaces and gilded domes, they should live in constant apprehensions of an attack from those who are, and who ought to be, their mortal enemies.

People of Illinois! to you belongs the decision of the important question; important as it relates to yourselves, but doubly so as it regards your posterity. Do not give them occasion to say, that through indolence, or through a mistaken zeal for public improvements, you have fixed upon them the curse of slavery—a curse which, when once fastened upon your land, cannot be removed. To you it belongs to say, whether this territory shal[l] be inhabited by freemen or by slaves—whether all its inhabitants shall live in simple and happy freedom, or one half of them shall be reduced to abject and cruel servitude to support the splendid misery and sickly pomp of the other half.

[12] *Intelligencer,* July 1, 1818.

As the love of liberty is dear to your hearts—as you would preserve yourselves and your posterity from the miserable fate of the once opulent inhabitants of St. Domingo—as you would respect the commands of Heaven and the dictates of your own consciences, let me beseach [sic] you be cautious to what persons you confide the important trust of framing your state constitution. Let no friend to slavery, however great his talents, enjoy your confidence. In particular, beware of those who, while they pretend opposition to slavery, are still desirous to uphold the present method of introducing slaves by indenturing. This half-way measure is satisfactory neither to the advocates of slavery, nor to the friends of liberty. Let no one enjoy your confidence who will not zealously advocate the entire exclusion of slavery from the state. Disregard the clamor by which the friends of slavery hope to divert your attention from the great question of slavery or freedom. Place your confidence in men who are in *practice*, as well as in *theory*, friends to liberty—men whose interests are blended with your own—who have no aristocratical desires to gratify; and whose information and talents enable them to act with benefit to their constituents, and with honor to themselves.

The third communication of "A friend to enquiry," published July 22, after the elections but before the meeting of the convention, is an argument against the exclusion of slavery from Illinois as "a principle fraught with cruelty and injustice." Admitting "the abominable principles of slavery," the writer desires "to call the attention solely to the most effectual mode of remedying this just stain in the political institutions of our common country. That this is the end to which our enquiries should at present be directed, and not to the mere policy of excluding slavery from this territory, will not, I presume be denied, by a single friend to humanity." Replying to "a modern writer of some celebrity," probably "Agis," he points out that "the mere act of exclusion, will not emancipate a single slave" and advocates a plan

which in itself, by remunirating [sic] the owner, and preparing the slave, for the right exercise of his liberty, would give to the system appearance of perfect justice and equity? That a plan of gradual emancipation might be rendered subservient to this purpose, will not be questioned after a moment's enquiry. And I have no hesitation in declaring, notwithstanding the opposition I may receive from a host of policy scriblers [sic], that under proper regulations, I would sooner see limited slavery introduced into our territory, though the limit should not take effect during the existence of the first generation, than this *exclusion* policy so much spoken of at present.

After quoting Dr. James Beattie in favor of gradual emancipation, he concludes:

Let us then, instead of excluding the slave from our territory, for surely that cannot be good policy which is not in unison with religion and humanity—let us, I say, provide by our political regulations, for his introduction and emancipation, under some such plan as that proposed by Beattie. And let it be remembered that it is no excuse for a dereliction of duty in this particular, to say that we have never yet tolerated slavery in our territory, and that the plan for its abolition has not been adopted by the slave holding states. On the contrary, may we not hope, if we set the example, it will become general. And would it not be a proud triumph to our posterity, after the business of universal emancipation shall have been effected, in tracing the effect to the cause, to find its origin in the benevolent policy of our territory?

In recommending the communication of "Agis" to their readers, the editors of the paper declared, "they are well worth, to those who are opposed to the toleration of slavery in this territory, an attentive perusal; and more especially, to those who are in favor of it." [13] This impartial attitude which the paper had endeavored to hold on the slavery issue was lost, however, in the comment on the third number of "A friend to enquiry." The arguments of this writer in favor of delaying the movement for statehood had been vigorously controverted by the editors, but his plan for the toleration of slavery met with their entire approval. "Our readers," the editorial runs,

are respectfully solicited to give the foregoing essay written by "A friend to enquiry", an attentive and candid perusal. It breathes the language of philanthropy, and is fraught with much meaning and benevolence of soul, and must flash conviction upon the mind of every person who feels a disposition to palliate the condition of the oppressed African, with so little injury to those, who by the laws of our government, have unfortunately become the owners of slaves. He pleads not for an everlasting bondage of the blacks—he pleads not for the perpetual security of that property guaranteed to him by the laws of the Union. No—he pleads for justice, in the emancipation of those unfortunate beings. . . . It would reflect much to the honor and humanity

[13] *Intelligencer*, July 1, 1818.

of the generous sons of Illinois, when the *grand object of universal emancipation* shall be effected, to hear it sounded from abroad, that this godlike and benevolent act of humanity originated with them.[14]

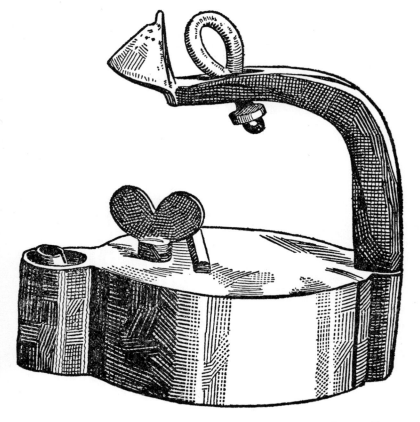

GREASE LAMP

The lower receptacle was filled with grease, a wick was inserted through the small opening, and it was the up-to-date lamp of 1818.

Not all of the readers of the communications from "A friend to enquiry" were so easily convinced that his motives were purely

[14] *Intelligencer*, July 22, 1818.

philanthropic, and the next issue of the *Intelligencer* contains
two replies. "Prudence" could see no good reason for bringing
"among us this class of men [negroes], to the exclusion of those
more beneficial to society . . . as well might we attempt to trans-
plant all the vices and diseases of the eastern states, that we
might have the credit of curing them—as to bring in these dusky
sons of Africa, to where the citizens do not want them, and too
where they are prohibited by the laws of the U. States." Especially significant is the statement that: "But few, I think who
read the labored essay of 'A Friend to Enquiry' will think, him
actuated *alone* by humanity. It is the *dernier resort* of an expir-
ing party, who finding that the naked hook of *unconditional slavery*, will not be swallowed by the people, have adroitly enough,
gilded it over with the form of general humanity." In conclusion
the writer expressed the wish that "the people in general, the
convention, and the convention's dictator, in particular," would
"take into view the serious evils arising from admitting among
us a host of free negroes; and that with their schemes of humanity they would mix a little PRUDENCE."

The other reply, by "Independence," was devoted mainly to
a rebuttal of the contention that the failure to show a population of 40,000 in June necessitated the abandonment of the movement for statehood. It contained one passage, however, significant
of the motives of the opposition: "Who are the '*disinterested*' so
much spoken of in a former piece by 'a friend to enquiry?' Who
have excited so much feeling in public as the advocates for the
continuance of our territorial dependency? What is the object in
abandoning the privileges of the act of Congress? Is it not for the
purpose of delay? Will delay benefit the many or the few?—As
for 'conclusive argument,' we have not heard any from the other
side—Of declamation, we have heard considerable." Another
writer, who signed himself "A citizen," makes a statement in the
Intelligencer of June 24 which throws additional light on what
was going on behind the scenes. "Some think," he declares, "that
the ordinance of Congress, and the law for our admission into the
union, excludes us forever, from being a slave state. Others, and
men of considerable investigation, think differently, and say that

this obnoxious feature, *in our bill of rights,* may be expunged by our next delegate. . . . I am thus particular, because I am one of those *unbelieving few,* who do not think that all, now, depends on the convention." Obviously "A citizen" was not in favor of the exclusion of slavery and was in favor of delay.

Some of those who advocated dropping the statehood movement for the time being may have hoped to discourage the voters from attending the elections. A letter from Shawneetown, dated June 17, indicates not only that this was the case and that the attempt met with little success, but also that the lack of 40,000 inhabitants must have been fully recognized some time before the returns were published. "I have made all the enquiry possible," the writer states, "as to the determination of the people on the subject of a convention; and from the best information I am able to get, the elections on this side will be general. The additional returns from some counties will be considerable—and a disposition is evinced by some, to form a constitution at all events." Two weeks after this letter was written and in the last issue before the elections, the *Intelligencer* announced a hopeful situation as concerned the census:

We are happy to learn from a respectable source, that the commissioner for taking the census in the county of Franklin, will probably return the number of two thousand inhabitants. We are also credibly informed, that the county of Gallatin contains one thousand inhabitants, not yet returned; and that the emigration to the eastern counties is astonishingly rapid. From the information we have received, it is probable, that if the commissioners for the several counties will be vigilant, that our numbers will increase to forty thousand by the first of August. We would therefore recommend to the commissioners to be industrious, and make returns of the additional settlers on the first Monday in August, that the convention may be enabled, if possible, to proceed to the formation of a constitution.

While slavery was without doubt the one great issue, it was by no means the only subject discussed in the convention campaign. These discussions as reflected in communications in the *Intelligencer* are of interest not only for the part which they played in the campaign, but also because of the effect which they may have had on the deliberations of the convention. Some time in May, while the campaign was in progress, a second paper was established, at Shawneetown, in which doubtless appeared similar communications affecting and reflecting the campaign in the eastern part of the territory. Unfortunately no issues of this paper earlier than October 17, 1818, are known to have been preserved.

The *Intelligencer*, in its editorial of March 11, urged the importance of electing to the convention "men who are versed in the science of government; men who have correct opinions of human nature, and who have an extensive acquaintance with the effects which the various forms of government have had upon the happiness of the human family." This opened up a long-drawn-out discussion of the qualifications which candidates should have and of the sort of men who should be sent to frame the constitution. Cook, as has been seen, urged the election of men of talents regardless of their position on the slavery question, while "Caution" thought there were not enough such men in the territory to frame the constitution and hold the offices. The most persistent writer on this subject, however, was "One of the people," whose first communication appeared on May 6. Urging the importance of having a constitution so framed "that no one class of citizens could be burdened by a future legislature more than any other class of citizens," a constitution that "should provide for an equitable and just system of taxation, which would prevent the poor from being taxed or burdened more than the rich, as they are in fact at present in this territory," he pointed out the necessity, in order to secure such a constitution, of having it "framed by men of intelligence, whose minds are expanded, whose views are liberal and who will be able to discover the practical operation of those things which may be engrafted into that important instrument." The tendency of unqualified candidates to come forward as volunteers was deplored and they were advised to give way and solicit others more qualified to accept the position.

In a second number, published May 13, the same writer declared that some opposed sending men of talents to the convention because "they could not be trusted." . . . If they are not of the same calling, that is another objection. "Their *interest*," they say, "may be different from ours." Therefore, "let us send men of our own calling, who will be governed by *interest*." That is coming to the point at once. And here it might be said with propriety, that the *pay* appears to be an object with some of them; for some have been known to enquire, whether the conventioners would receive any *pay!* before they offered to volunteer their services. Men of narrow contracted minds, who will be governed by the corrupting principle of *self-interest*, are the last men in the world, who ought to be elected to form a happy constitution for a free people. Yet such it is believed, are many of the persons who claim the right to form for us a constitution. They claim it upon the ground that they are the oldest settlers. Many old settlers of the class of candidates, appear to consider all who have not been here *quite* so long as themselves, as *aliens*; who have no more rights here than *aliens* enjoy under the English Monarchy.

Still a third number, appearing the following week, presented a series of searching questions beginning with *"Can I* do anything more in a convention than to give my vote?" which each of the would-be candidates was advised not only to answer but to submit to the "best informed men in the county" before deciding to stand for election.

Immediately after these articles were published, another writer, who called himself "Anticipator," appeared on the scene with a number of concrete suggestions as to articles which should be included in the constitution. Among these were provisions against plural officeholding, against a religious test for officeholders, for the punishment of bribery or the soliciting of votes, and for allowing "all widows and unmarried females over the age of 21 years . . . to vote at popular elections." The argument in favor of this latter provision has quite a modern ring, although few advocates of women's suffrage today would confine it to "widows and unmarried females." "We frequently see widows," he wrote, "administering on estates and having charge of large families. It is reasonable to suppose that they are some times interested in the passage of particular laws, which affect themselves, their children, or their property. They know before an election, who will and who will not advocate particular measures.—A single vote may preponderate the election either way. Why deprive them of acting in this *case,* where they are particularly interested, when their peculiar circumstances had made it necessary for them to act in *others,* which arbitrary habit, has made the province of men?" In a second number "Anticipator" took occasion to con-

SHAVING HORSE
A kind of vise that held barrel staves, axe handles, etc., for the knife.

demn "the old ritual of the English common law, handed down with little variation, from the barbarous age of Edward IV," and to advocate the substitution of arbitration of disputes for trial by jury in all civil cases.[15]

[15] *Intelligencer,* May 27, June 10, 1818.

About the same time appeared two communications from "A friend to equal justice," who considered the existing system of taxation, together with the requirements of road work and muster service, very oppressive to poor men and to young men. A rich man with 1,000 acres of valuable land paid only $10 in taxes a year, he claimed, while the poor man was obliged to contribute the equivalent of $28.50 in money or service. This he believed to be due to the fact that the wealthy farmers "have heretofore been our *law makers*," and now they "are offering to go and *adopt* a constitution for us." Congress having given the vote to all without regard to property qualifications, the young men and the poor men were urged to improve the opportunity by sending "enlightened men" to the convention instead of "ignorant wealthy men" who would insist on a property qualification for members of the legislature and thus ensure the continuance of the "oppressive system of taxation."

The arguments of "One of the people" and "A friend to equal justice" called out a reply from "An old farmer," who believed that the articles over these signatures were written by the same hand. The protest against "unqualified candidates" he considered to be a recommendation to the old men of the different counties of the territory, farmers in particular, who had formerly been representatives, "to stay at home, and let the young ones (who are always the wisest) go and make a constitution for them." Much as I admire the modesty of this young stranger, I cannot, altogether, come into his measures. I presume he means that it is lawyers who ought to represent us.—I agree that the avocations of the bar, and a classical education, [in] particular the latter, (which some of them may have,) contribute greatly to store the mind with extraneous knowledge; but that the continual practice of chicanery, will qualify a man for forming laws, I deny. Certainly, the constant habit of public speaking, will give the muscles of his mouth more elasticity, and he can learn to associate his ideas with more ease. But, at the same time, the little, dirty quarrels, and disputes, which his profession impels him continually to take part in, or starve, will have a tendency to contract and Yankeefy a mind that might be otherwise liberal and generous.

The complicated system of the law was then attacked and the writer declared himself "for trusting to the enlight[en]ed farmers and others, who have the same object in view, to simplify our laws, and lop off from them that load of technicalities which make pack horses of our memories." To the "two lamentable tales about taxation" he replied only with ridicule.[16]

Still another writer, who used the name of "Erin," in the paper of June 24, called upon "One of the people" to cease harping on the self-evident proposition that able men should be sent to the convention and instead to discuss the principles which should be incorporated into the constitution; "then let the people find men enough learned in those principles to adopt them into being." One of the subjects which he wanted discussed was "whether the preachers of the gospel of Christ ought to have a seat in the convention or not. Whether in all respects, good men, merely for their entering on that most interesting business to mankind, should be excluded from a seat in the convention, and the legislatures arising therefrom. Or whether men, who say often themselves, they are called to the pulpit by the Almighty God, ought to degrade themselves by entering into politics." Another "subject of much concern to the territory" was that of slavery: "whether it would not be most consonant to true religion and freedom, to allow the half starved blacks of the south to partake of Illinois plenty; and whether it would not be to the advantage of the new state to permit those unfortunate subjects of the southern states a place in the 'land of promise:' and devise some mode of their gradual emancipation; or whether it would not be better for the negroes of the United States, and our new state to stay as they are."

"One of the people" decided to ignore the challenge of "Erin" because it was "too late to reply, in time to answer any of those purposes which he appears to have had in view," the elections then being over. To "An old farmer," however, he replied with vigor, accusing him of being no farmer at all but a doctor who had "been in the territory about six or eight weeks." Denying that he had written the articles signed "A friend to equal justice," he accused "An old farmer" of having written those signed "Anticipator," and of having "commenced 'anticipating' a con-

[16] *Intelligencer,* June 17, 1818.

stitution for us" two weeks after he came to Illinois. So much of this reply as was not devoted to ridicule and personalities was a defense of the law and lawyers.[17] The character and value of the common law, however, were much more ably discussed in a communication signed "Common Sense," which appeared in the previous issue of the paper:

Let us enquire what this law is, so much detested by the learned Anticipator. It is in the words of an able judge the perfection of reason; it has for its foundation the general customs of the kingdom, the law of nature and the law of God; it is founded upon reason and is said to be the perfection of reason acquired by long study, observation, and experience, and refined by learned men in all ages. . . . Its continuance, therefore, the warmth with which it has always been supported, and its general adoption throughout the U. States is the best evidence of its utility and excellence; it is the birthright of every citizen, the only safeguard he hath for the protection, not only of his property but his family.[18]

All these various communications, considered together, would indicate that there were in Illinois in 1818 two sorts of politicians. One type consisted of young ambitious lawyers, with a fair amount of education, many of whom had come to the territory only a few years before in the hope of finding there a road to wealth and political preferment. The other class, more numerous, was made up of those among the old established citizens who, having come in the front ranks of the pioneers, had acquired a competence by land operations or business enterprises and had become the social and political leaders of their fellows. Lacking the advantages of education and wide experience, the men of this latter class were provincial in their views and ignorant of the science of government, but they were in no hurry to withdraw in favor of the more competent newcomers.

In spite of the importance of the issue of slavery in the election of members of the convention, it seems probable that personal popularity played a very large part in determining the outcome, just as had been the case with territorial elections.

[17] *Intelligencer,* July 8, 1818.
[18] *Intelligencer,* July 1, 1818.

Relying on this popularity, some of the candidates evidently tried to evade the issue. In the *Intelligencer* of May 27, a writer who signed himself "The people" declared: "The object which most interests the public mind, with regard to the approaching election, for members to the convention, is to know whether they are in favor of the toleration or the prohibition of slavery. Several have offered, in different parts of the territory, who have made their sentiments known on that head, and pledge themselves to one or other of the parties to support their favorite measure:— Others again conceal their real opinions, and measurably give both parties hopes of being successful through their means." Still more objectionable to this writer were those who claimed to be ready to obey the instructions of their constituents regardless of their own views and thus made "so light of their opinions as to barter them for an office." This communication was probably from an opponent of the toleration of slavery, but a month later "A citizen," who seems to have been on the other side, called for the "candid and impartial sentiments" of the candidates on the subject. "On this important point," he wrote, "it will be well for every man to inquire before he gives his vote —and to enquire of the candidate, in the presence of those of an opposite opinion to himself, so that he may not flinch, and act the *camelion*, as, I fear, some of our candidates are doing." [19]

The complicated nature of the slavery question doubtless enabled many of the candidates to evade the vital issues of existing slavery and the indenture system by merely declaring themselves opposed to the admission of slavery. In Madison County, according to a contemporary writer many years later, the "candidates all professed to be opposed to slavery. One of them said he was opposed to it because he believed it would be a disadvantage to the State,—if he had thought it an advantage, he would have been in favor of it." One of the successful candidates in this county was Benjamin Stephenson, who in the convention voted for all the proslavery clauses. Probably he had declared himself opposed to the introduction of slavery but did not feel

[19] *Intelligencer,* May 27, June 24, 1818.

under any obligation to aid in wiping out existing slavery or the indenture system. For the attitude of candidates in the other counties little evidence is available except the votes in the convention of those who were successful. The representatives of three counties, Union, Johnson, and Edwards, all voted on the antislavery side at every opportunity, and it is quite likely that the slavery issue played a considerable part in their elections. Of the four unsuccessful candidates in Union County, two held slaves. In Johnson, the only known candidate who was not elected was a slaveholder and an active advocate of the toleration of slavery in Illinois. He is said to have been defeated by only a few votes.[20] In Edwards it is possible that Birkbeck may have exerted an influence against slavery even as early as this election.

All the representatives from Gallatin, Randolph, and Jackson counties voted consistently for the recognition of the indenture system and existing slavery. The importance of the saline, the operation of which depended upon slave labor, is sufficient to explain the situation in Gallatin. In Randolph, Kane is said to have declared that "if Doctor Fisher should be elected as his colleague, he, Mr. Kane, would consider himself instructed to vote for the introduction of slavery, but if Mr. McFerron was elected as his colleague, then he would consider himself instructed to vote against slavery." [21]

From this it would seem that Kane expected to be elected himself, regardless of the issue, because of his prominence in the county. The situation was somewhat similar in Jackson County, where it was only a question of whom the voters should "select as the other delegate to accompany Conrad Will; for the doctor's ability and prominence made him pre-eminent in all their public affairs. Their choice fell upon James Hall, Jr., an intelligent and enterprising citizen, though having but moderate education."

---

[20] His name was John Copeland. See *Biographical Review of Johnson, Massac, Pope, and Hardin Counties,* 354; Churchill, "Annotations," no. 7.

[21] Churchill, "Annotations," no. 7; see also pp. 199-200. For the situation in Jackson County see Illinois State Historical Society, *Transactions,* 1905, pp. 358–359; Patterson, "Early Society in Southern Illinois," in *Fergus Historical Series,* no. 14:122.

R. E. Heacock, a lawyer who in 1816 ran against Pope for the position of delegate, was the only one of the five known candidates in this county who was not a slaveholder. Here again the salt works were an influential factor. The election in the other counties of men who opposed each other on the slavery issue indicates that the question was not the determining factor in these cases.

The methods of campaigning adopted by the candidates in this election were those customary on the frontier at the time. The two newspapers must have reached only a small proportion of the voters, but it is probable that handbills were circulated and these may have been more specific in their discussion of the merits of the respective candidates than were the articles in the *Intelligencer*. To a large extent, however, the campaign probably took the form of a house-to-house canvass, the character of which is admirably delineated in a poem entitled "Candidates" which was published in the *Intelligencer* of July 1, five days before the elections began:

> In dreary woods, remote from social walks
> I dwell. From year to year, no friendly steps
> Approach my cot, save near election days,
> When throngs of busy, bustling candidates
> Cheer me with their conversation so soft and sweet—
> I list' with patience to their charming tales,
> Whilst gingerbread and whisky they disperse,
> To me, my wife and all the children round.
> Some bring a store of little penny books
> And trinkets rare for all my infants young.—
> My health and crops appear their utmost care,
> Fraternal squeezes from their hands I get—
> As tho' they lov'd me from their very souls:—
> Then—"Will you vote for me my dearest friend?
> Your laws I'll alter, and lop taxes off;—
> 'Tis for the public weal I stand the test,
> And leave my home, sorely against my will:
> But knowing that the people's good require
> An old substantial hand—I quit my farm
> For patriotism's sake, and public good;"
> Then fresh embraces close the friendly scene,
> With protestations firm, of how they love.
> But what most rarely does my good wife pleate,

Is that the snot nos'd baby gets a buss!!
O that conventions ev'ry day were call'd,
That social converse might forever reign.

It would seem that those candidates who most diligently followed this method of house-to-house canvass were the most
likely to be elected. No one had a better opportunity for such a
canvass than the commissioners who took the census, and five
of them, or one-third of their number, were elected to the convention. Among the other successful candidates were the father
of one and the brother of another of the commissioners. Doubtless the latter had availed themselves of the opportunity to speak
a good word for their relatives while collecting the census data.

In such a campaign it is probable that personalities played a
large part. One of the candidates in Monroe County was Andey
Kinney, an early settler in the country. His opponents first
charged him with "offering to purchase votes on such and such
terms" and then dug up an old charge that he had once rebelled
against his country "and had taken a captain's commission under
a French officer." They specified, moreover, that he "had been
tried by a court of justice, fined in a sum of forty dollars, and
never to hold a commission in the territory afterwards."

Kinney denied the charge in the *Intelligencer* of June 10, and
presented several certificates to prove that he had been acquitted
at the trial. He also pointed to the fact that he had "valiently
[*sic*] assisted in defending my country . . . in an engagement
above Cahokia, under the Bluff . . . where we killed seven men,
and wounded some more, in the year 1794." The sole cause of
his "embarking in this important case of the convention, was
for the express purpose of being an advocate for our inherent
rights which naturally belong to a free and independent people.—Slavery is an abomination which we ought to guard against
in every sense of the word. High salaries which are oppressive
to the people, ought never to be sanctioned. So I shall conclude,
stating that if I should be elected, that according to the best of
my abilities, I will use every exertion in my power, to promote
the general interest of the people." Kinney was not elected.

The elections took place on July 6, 7, and 8. The only polls in each county were held at the county seat and the voting was *viva voce*. The vote of each elector was recorded and proclaimed aloud by the sheriff. This system, which was used in several of the southern states, had been substituted for election by ballot by a law passed by the territorial legislature on December 8, 1813. The preamble of this act declared:

Whereas voters have hitherto been obliged to vote by ballot, and the ignorant as well as those in embarrassed circumstances are thereby subject to be imposed upon by electioneering zealots.

And whereas it is inconsistent with the spirit of a representative republican government since the opening for bribery and corruption is so manifest, which should ever be opposed and suppressed in such a government, for remedy whereof.

One of the communications of "Agis," published July 1, 1818, was a protest against the *viva voce* system of voting and against the regulation requiring "all the electors of a county to give their votes in one place." The writer showed that voting by ballot, instead of giving opportunity for corruption and undue influence, was the best means of preventing it. "These hints," he concluded, "are suggested at this time in order that, when the all-important selection of members of the convention for framing your state constitution, your choice may be directed to such men as will support the equal rights of the people." [22]

No statistics are available regarding the number of ballots cast in any of the counties except Madison. The census shows 1,012 men of voting age in that county, and there were 517 votes cast in the election.[23] Taking into consideration the fact that only those who had been in the territory since the first of the year were qualified to vote and the long distances which many of the voters must have had to travel, this indicates a very active interest on the part of the electorate.

News of the result of the election was slow in coming in. On July 15, the *Intelligencer* printed the names of the successful candidates in Randolph and the nearby counties of Monroe, St. Clair, Madison, and Jackson. The next week the list was com-

[22] *Pope's Digest*, 1:154-155; *Intelligencer*, July 1, 1818.
[23] Churchill, "Annotations," no. 7.

pleted for all except Bond, Edwards, and Crawford counties, but the names of the representatives from these counties were not printed until August 5, two days after the convention assembled.

The issue of the *Intelligencer* in which were printed the first proceedings of the convention contained the following address:

The undersigned happening to meet at the St. Clair Circuit Court have united in submitting the following address to the friends of Freedom in the state of Illinois:

Feeling it a duty in those who are sincere in their opposition to the toleration of slavery in this territory, to use all fair and laudable means to effect that subject, we therefore, beg leave to present to our fellow-citizens at large, the sentiments which prevail in this section of our country on that subject. In the counties of Madison and St. Clair, the most populous counties in the territory, a sentiment approaching that of unanimity against it seems to prevail. In the counties of Bond, Washington and Monroe, a similar sentiment also prevails. We are informed that strong exertions will be made in the Convention to give sanction to that deplorable evil in our state; and least such should be the result at too late a period for any thing like concert to take place among the friends of freedom in trying to defeat it; we therefore, earnestly solicit all true friends to freedom in every section of the territory, to unite in opposing it, both by the election of, a Delegate to Congress who will oppose it, and by forming meetings and preparing remonstrances to Congress against it. Indeed, so important is this question considered, that no exertion of a fair character should be omitted to defeat the plan of those who either wish a temporary or unlimited slavery. Let us also select men to the Legislature who will unite in remonstrating to the general government against ratifying such a constitution. At a crisis like this, thinking will not do, *acting* is necessary.[24]

In this address, the leaders of the extreme antislavery party acknowledged their defeat.

[24] *Intelligencer*, August 5, 1818. The address was signed by Risdon Moore, Benjamin Watts, Jacob Ogle, Joshua Oglesby, William Scott, Sr., William Biggs, George Blair, Charles Matheny, James Garretson, and William Kinney from St. Clair County; William Whiteside from Madison; James Lemen from Monroe; and William Bradsby from Washington.

Chapter 10

Framing the Constitution

It must have been a great event for the quaint old town of Kaskaskia when the constitutional convention assembled on the first Monday in August, 1818. Composed of 33 members, this body was almost twice as large as the council and house of representatives combined of the last territorial legislature. Doubtless many who were not members of the convention but were interested in the outcome of its deliberations visited Kaskaskia during the session; Bennett's tavern was filled to overflowing. Among the distinguished men known to have been present were the Reverend John Mason Peck, Baptist missionary, who disclaims any business with the convention, and Edward Coles, afterwards governor and leader of the antislavery party, who asserts that he not only attended the convention but also "made the acquaintance and learned the opinions, views and wishes of many of its prominent members." Neither of these men, unfortunately, left any detailed account of his observations, and practically the only available sources of information about the convention are the recently discovered "Journal" and the very inadequate and colorless reports in the *Intelligencer*.[1]

All the representatives elected to the convention except the four from the nearby counties of Washington and Jackson

---

[1] Babcock, *Memoir of Peck*, 97; Washburne, *Edward Coles*, 44; Coles to Lippincott (n.d.), copied as a manuscript note in Lippincott's copy of his "Conflict of the Century." The only copy of the "Journal" of the convention known to be in existence was presented to the secretary of state in 1905 by J. W. Kitchell, a nephew of Joseph Kitchell, one of the members of the convention from Crawford County. A page-for-page reprint of this copy can be found in the Illinois State Historical Society, *Journal*, 6:355-424. [The following narrative is based mainly on this "Journal" and on the text of the constitution. Since both are comparatively brief documents, it has not been thought necessary to give detailed citations, except in a few cases where it seemed advisable to fix the source of the quotation.—Ed.]

were present on August 3, the date set by the enabling act for assembling. A temporary organization having been effected, the "representatives from the several counties were then called" and the members present took their seats. Permanent organization followed immediately: Jesse B. Thomas was elected president, William C. Greenup, secretary, and Erza Owen, sergeant at arms. Judge Thomas was the most prominent man who had been elected to the convention so that his choice as president was a natural one and may have had no political significance. Greenup had held various clerkships in the territorial legislature and in the courts of Randolph County, and in spite of his hostility to the governor had been appointed clerk of the circuit court and reappointed clerk of the county court the preceding January. Doubtless he was one of the few men available who were qualified for the position. The "Journal" gives no information about the balloting for officers, except the names of the men elected, but it is clear that, if there was any contest be-

SICKLE

tween the old political factions over the organization of the convention, the Edwards faction certainly was not in control.[2] The only other business transacted the first day was the appointment of three committees, one to examine the credentials of the

[2] "Journal," p. 3, in Illinois State Historical Society, *Journal,* 6:355; James, *Territorial Records,* 55; letter of Edwards, January 18, 1818, and one with no date in Chicago Historical Society Manuscripts, 49:235; 51:484.

members, one to frame a set of rules, and one to secure a minister to open the next meeting with prayer.

The first real work of the convention was necessarily to ascertain officially the result of the census in order that it might know whether or not it was authorized, under the enabling act, to proceed with the framing of a constitution. On the second day, August 4, after the representatives from Jackson and Washington counties had been admitted, Mr. Kane moved the appointment of a committee "to examine the returns made to the secretary's office of this territory . . . and make report thereon. And also, to receive and report such other evidence of the actual population of the territory as to them shall seem proper." Kane himself was made chairman of this committee as he had been also of the credentials committee. On the following day he reported first for the latter committee, a simple matter as there appear to have been no contests over seats, and then presented the census returns by counties as ascertained from the secretary's office. The lists totaled 40,258, an increase of 5,638 over the first reports in June. Besides the 1,281 for Franklin County which had not been reported on before, this increase was divided among the different counties in numbers varying from 16 to 1,847. In Bond, Randolph, Johnson, and Pope the increments were less than 100, while in Madison, St. Clair, Gallatin, and Crawford they were above 500. These additions were, in general, the results of the supplementary census, which appears to have been taken in all but two counties at least.[3] Only four of these additional returns are now available but they throw some light on the character of the census. The Washington County commissioner evidently went into outlying districts where the people had not previously been counted, and even visited and counted those in the western part of Edwards County, who were widely separated from the main settlements near the Wabash. In the returns from

---

[3] In 1819 the legislature passed *"AN ACT for the relief of persons taking additional census,"* which provided extra payment ranging from $5 to $30 for the commissioners of all the counties except Bond, Johnson, and Edwards. *Laws of Illinois*, 1819, p. 347.

Jackson, Gallatin, and Crawford, however, it is clear that it was the newcomers who were being counted, and the fact that very few among the additional names are to be found in the lists of old settlers in the county histories would indicate that many were included who were merely passing through the county. Among the names in the additional census of Gallatin is that of C. Trimmer, who figures as the head of a family of 50. This entry refers to a party of English emigrants on its way to Birkbeck's colony in Edwards County. The discrepancy for several of the counties between this census and that of the United States in 1820 is of course increased by the supplementary figures.

The convention appears to have raised no question as to the adequacy of the census. At any rate, the "report was read, considered and concurred in." After postponing the consideration of rules until the following day, the convention was ready to decide the all-important question of the expediency of advancing to statehood. Mr. Prickett offered a resolution declaring that as "there are upwards of 40,000 inhabitants" in the territory, "it is expedient to form a constitution and state government." A motion by Kane to postpone consideration of the resolution until the following day was voted down; the resolution was then considered and passed. Judging from this prompt action it would seem that the opponents of statehood, if there were any in the convention, must have numbered only a small minority and must have recognized the futility of any opposition. It is doubtful if Kane's motion to postpone consideration of the resolution for a day was due to any desire to check the statehood program. Had he entertained any such designs, he was too shrewd to have missed the opportunity afforded by the character of the census and especially by the inclusion of the estimated population at Prairie du Chien. Had these figures been omitted, as they should have been under the provisions of the enabling act, the totals would have been below the requisite 40,000.[4] As chairman of the committee on the census, Kane might, had he so desired, have

[4] On this whole discussion of the census see above, pp. 239-242; compare "Journal," pp. 6, 7, and Flower, *English Settlement,* 96, 99.

presented a report which at least would have made the convention hesitate.

The alternative procedure of providing for a second convention to frame the constitution does not appear to have been considered at all, for immediately after the adoption of the "expediency" resolution, provision was made for "a committee of fifteen, one from each county . . . to frame and report to this convention a constitution for the people of the territory of Illinois." The chairman of this committee was Leonard White of Gallatin but, according to all the evidence, the directing spirit was Elias Kent Kane. The report of the committee, however, certainly did not represent the latter's wishes in all particulars. The committee took a week in which to prepare its draft of the constitution; the convention in the interval considered and adopted an elaborate body of rules of procedure, provided for the printing of the journal and the draft, and contracted for stationery.[5] On the sixth Mr. Gard offered a resolution for a committee "to draft an ordinance to establish the bounds of the state of Illinois and for other purposes"; and Mr. Hubbard offered another for a committee "to draft an ordinance acknowledging and ratifying the donations made by an act of congress passed in April, 1818." On motion of Mr. Kane consideration of both of these resolutions was postponed until the following day, when the first was dropped and for the second was substituted, again on motion of Mr. Kane, another resolution directing the committee of 15 "to consider the expediency of accepting or rejecting the propositions made to this convention by the congress of the United States, and if in their opinion it shall be expedient to accept the same, it shall be their further duty to draft an ordinance irrevocable, complying with the conditions annexed to the

---

[5] Reynolds, *My Own Times,* 211; Ford, *History of Illinois,* 24; Brown, "Early History of Illinois," in *Fergus Historical Series,* no. 14:86-87; John F. Snyder is an authority for the statement that "Judge Breese, who was then a law student in Elias K. Kane's office in Kaskaskia, said the Constitution . . . was written in Mr. Kane's office some time before the meeting of the convention." Illinois State Historical Society, *Transactions,* 1905, p. 360n. Breese did not arrive in Illinois, however, until several months later. Samuel Breese to Kane, October 20, 1818, in Chicago Historical Society Manuscripts, 52:33; Moses, *Illinois,* 1:455.

acceptance of such propositions in the act for the admission of this territory in the union, and report thereon." [6]

On the same day, the seventh, "Mr. Kane presented two petitions signed by sundry inhabitants of Randolph county, one praying that this convention shall declare in the constitution to be formed that the moral law is the basis of its structure, and acknowledge therein an universal parent. The other praying that this convention may declare the scriptures to be the word of God, and that the constitution is founded upon the same." These petitions emanated from a sect of Covenanters who had established themselves in Randolph County. They were referred to a select committee but no attention was paid to them in the framing of the constitution and, according to Governor Ford, the Covenanters for many years "refused to work the roads under the laws, serve on juries, hold any office, or do any other act showing that they recognize the government." The only exception was in the convention election of 1824, "when they voted for the first time, and unanimously against slavery." [7]

On Saturday and Monday, the eighth and tenth, the convention marked time. On the eleventh Mr. Bankson announced the death that morning of his colleague, John K. Mangham of Washington. The members of the convention agreed to wear crepe on the left arm for 30 days in testimony of their respect for Mr. Mangham's memory, and a committee was appointed to make arrangements for the funeral. This took place late in the afternoon "attended by the members of the Convention and the citizens of the place generally." Two days later a committee was appointed to inquire into the expediency of ordering an election to fill the vacancy, but the committee reported "that an election could not be effected in time to answer the purpose of giving the said county their full representation in this convention before the same will have risen." This report was concurred in by the convention and no election was held.

[6] "Journal," p. 13, in Illinois State Historical Society, *Journal,* 6:365.

[7] Ford, *History of Illinois,* 25; "Journal," p. 13, in Illinois State Historical Society, *Journal,* 6:365. See also p. 66 of the "Journal" on a similar petition, presented near the close of the session of the convention.

The draft of the constitution was finally reported by the committee of 15 on Wednesday the twelfth. It consisted of a preamble and eight articles, the greater part of which had been copied from the constitutions of neighboring states. Periods of time, ages, and amounts of salary were left blank to be filled in by the convention. Accompanying the draft was an ordinance accepting the federal donations and agreeing to comply with the requisite conditions; this was adopted by the convention without change. The day after the introduction of the draft of the constitution the convention took it up for consideration, section by section, and made various changes. This "first reading" took two and a half days and at its conclusion a committee of five was appointed, none of whom had served on the committee of 15, to suggest additional articles or sections which it might consider necessary to complete the draft of the constitution. The work of this committee was primarily to prepare a schedule for putting the new government into operation and that same day presented its first report on the temporary apportionment of senators and representatives.

On Monday the seventeenth, the second reading of the constitution was begun and the first five articles were considered. Tuesday morning the apportionment proposed by the committee of five was read the second and third times, amended, and adopted, after which the second reading of the constitution was continued and completed. A schedule of 16 sections was then reported by the committee, read the first time, and considered section by section. The committee also presented at this time a "separate report relative to a permanent seat of government." The morning of the nineteenth was taken up with various reconsiderations, and in the afternoon the convention began the third reading of the draft "as amended and engrossed." Some time was spent the next morning considering resolutions relative to the location of the capital, after which the third reading of the constitution was continued and completed. Various additional sections proposed from the floor were then considered. On August 21 a "committee of enrolments" was appointed, consisting of Kane, Stephenson, and Cullom, the schedule received its second and third readings, and various resolutions relating to qualifications for voting at the first election and to the location of the seat of government were considered. "A committee of revision" consisting of Lemen, Omelveny, and Kane was appointed the next day, Saturday the twenty-second, "to examine the draft of the constitution as amended and passed, and make report to this convention on next Monday morning." This committee "corrected sundry inaccuracies" and recommended the expunging of one entire section. Its report, presented by Kane, was concurred in by the convention, but even after that several changes were made in different sections by reconsideration. A resolution relative to the seat of government was adopted on the twenty-fourth, and finally on Wednesday, the twenty-sixth, the constitution was signed and the convention adjourned.

The preamble of the draft and article one, which deal with the distribution of the powers of government into three departments, follow in the main the wording of the constitutions of Indiana and Kentucky; the preamble contains the statement of the boundaries assigned by Congress. These sections were adopted by the convention with only slight changes.

The second article, dealing with the legislative department, follows very closely the constitution of Ohio. Section one provides for a bicameral legislature, and sections two to six inclusive deal with the election and qualifications of members. At the first reading the blanks were filled in to make the elections biennial on the first Monday in August but this necessitated a special provision for the date of the first election. At the second reading the first Thursday of September, 1818, was selected, but some of the members felt that this was too early. As a compromise the third Thursday was finally adopted almost unanimously. Representatives were required to be 21 years of age, citizens of the United States, and residents in the district represented for 12 months preceding the election. For senators, the requirements were the same except that the age limit was 25 and they were required to "have paid a state or county tax." The convention added the latter qualification for representatives also, at the third reading. The terms of senators were fixed at four years, one-half to be elected biennially. Both senators and representatives were to be apportioned according to the number of white inhabitants. The number of representatives was to be not less than 27 nor more than 36 until the population should reach 100,000, and the number of senators was never to be less than one-third more than one-half the number of representatives.

The seventh section of article two originally provided that each house should choose a speaker, but this was changed on third reading to except the senate, after sections establishing the office of lieutenant governor had been added to another article. Sections eight to seventeen, inclusive, dealing with procedure in the legislature, were of the usual sort and received only verbal changes at the hands of the convention. Section eighteen, however, which dealt with salaries, caused a bitter contest. After the blanks had been filled, at first reading, the section prohibited the legislature from allowing, before 1824, annual salaries greater than $1,250 for the governor and $500 for the secretary of state, while the pay of members of the legislature was not to exceed $2 per day. On a second reading the limit for the secretary of state was raised to $600 and that for the members of the legislature to $3 per day, but at third reading, on motion of Kane and Messinger, all reference to the salaries of members of the legislature was dropped. Had it not been for a controversy over the salaries of justices of the supreme court, provided for in section five of article four, it is probable that no further changes would have been made in this section. At second reading the salaries of justices were fixed at $1,250, the same amount as had been allowed the governor, but at third reading this sum was reduced to $1,000. The following day a motion for reconsideration of the section limiting the governor's salary was defeated by a tie vote but three days later it was carried, 16 to 14. The limit was then reduced from $1,250 to $1,000 by a vote of 17 to 14. That this action was taken in retaliation for the reduction of the salaries of justices is evident from the fact that nine men who voted for reduction in each case opposed it in the other. Enough other members, however, were in favor of economy to carry both votes.

Two sections of article two of the draft dealing with "ministers of the gospel" are of special interest because of the extensive discussion in the *Intelligencer* of the political activities of clergymen during the later territorial period. A writer who signed himself "A foe to religious tyranny" had roundly denounced the political sermons of certain ministers and their theory that only "professors of religion" should be elected to office. In the first draft of the constitution, section twenty-six provided that: "Whereas, the ministers of the gospel are by their professions, dedicated to God and the care of souls, and ought not to be diverted from the great duties of their functions: Therefore, no minister of the gospel or priest of any denomination whatever, shall be eligible to a seat in either house of the legislature." As a corollary to this was section thirty-three: "No minister of the gospel, or priest of any denomination whatever, shall be compelled to do militia duty, work on roads or serve on juries." The introduction of these sections called forth a communication in the paper of August 12, addressed to "The members of the Illinois Convention, now in session." "It is with peculiar pleasure," said the writer,

I learn that the committee appointed to draft a Constitution have embodied in it a provision to exempt *ministers of the Gospel* from the servile and arduous drudgery of legislation, and of electioneering to procure themselves seats in the legislature. This provision is extremely humane and is not without precedent in other constitutions.[8] The *flesh* of many of these preachers is very willing but their *spirit is truly weak.* There did appear amongst them a spirit that would have enabled the people to have filled the Convention with *ministers*, MINISTERS of the GOSPEL!! . . . But I would humbly suggest that said provision is not sufficiently extensive to administer complete relief. . . . Why not disqualify preachers of the gospel from holding any civil office?

A motion to strike out section twenty-six which was made during the first reading was voted down, but on later reconsideration both sections were dropped from the constitution.

Another section of the second article of the draft which failed

[8] Similar sections are to be found in the New York constitution of 1777, section thirty-nine, and the Kentucky constitution of 1799, article eight, section one. Thorpe, *Constitutions,* 5:2637; 3:1280.

to meet with the approval of the convention was number thirty-five. This prohibited the removal of county seats without "full compensation . . . to the persons injuried [*sic*] by such removal" and also prohibited the organization of new counties "unless a petition shall be presented to the legislature, signed by at least two hundred qualified voters, residing in the bounds of the district applying to be laid off." At the first reading this whole section was stricken out, and an attempt later to introduce into the schedule a section dealing with the organization of counties was also a failure.

Section twenty-four of article two as originally drawn provided for annual sessions of the legislature but at second reading these were changed to biennial. The first session was to begin "on the first Monday of October next" and others "on the first Monday of December next ensuing the election." Reasons which may have influenced the convention to decide on biennial instead of annual sessions are indicated in a "letter from an inhabitant of St. Clair county, to a Member of the Convention," an extract from which was published in the *Intelligencer* of August 19. After declaring "that the lapse of a few months will not furnish a sufficient test of the qualities of the theory or practicable operation of the laws passed at any one session," the writer illustrated his point by calling attention to the activity of the territorial legislature "enacting at one session and repealing at the next, until our laws on some subjects have become so confused, that to use a common adage, 'a Philadelphia lawyer' could not tell what these acts mean, nor even how much of them is in force." Another advantage pointed out was the saving of expense and this was probably the one which appealed most strongly to the members of the convention.

A census of all "white male inhabitants above the age of twenty-one years" to be taken periodically was ordered by section thirty-two of article two of the draft. At first reading this provision was amended so as to require an enumeration in 1825 "and every fifth year thereafter . . . of all the free white inhabitants." At second reading, 1820 was substituted for 1825 as the date of the first census, and the superfluous word "free" before "white" was stricken out. In this form the section became number thirty-one of the final constitution. Just why the convention chose to order a duplication of the decennial census of the United States it is difficult to understand.

Two other sections of article two dealing with elections are of special interest. Section twenty-eight gave the suffrage to "all white male inhabitants, above the age of twenty-one years, having resided in the state six months next preceding the election"; the second provided that "all votes shall be given vive voce until altered by the legislature." Opposition to *viva voce* voting on the part of "Agis" has already been noted and the adoption of this section was followed by appeals to the legislature to change the system to voting by ballot—appeals which were heeded at the second session of the first general assembly in 1819. The provision allowing "inhabitants" to vote regardless of whether or not they were citizens may have been a result of thoughtless copying of the Ohio constitution. Indiana two years before had limited the franchise to citizens, probably as a result of the increase in the number of foreign-born inhabitants in the 14 years which had passed since the Ohio constitution was drawn up. Aliens had been allowed to vote and even to hold office in Illinois during the territorial period and it is possible that the convention deliberately decided to continue the practice. The adoption of this section stored up trouble for the future, and called forth the following request from a critic of the convention: "We would wish every member of the late convention of Illinois to declare publicly in some newspaper printed in the state whether it was his intention to extend the elective franchise in this state to the subjects of foreign powers who had never complied with the naturalization laws of the U. S." [9]

Article three of the constitution, dealing with the executive, was also copied largely from the constitution of Ohio. Sections two and three as finally adopted provided that the governor should "be chosen by the electors of the members of the general

[9] "Journal," p. 21, in Illinois State Historical Society, *Journal*, 6:373; *Intelligencer*, October 14, November 11, 1818.

assembly," and should hold office four years but be ineligible for "more than four years in any term of eight years." He was required to be 30 years of age, a citizen of the United States for 30 years, and a resident of the state for two years preceding the elections. When the blanks were filled in at the first reading, the period during which the governor must have been a citizen was fixed at 10 years but at second reading this was lengthened to 30 years. Sections four to ten inclusive, giving to the governor the usual powers and duties, remained essentially as they were in the draft.

Section eleven of article three provided for a sheriff and a coroner in each county to be elected biennially by those "qualified to vote for members of the general assembly." The draft provided that no sheriff should be eligible for more than "four years in any term of six years," but this feature was stricken out at third reading.

The "speaker of the senate" was empowered by section thirteen of article three of the draft to exercise the powers of governor in case of a vacancy in that office, "unless the general assembly shall provide by law for the election of a governor to fill the vacancy." When the committee of five drew up its schedule, however, it embodied therein five sections copied from the Indiana constitution providing for a lieutenant governor who should be elected in the same manner and have the same qualifications as the governor, and who should be speaker of the senate. An unusual provision allowed him to debate and vote in committee of the whole, "and whenever the senate are equally divided, to give the casting vote." On motion of Mr. Kane, these sections were taken from the schedule and inserted in article three just before section thirteen. That section was then renumbered eighteen and the words "lieutenant-governor" substituted for "speaker of the senate."

Instead of giving a veto power to the governor as had been done in most other state constitutions, the draft provided in section fifteen of article three for a council made up of "the judges of the supreme court or a major part of them together with the governor," which should "revise all bills about to be passed into laws" and return those of which it disapproved, together with its objections, to the house in which they had originated. This section was copied almost verbatim from section three of the New York constitution of 1777. At first reading a substitute was adopted by which the veto power was given to the governor with the provision that bills might be passed by a two-thirds vote in spite of his objections. Between the first and second readings, however, the convention was won over to the New York system and at second reading the original section was restored with a provision allowing bills to be passed over the objections of the council of revision "by a majority of all the members elected." This was an important departure from the New York arrangement, which required a two-thirds vote and thus allowed the judges to interfere seriously with legislation. The incorporation of this system in the Illinois constitution probably reflects the feeling against the absolute veto power of the territorial governors. The suggestion doubtless came from Kane, who was a native of New York and must have been familiar with its constitution.

The last section of article three of the draft directed the governor to "nominate and by and with the advice and consent of the senate appoint a secretary of state." It was accepted without a change by the convention, and at the close of the third reading, two other sections, twenty-one and twenty-two, were added, providing for additional officers. The state treasurer and public printer were to be elected biennially by joint vote of both houses of the legislature. All other officers whose appointments were not otherwise provided for were to be appointed by the governor, except that "inferior officers whose jurisdiction may be confined within the limits of the county, shall be appointed in such manner as the general assembly shall prescribe." With the exception of the provision for a public printer, all these sections were copied from the Kentucky constitution. The general appointive power granted to the governor by section twenty-two was largely nullified by section ten of the schedule, which, as amended and adopted the following day, provided that: "An auditor of public accounts, and an attorney general and such

other officers as may be necessary may be appointed by the
general assembly, whose duties may be regulated by law." The
effect of this provision was to allow the legislature to play
fast and loose with the appointive power of the governor. The
explanation, according to Governor Ford, is that "the Convention wished to have Elijah C. Berry for the first auditor of
public accounts, but it was believed that Governor Bond [whose
election was assured] would not appoint him to office."[10]

The subject of the judiciary had been so extensively discussed
during the territorial period that the committee of 15 apparently felt competent to draft article four dealing with it without
reference to other state constitutions. The judicial power was
vested in a supreme court and such inferior courts as the legislature might establish. The supreme court, consisting of a chief
justice and three associate justices,[11] was to have appellate jurisdiction only, except in certain special cases. All justices and
judges were to be appointed by joint ballot of the two houses
of the legislature. The first appointees were to hold office during good behavior until the end of the first legislative session
begun in 1824, and until that time the supreme court judges
were to "hold circuit courts in the several counties." After that
period the justices were to "be commissioned during good behavior" and were not to "hold circuit courts unless required
by law." The provision for new elections by the legislature of
1824 was doubtless inserted in order that advantage might be
taken of "any accession of talent" during the interval.[12] The
salaries of justices during the temporary appointment were
first fixed at $1,250 and then reduced to $1,000. For the later
permanent appointments, all the judges were to "have adequate
and competent salaries." Apart from the question of salaries
the only change made by the convention in the article on the
judiciary was in the last section. This provided in the draft that
the governor should "nominate, and by and with the advice

[10] "Journal," p. 63, in Illinois State Historical Society, *Journal*, 6:415;
Ford, *History of Illinois*, 26.

[11] The number of associate judges might be increased after 1824.

[12] *Intelligencer*, August 26, 1818.

and consent of the senate, appoint a competent number of justices of the peace in each county." At the third reading, however, the section was stricken out and a substitute was finally adopted providing for the election of justices of the peace in each county. Four days later, August 24, this action was reconsidered, "on the motion of mr. Kane," and another substitute was adopted arranging for the justices to "be appointed in each county in such manner . . . as the general assembly may direct."

Article five dealing with the militia directed that it should consist of "all free male able bodied persons, negroes, mulattoes and Indians excepted, resident in the state, between the ages of 18 and 45 years, except such persons as now are or hereafter may be exempted by the laws of the United States, or of this state." Persons "conscientiously scrupulous of bearing arms" were not to "be compelled to do militia duty in time of peace, provided such person or persons shall pay an equivalent for such exemption." Regimental officers and all officers below them, staff officers excepted, were to be elected by the men of their several organizations, and brigadier and major generals "by the officers of their brigades and divisions respectively." This article, which was abridged from the militia article of the Indiana constitution, received only verbal changes at the hands of the convention, with the exception of the addition at the third reading of a section declaring the militia except in certain cases exempt "from arrest during their attendance at musters and elections of officers, and in going to and returning from the same."

The article of the draft which suffered the most radical changes at the hands of the convention was the sixth, dealing with slavery, and in view of the character of the campaign for members of the convention and the great importance of the issue, the consideration of this article is of special interest. The discussions of slavery in the *Intelligencer* had not ceased with the elections, or even with the assembling of the convention. The issue of August 12, the day on which the draft was reported, contained a long communication from "Pacificus" addressed "To the honorable members of the convention of the Illinois Territory." This writer professed to be opposed to absolute slavery but was very solicitous about the welfare of "a large and respectable portion of the inhabitants of this territory who are anxious to be permitted to live as they have hitherto done—to retain in their families those whom they have brought with them into the country, perhaps raised among their children, or purchased with their money for the purpose of relieving the toils and burdens of domestic life." After dwelling upon "the blessing of being surrounded by good and faithful servants," he proceeded to suggest "the outlines of a plan which might gratify the wishes of those who are in favor of slavery, and not materially, if at all, affect the future prosperity of our infant state." This plan contemplated the toleration of a modified form of slavery. All slaves introduced were to be registered by their owners, taught to read, and given "correct ideas of the general principles of the christian religion." Then they were to become free, males at the age of 40 and females at 35. Children of slaves and indentured servants were also to be registered and should be freed, males at 32 and females at 28. "The constitution also to declare, that from and after the first day of January, one thousand eight hundred and sixty, slavery of every kind or character should then and from thenceforth cease:—the proprietors being liable upon their bonds, that no slave at that time, infirm or over fifty years of age, should become in any manner chargeable to the public."

The members of the Illinois convention had before them the slavery provisions of two constitutions framed for states which, like Illinois, had been under the obligation of making their constitutions harmonize with the Ordinance of 1787. Section two of article eight—the bill of rights—of the Ohio constitution of 1802 reads:

There shall be neither slavery nor involuntary servitude in this State, otherwise than for the punishment of crimes, whereof the party shall have been duly convicted; nor shall any male person, arrived at the age of twenty-one years, nor female person, arrived at the age of eighteen years, be held to serve any person as a servant, under the pretense of indenture or otherwise unless such person shall enter into such indenture while in a state of perfect freedom and on condition of a *bona-fide* consideration, received, or to be received, for their service, except as before excepted. Nor shall any indenture of any negro or mulatto, hereafter made and executed out of the State, or, if made in the State, where the term of service exceeds one year, be of the least validity, except those given in the case of apprenticeships.

The Indiana constitution of 1816 ignored the question of existing indentures and merely declared: "There shall be neither slavery nor involuntary servitude in this State, otherwise than for the punishment of crimes, whereof the party shall have been duly convicted, nor shall any indenture of any negro or mulatto, hereafter made and executed out of the bounds of this State be of any validity within the State." Both constitutions, moreover, declared that no alteration should ever be made so as to introduce slavery or involuntary servitude, the Indiana constitution stating as reason therefore that "the holding any part of the human creation in slavery or involuntary servitude can only originate in usurpation and tyranny." [13]

The members of the committee of 15 which framed the draft of the Illinois constitution appear to have been unwilling to leave the question of existing indentures to the courts and so they selected the provision from the Ohio constitution, leaving blanks to be filled in for the age limits. Instead of inserting the section in the bill of rights, however, it was presented as the single section of a separate article numbered six. This might be taken to indicate that the committee expected additional sections to be added by the convention. At the first reading of this article the blanks were filled as they had been in the Ohio section and "further consideration was postponed until the second reading." The first real consideration of the question took place on August 18. The issue of the *Intelligencer* for the nineteenth, which doubtless went to press before any action had been taken, stated that "the question of *slavery* is not yet decided; a majority however, are said to be opposed to it." The same issue contains also a communication which indicates the kind of argument which was being brought to bear upon the members of the convention. After lamenting the burden of taxation which would

[13] Thorpe, *Constitutions*, 5:2909; 2:1070, 1068.

be necessary in order to carry on the state government "even upon as economical a scale as can safely be established," the writer declared: "It is thought the exclusion of slavery will annihilate a lucrative source of public revenue. I mean the United States' salines, as white men cannot be procured in sufficient numbers to convert these salines to any extensively valuable purposes." Undoubtedly the problem of the salines was a considerable factor in determining the convention's attitude on the slavery question.

When article six came up for second reading, on August 18, the first clause was changed to read: "Neither slavery nor involuntary servitude shall hereafter be introduced into this state"; for the words "under pretence of indenture or otherwise" were substituted "under any indenture hereafter made"; and a second section was added as follows: "Nor shall any person bound to labor in any other state, be hired to labor in this state, except within the tract reserved for the salt works near Shawneetown, nor even at that place for a longer period than one year at one time; nor shall it be allowed there, after the year—any violation of this article, shall effect the emancipation of such person from his obligation to service." [14] The changes in the first section and the additional section appear to have been proposed together but they were voted on separately. The vote on the amendments to the first section would appear to be the most significant of any of the votes on the slavery question in the convention. Those in favor of the changes were Morse of Bond; Borough, Prickett, and Stephenson of Madison; Messinger of St. Clair; Cairns of Monroe; Fisher and Kane of Randolph; Hall and Will of Jackson; Omelveny of Pope; Harrison of Franklin; Jones, White, and Hubbard of Gallatin; and Cullom and Kitchell of Crawford—17. Opposed to them were Kirkpatrick of Bond; Lemen of St. Clair; Bankson, the sole representative from Washington; Moore of Monroe; M'Fatridge and West of Johnson; Ferguson of Pope; Echols and Whiteaker of Union;

---

[14] An act passed by the territorial legislature on December 22, 1814, had permitted the hiring of slaves anywhere in the territory for periods not to exceed one year. *Pope's Digest,* 2:472.

Roberts of Franklin; Hargrave and McHenry of White; and Gard and Compton of Edwards—14. This vote would indicate that the issue was by no means a sectional one between the northern and southern parts of the settled area.

The object of the changes in section one of the slavery article was undoubtedly to prevent the section from being interpreted in such a way as to interfere either with the so-called "French slaves" or with the indentured servants who had been introduced during the territorial period. After the adoption of these changes, the proposed second section was accepted without a division. There were some members of the convention, however, who were not satisfied with a merely negative position on the existing indentures, and on the following day, without waiting for the third reading of the article, Leonard White of Gallatin offered an additional section declaring that "each and every person who has been bound to service by contract or indenture, in virtue of the laws of the Illinois territory, heretofore existing, and in conformity with the provisions of the same, without fraud or collusion, shall be held to a specific performance of their contracts or indentures; and such negroes and mulattoes as have been registered in conformity with the aforesaid laws, shall serve out the time appointed by said laws:—Provided however, that the descendants of such persons, negroes and mulattoes, shall become free at the age of twenty-five years." This section was adopted by the same vote as that on the amendments to section one, 17 to 14, but the alignment was not the same. Four men, Ferguson of Pope, Hargrave and McHenry of White, and Roberts of Franklin, who had opposed the changes in section one, voted for this additional section; and four others, Borough and Prickett of Madison, Cairns of Monroe, and Cullom of Crawford, who had supported the changes, opposed this section. What the motives of these men were can only be conjectured, but one of them, Prickett, had apparently experienced a change of heart, for he at once moved a reconsideration of the whole article. The motion was defeated, however, without a division.

When article six came up for third reading, the first section was adopted, apparently without protest. An attempt was made, however, to strike out the second section, permitting the hiring of slaves in the salines, but this was defeated by a vote of 10 to 21. Among the ten were three of the men who had voted for the changes in section one and against section three—Borough, Cairns, and Prickett. All four of the men who had voted against the changes in section one and for section three opposed striking out section two, as did also three who had voted on the anti-slavery side on each of the other propositions—Bankson of Washington, Kirkpatrick of Bond, and Moore of Monroe. The conclusion of section three was amended to read: "Provided, however, that the children thereafter born of such persons, negroes and mulattoes, shall become free; the males at the age of twenty-one years, the females at the age of eighteen years. Each and every child born of indentured parents shall be entered with the clerk of the county in which they reside, by their owners within six months after the birth of said child." The section was then adopted without a division.

The article on slavery as a whole is not easy to interpret. It would seem to have been the purpose of the convention to make Illinois ultimately a free state and to wipe out the territorial indenture system for the future, but to interfere in no way with existing property rights in slaves or indentured servants.[15] The only vestige of the indenture system left was the right to bind negroes "while in a state of perfect freedom, and on condition of a bona fide consideration" to serve for not more than one year, and such indentures were to be valid only if made within the state. The action of the convention has usually been represented as an antislavery victory but the members who are known to have favored slavery were on the winning side in all three of the record votes. It has also been called a compromise between the opponents and the advocates of slavery but it would probably be more accurate to consider it a victory for those who

[15] The constitution did reduce the age to which children of indentured servants could be held, from 30 and 28 to 21 and 18 for males and females respectively. See *Pope's Digest*, 2:472.

occupied middle ground on the subject. The solution may well have embodied the views of a majority of the convention and also of a majority of the people of the state as well. On the other hand the possibility of the refusal of Congress to admit the state if the constitution should lean too strongly toward the proslavery side was doubtless kept in mind. In this connection it should be noted that the section on amendment contained no prohibition of a change in the constitution to allow the introduction of slavery, as had been the case in the constitutions of Ohio and Indiana. This may be significant of the hopes and expectations of some of the members of the convention.

The method of amending the constitution was set forth in article seven and was copied from the Ohio constitution. It provided, in the draft, that two-thirds of the general assembly might recommend to the electors "to vote for or against a convention." If "a majority of all the citizens of the state voting for representatives" voted in the affirmative, the next legislature was to call such a convention consisting of the same number of members as there were in the general assembly, which should meet within three months after the election, "for the purpose of revising, amending or changing the constitution." At first reading, a provision was inserted requiring two-thirds of all the members elected to the general assembly to join in ordering the election. The last article of the constitution, number eight, was the usual bill of rights. Here again the Ohio constitution was followed in the main, with occasional preferences shown for sections in the constitutions of Kentucky, Tennessee, or Indiana. A section which appears to have been original is number twenty; it provided "that the mode of levying a tax shall be by valuation, so that every person shall pay a tax in proportion to the value of the property, he or she has in his or her possession." Possibly this section was inserted in response to the complaints of "A friend to equal justice" about the "oppressive system of taxation" in existence in the territory. Section twenty-one also dealt with a matter of vital interest at the time not only in Illinois but throughout the country and especially in the west—the subject of banking. There had been much discussion of this subject in the paper during the latter years of the territorial period, a number of banks had been chartered by the legislature, and one had actually been established.[16] The section in the draft provided "that there shall be no other banks nor monied institutions in this state, but those already provided for by law, except a state bank and its branches, which shall be established and regulated by the legislature of said state, as they may think best." The convention at first reading changed the second "shall" to "may." It is possible that one object of this section was to prevent the establishment in Illinois of a branch of the United States Bank. Section twenty-two of the draft of the bill of rights declared that "to guard against the transgressions of the high powers which we have delegated, we declare that all powers not hereby delegated, or well understood, remain with the people." After having run the gauntlet of three readings, this section, for some unknown reason, was stricken out on the recommendation of Kane's committee on revision. At the close of third reading, two sections, numbers twenty-two and twenty-three of the final constitution, were added to article eight. These were taken from the Indiana constitution and provided for freedom of the press and of opinions and for the right to offer the truth of the charges as evidence "in prosecutions for the publication of papers investigating the official conduct of officers, or of men acting in a public capacity or where the matter published is proper for public information."

The deliberations of the convention on the schedule and on various resolutions which were ultimately incorporated in it occupied a large amount of time and are of considerable interest, but unfortunately they are difficult to follow because the reports of the committee of five were not printed in full as was the draft

[16] "Journal," pp. 28, 40, 49, 60. The words added to the article on amendments do not appear in the enrolled copy of the constitution in the office of the secretary of state. They must have been stricken out shortly before the convention adjourned, and the action upon it was doubtless recorded on one of the last pages of the "Journal," which unfortunately are lacking in the only available copy. See also Dowrie, *Development of Banking in Illinois, 1817-1863*, ch. 2; "Journal," pp. 31, 40; *Intelligencer*, October 28, 1818.

of the constitution proper. The principal purpose of the schedule was to provide for the transition from territorial to state government. Thus it directed that the governor and all other territorial officers should continue to exercise their functions until superseded, and that all suits should be continued "as if no change had taken place." One of the sections which was evidently the subject of dispute in the convention was number twelve, dealing with the qualifications of voters at the first election. Section twenty-seven of article two, as has been noted, restricted the franchise to those who had "resided in the State six months next preceding the election." The schedule reported by the committee apparently proposed no modification of this for the first election, but on August 21, Borough of Madison offered a resolution to extend the right to vote on that occasion to all those "who are actually residing in the state at the time." This resolution received its second reading the following day and was then rejected by vote of 3 to 28. It is significant that the affirmative votes were cast by the three delegates from Madison, the county which was growing most rapidly and was thus most interested in the proposed concession. Three days later Borough made another attempt with a resolution extending the franchise at the first election to those "who shall be actual residents of this state at the signing of this constitution," a three weeks' residence. The Madison County delegation must have won over many of the members to their views in the interval, for this resolution was carried by vote of 18 to 12. The affirmative votes were cast, in the main, by the representatives from those counties in which the population was increasing most rapidly.

The question of apportioning members of the legislature until the first state census should be taken was the subject of the first report of the committee of five, presented August 15; it ultimately became section eight of the schedule. This provided for 14 senators and 26 representatives specifically assigned to the different counties. One senator was allowed to each of the counties except Johnson and Jackson, which were to form a single senatorial district. An analysis of the apportionment of representatives, however, shows that it was based on the returns of the census just taken. One representative only was given to each county having less than 2,000 inhabitants, two to each having between 2,000 and 3,000, three to each having over 3,000. When this report was finally adopted on the eighteenth, the only change was to link Johnson County with Franklin instead of Jackson for the election of a senator. This was a logical change as Franklin, next to Johnson, had the smallest population and, moreover, was contiguous to Johnson, whereas Jackson was not. The schedule contained also four sections of a miscellaneous character, which might more logically have been incorporated in the constitution proper. One of these, relating to appointments, has already been considered. Another, section fourteen, also nullified one of the provisions of the constitution proper—the provision requiring the lieutenant governor to have the same qualifications as the governor, including citizenship for 30 years. The section reads "any person of thirty years of age who is a citizen of the United States and has resided within the limits of this State two years next preceding his election, shall be eligible to the office of lieutenant-governor; anything in the thirteenth section of the third article of this constitution contained to the contrary notwithstanding." [17] Governor Ford's explanation of this section, doubtless correct, is that "Col. Pierre Menard, a Frenchman, and an old settler in the country, was generally looked to to fill the office of lieutenant governor; but . . . he had not been naturalized until a year or so before." [18] The legal complications which might have arisen, had Menard been called upon to fill the governor's office, would be an interesting subject for speculation.

Section four of the schedule determined the form of county government, which had been subject to frequent change during the territorial period; [19] it directed that "there shall be elected

---

[17] Thorpe, *Constitutions*, 2:985. This section must have been incorporated just at the close of the convention as there is no record of it in the only available copy of the "Journal."

[18] Ford, *History of Illinois*, 26.

[19] See ch. 7, above, pp. 193-194, 196-198.

in each county three county commissioners for the purpose of transacting all county business, whose time of service, power, and duties shall be regulated and defined by law." Section eleven made it obligatory upon the legislature "to enact such laws as may be necessary and proper to prevent the practice of duelling." This was proposed by Mr. Cairns in the form of a resolution on August 20 and later was incorporated in the schedule. Earlier in the same day Cairns had proposed another resolution directing the legislature to pass laws permitting the decision of differences by arbitrators. The settlement of all civil disputes in this manner had been advocated in one of the communications published in the *Intelligencer* before the convention assembled, but the resolution was rejected without a division. In this connection it is interesting to note that the first general assembly not only complied with the direction of the convention by passing a stringent law to prevent dueling, but also enacted another law *"authorizing and regulating Arbitrations."* [20]

The subject of the location of the capital of the state, which was dealt with in section thirteen of the schedule as finally adopted, occupied a large amount of the convention's time and was more bitterly contested than any other question, excepting that of slavery. The decision of this question was no necessary part of the convention's work and might well have been left to the future. As has been noted, the memorial asking for statehood failed to request, and the enabling act failed to grant, land for a capital site, and there is no evidence that the question was raised at all during the convention campaign. A writer well versed in the traditions which have come down from that period of Illinois history claims that "there was no demand for that change at that time by the people, or by any public exigency. It was premature and unnecessary, and was concocted and consummated by a lot of speculators who expected to reap large

[20] *Laws of Illinois,* 1819, pp. 32, 71-73. The former was modeled on an act passed by the governor and judges on April 7, 1810; the latter was copied from the Indiana code of 1807. Alvord, *Laws of the Territory,* 25-27; *Laws of Indiana Territory,* 1807, pp. 175-179; *Pope's Digest,* 1:122-127; *Intelligencer,* July 10, 1818.

profits in building up the new capital." [21] The question appears to have come up as a result of "sundry propositions in writing, offering donations to the state of land &c. from the proprietors of Pope's bluff, Hill's ferry, and Covington." [22] These places were all situated on the Kaskaskia River and north of the base line of the government surveys. No attempt was made in the convention to remove the capital to any other specific place, although the proprietors of other towns undoubtedly entertained or had entertained designs upon it. An example is Ripley, situated in Bond County on Shoal Creek, a branch of the Kaskaskia, which had been advertising its advantages in the *Intelligencer*. Among the attractions enumerated was this: "Its central and eligible situation in the territory gives rise to a strong presumption, that it will at no distant period become the seat of government." [23] Ripley appears to have withdrawn in favor of Hill's Ferry, for one of the men connected with the speculation was Abraham Prickett, the member of the convention who proposed that Hill's Ferry be selected as the capital site.

Of the three towns presenting proposals, the only one which apparently had any population at the time was Covington, the county seat of the recently organized Washington County. Since May a prospective sale of town lots had been advertised by the proprietors, who called attention especially to the situation of the town

near the centre of the territorial population, and . . . surrounded by a rich beautiful and extensive tract of country; the site is high, dry and healthy, extending one mile on the margin of the Kaskaskia river, the navigation of which, is good from thence to its confluence with the Mississippi, a distance of one hundred and twenty miles. The roads from any landings on the Ohio river, between the mouth of the Wabash and Frazier's ferry to Edwardsville, St. Louis, and the principal settlements in the Missouri territory, must inevitably pass through this town, by which the advantage of excellent roads will be obtained, and the distance in comparison with the roads now in use diminished more than 15 miles.

With the issue of the *Intelligencer* of July 29, the advertisement

[21] Snyder, *Adam W. Snyder*, 39-40.
[22] "Journal," p. 51, in Illinois State Historical Society, *Journal*, 6:403.
[23] *Intelligencer*, June 3, 1818.

announced that an auction of town lots would begin the fourth Monday in September. No mention was made, however, of any possibility that the town might be selected for the state capital.

Hill's Ferry was located where the Vincennes road crossed the Kaskaskia River in what is now Clinton County—the site of the present town of Carlyle. In 1818, the log cabin of the man who kept the ferry is said to have been the only house on the site. The desirability of the location had been recognized, however, and the land on both sides of the river had been entered by non-resident speculators. In 1816 Charles Slade bought from John Hill the quarter section on which the ferry was located and before 1818 he entered the remainder of that section and a large part of the adjoining one. Not until September was the place advertised under the name Carlyle. Then its attractions were set forth as follows:

THIS TOWN is beautifully situated on the west bank of the Kaskaskia river, at the well known crossing of *Hill's Ferry*—The great notoriety of this situation renders it necessary for the proprietors to state but a few facts relative thereto—That the site is singularly advantageous, being at the head of navigation for boats of any considerable burthen, the river diminishing in size after losing the Hurricane and east forks which empty themselves into the Kaskaskia a few miles above, having the great United States road from Vincennes to St. Louis, the roads from Shawneetown, the Saline and the Ferries on the lower Ohio, to the mouth of Missouri and the great Sangamo country passing thro' its principal street, being high and airy, affording most excellent spring and well water, and being surrounded by a country so rich and so equally diversified with wood and prairie as at once to invite and insure a crouded populatron [*sic*].[24]

Pope's Bluff was still farther north on the Kaskaskia River, in the southwestern part of Bond County. The southern half of the section was entered in 1816 by Nathaniel Pope, and just two days after the site was proposed for the capital in the convention, sections thirteen and fourteen and the remainder of section fifteen were entered by the firm of "Pope, Messenger and Stephenson." The motion to accept the propositions of the pro-

[24] *History of Marion and Clinton Counties*, 52, 174; land records, auditor's office, Springfield; *Intelligencer*, September 9, 1818.

prietors of Pope's Bluff came from Leonard White, who, though a representative from Gallatin County, was in close touch with these members of the Edwards faction. The place was not advertised in the *Intelligencer* either before or after the convention.

The offers of land from the proprietors of each of these three places were laid before the convention by the committee of five on Tuesday, August 18. At the opening of the session on Thursday, it was resolved, on motion of Mr. Kitchell, "that it is expedient at this time to remove the seat of government from the town of Kaskaskia." Mr. Gard of Edwards County at once offered a resolution for the appointment of a committee of five "to view the sites on the Kaskaskia river, above the base line, and report . . . to the next general assembly." The convention had no intention of leaving the decision to the legislature, however, and the resolution was voted down. Bankson of Washington then offered a resolution for the location of the capital at Covington but that also was rejected. Then Kane proposed, with no more success, "that the seat of government be located at the town of Kaskaskia five years." After resolutions in favor of Pope's Bluff and Hill's Ferry had been offered and rejected, Kane tried again with a resolution "that the seat of government be located for four years at the town of Kaskaskia, after which time, the general assembly shall have power to remove the same." This was also rejected, as was another resolution, proposed by Hubbard, for the appointment of commissioners "to examine the geographical situation of the state, taking into view the population therof, and the eligibility of the most prominent, and as they may conceive the most convenient places and report the same to the next session of the general assembly, who may either reject the whole or select some one from among the places reported, for the seat of government for this state." It seemed to be impossible to reach an agreement and the convention, in desperation, postponed further consideration of the question.

The next day, Friday the twenty-first, Gard offered a resolution evidently designed to take the whole question of the location of the capital out of the field of private speculation. He proposed to make it

the duty of the general assembly at their first session to petition congress for the right of pre-emption of four sections of land on the Kaskaskia river as near as may be, east of the third principal meridian on said river, to be selected by five commissioners. If the grant should be made, it shall be the duty of the aforesaid assembly, at their next session after the grant is made, to lay out a town, which shall be the permanent seat of government for the state of Illinois, but if the grant should not be made by congress, in that case it shall be the duty of the general assembly to fix on some other place, that they shall think best for that seat.

This resolution was carried by vote of 18 to 13, and on Saturday it passed second reading without a division. At third reading on Monday Gard offered a substitute elaborating some of the details and directing that Congress be requested either to grant the land to the state or to allow it the right of pre-emption. White then moved to strike out all except the first sentence of the substitute, which read: "The seat of government for the State shall be at Kaskaskia until the general assembly shall otherwise provide." This would have given the speculators another chance before the legislature, but the motion was lost by vote of 15 to 16, "the president refusing to vote in the affirmative." Kane then moved to amend the substitute so as to make the proposed site the seat of government for 20 years, instead of permanently, and this was carried by vote of 25 to 6, after which the substitute was adopted and incorporated in the schedule without a division.

The reason for requiring the proposed site of the capital to be located east of the meridian seems to have been to get it on unsurveyed and unentered lands so that the state instead of individuals might reap the profits from the sale of lots. Such a location would be far from the settled parts of the state for some time, however, and it is not strange that the scheme called forth protests. One of these took the form of a remonstrance counter to the petition which the first legislature sent to Congress in conformity with the instructions of the convention. This declared that

the proposed seat of government is not in a central situation. Neither
is it in the centre of the population, nor is there any probability that it
ever will be so. Situated on the Kaskaskia river, far above the head of
navigation, in a part of the country, which, as we are credibly informed,
is naturally unhealthy, the only inducements which people can have to
settle in such a town must be derived from a *biennial session* of a General Assembly composed of *forty-two* members! Is it possible, we ask,
that the legislature can be accommodated at such a place and under
such circumstances, without putting the state to an expense which will
greatly outweigh all the profits to be derived from a beggarly speculation in village lots? [25]

The contest in the convention over the location of the capital
is the only one in which the territorial factions appear to have
played a part. An examination of the votes does not show, as
might have been expected, an alignment of the northern against
the southern counties. It shows, on the other hand, such men
as White, Stephenson, and Messinger, recognized members of
the Edwards faction, working together to promote a scheme for
land speculation, in which they were defeated by the votes of
such men as Kane, Thomas, and Jones, well-known opponents
of the Edwards group. The contest, moreover, illustrates clearly
the fact that the leaders of one of these factions at least were
bound to each other by business as well as by political ties.

When the first constitutional convention of Illinois completed
its work on August 26, 1818, it had been in session 21 days.
Nine days had passed before the draft of the constitution was
available for consideration. In the 12 remaining days much
time was devoted to a question which did not concern the
frame of government, yet in that short period the representatives of the people of Illinois discussed and determined the
varied features of the instrument which was to be the fundamental basis of the government of the state for 30 years. It
was not customary at that time to submit constitutions to a
vote of the people and no suggestion of such a procedure appears to have been made. On the whole, however, the people
were probably satisfied with the work of the convention. The
inhabitants of Kaskaskia indicated their approval by a cele-

[25] House Files, December 9, 1818.

bration which the *Intelligencer* of September 2 described as
follows:

On Wednesday last, the constitution for the state of Illinois, was
signed, and the convention adjourned sine die. On this important occasion, the citizens of the town assembled to fire a federal salute to per-
petuate the remembrance of the day when our constitution was signed
and sealed. As many of the independent company of the town as were
requisite to man the field piece, appeared at the capitol, in uniform,
with their colours flying, (being the flag of the union as adopted by the
last act of congress,) accompanied by the principal field officers. Upon
the signing of the constitution, and the convention being about to ad-
journ they were invited by the committee of arrangements to join in
the feu de joie.

The field piece was placed in front of the capitol, the military officers
a few paces in its rear—the governor, secretary, delegate to congress,
and most of the territorial officers, accompanying the members of the
convention, took their positions a few paces in the rear: The salute was
commenced—20 rounds were fired, and one for the new state of Illinois,
which was accompanied by the following pledge, from the independent
corps:

"Under these colours, we pledge ourselves to support the constitution
of Illinois."

This was truly a proud day for the citizens of Illinois—a day on
which hung the prosperity and hopes of thousands yet to follow—a day
which will long be remembered & spoken of with enthusiastic pride; as
a day connected with the permanent prosperity of our literary, political
and religious institutions—as the main pillar in the edifice of our state
independence, and justly the basis of our future greatness.

The united exertions of our representatives have furnished us with a
wise and republican constitution—distributing to all classes their just
rights. It now beho[o]ves us as faithful citizens to protect it from en-
croachment: And in the language of the immortal Washington, to cher-
ish a cordial and immovable attachment to it—accustoming ourselves
to think and speak of it as the palladium of our political safety & prosperity—watching for its preservation with jealous anxiety—discounte-
nancing whatever may suggest even a suspicion that it can in any event
be abandoned.

Chapter 11

A State in the Union

The first election of state and county officers in Illinois took place on September 17-19, 1818, as provided for in the constitution. The campaign for state officers was necessarily a brief one, for not until the convention met was it known whether or not it could or would proceed to form a state government, and not until the convention had accomplished its work was it known just what officers were to be elected. The interest in the election, however, centered not in the choice of state and county officers but in that of a representative to Congress, and for this there had been a long campaign. The *Intelligencer* of April 22, 1818, announced for Mr. Pope "his determination to retire from public life." Two weeks later, May 6, the paper announced Daniel P. Cook "a candidate for Congress to represent us in the Lower House," and on May 20 it stated that John McLean of Shawneetown was "a Candidate for Congress to represent the people of this territory in the next Congress of the United States." The form of the announcements would indicate that these men were candidates for either territorial delegate or state representative as events might determine, and on June 10, when it was very doubtful if the requisite population for statehood could be found, the paper made an authorized statement that Cook would "cheerfully serve" in the capacity of delegate. The following week Shadrach Bond was announced as "a Candidate for Delegate to Congress from this territory."

Cook and McLean, although they had been in the territory but three or four years, were identified with the Edwards and anti-Edwards factions respectively. Both were young and clever lawyers. Bond, on the other hand, was at least 20 years older than either of his opponents and had been in Illinois for 24 years. He was a farmer, with only average education and ability, but from an early period he had been popular with the voters.

They had kept him in the Indiana legislature as long as Illinois was a part of that territory, and at the first election in Illinois they gave him the highest office in their power, that of delegate to Congress. Although identified with neither of the territorial factions, he was better known on both sides of the territory than either Cook or McLean and his chances for election were very good. Cook's address "to the electors of Illinois," written July 1, indicates that he considered Bond the most dangerous rival. In one place he says: "You are gravely told, fellow citizens, that I am too young to represent you . . . if men who have but just passed the age of 25, are better qualified than men of 45, the public interest is consulted and promoted by their election," and in another: "A distinction fellow citizens, is attempted to be made, between farmers and lawyers." A month later he wrote to Edwards from Golconda: "McLean it is said, will beat Bond four to one in Crawford, Edwards, White, and Gallatin." [1] Evidently the wish was father to the thought and Cook preferred that the voters of the eastern counties, where he could expect little support, should cast their ballots for McLean rather than for Bond.

In the middle of August, when statehood was practically assured, election to Congress became much more desirable. Yet it was just at this time that Bond dropped out of the race. In the *Intelligencer* of August 19 he addressed "The Citizens of the Illinois Territory" as follows: "The formation of a constitution, and the organization of a state government, will put an end to the office of delegate to the Congress of the United States: I wish therefore, no longer to be considered a candidate for that appointment. Repeated and numerous applications have been made to be [*sic*] me, to become a candidate for the office of Governor of the NEW STATE. It is my pleasure and duty to yield to this expression of the public wish. Should my fellow-citizens, therefore, think proper to elect me to this important station, I promise them diligence and fidelity in the performance of the duties thereby enjoined." While no positive evidence is available

[1] *Intelligencer,* July 8, 1818; Washburne, *Edwards Papers,* 145.

on the subject, it is fair to assume that the "repeated and numerous applications" came in part at least from friends of Cook and McLean who were anxious to get Bond out of the race for Congress. The failure of either of the factions to put up a candidate for governor against Bond would indicate that there was an understanding on the subject.

BUILDING IN WHICH TERRITORIAL LEGISLATURE FIRST MET IN KASKASKIA
(Drawing owned by Chicago Historical Society)

With Bond out of the race, the congressional campaign became not only a contest between the rival factions but also one between the east and west. This was due not so much to antagonism between the two sections as to the propensity of the voters to cast their ballots for the man they knew personally. Neither candidate was well known except on the side of the territory in which he resided.[2]

Earlier in the campaign the slavery question had played a

[2] On June 12, John Law of Vincennes wrote Kane: "Is there a probability of McLeans election . . . he is considered as a popular candidate on this side of the Territory." Chicago Historical Society Manuscripts, 54:57.

considerable part. Cook's opposition to slavery as an institution was made known by his communications in the *Intelligencer* of February 4 and April 1, over the recognized signature of "A republican," while McLean was at a later period an out-and-out proslavery man and doubtless favored the institution at this time. In the *Intelligencer* of June 24, however, "A citizen" expressed a desire to know the "candid and impartial sentiments" of the candidates for Congress "as it respects *the toleration of slavery.*" "On this important point," he continued, "it will be well for every man to inquire before he gives his vote—and to enquire of the candidate, in the presence of those of an opposite opinion to himself, so that he may not flinch, and act the *camelion,* as, I fear, some of our candidates are doing." Late in July Cook issued a statement over his own name, which begins: "In pursuance of a wish expressed by many who are opposed to slavery, and who wish for an expression of the public sentiment on that subject in the Congressional election, I beg leave to state through the medium of the Intelligencer, that I am decidedly opposed to the toleration of slavery in this territory." In his letter of August 3 from Golconda, already referred to, Cook wrote: "I made a speech and excited warm opposition from *slavemen,* but still warmer support from *freemen.*" [3]

The action of the convention narrowed the slavery issue in the congressional campaign to the question of whether or not the candidates, if elected, would support the application for statehood under the constitution as adopted. The antislavery men, in their address to the "friends of freedom," published just as the convention was assembling, appealed to them to elect a delegate opposed to slavery and to use every possible means to prevent the ratification by Congress of a proslavery constitution. The more radical of these men undoubtedly considered the slavery article of the constitution unsatisfactory and would gladly

---

[3] *Intelligencer,* June 24, July 29, 1818; Washburne, *Edwards Papers,* 145. Lippincott, in his "Early Days in Madison County," no. 13, says: "All I knew or heard of the candidates in their first canvas was that Mr. McLean was in favor of slavery and Mr. Cook opposed to it." See also Churchill, "Annotations," no. 3.

have voted for a candidate who would oppose ratification. On the day after the constitution was signed, Cook prepared a statement in which he said: "It is questioned by some, whether I will support the constitution of our state in congress if elected. When it is known that I was the first person in the state who urged the propriety of petitioning congress for leave to form a state government, by an address to the legislature thro' the public print; it can scarcely be supposed that I am unfriendly to a change of the government." He would, he declared, use his "best exertions to procure a ratification of the constitution." [4]

That the opposition of the Edwards men to the plan adopted by the convention for locating the state capital was being used against Cook is indicated by another part of the same statement. "It is insinuated," he wrote, "that I will not wish the seat of government to be fixed as the Convention has provided; to this insinuation I will remark that it can only have grown out of a wish to defeat my election.—I shall endeavor if elected, to procure the grant which it is made the duty of the legislature to petition for." In this connection it is interesting to note that when Edwards came up for re-election to the United States Senate in 1819, he was charged with being opposed to the donation of land for a capital site.

When the election was over, it was found that McLean had carried two western counties, Randolph and Washington. In the eastern counties, where Cook thought that McLean would beat Bond 4 to 1, he beat Cook himself 8 to 1. Yet so large was Cook's vote in the populous counties of the northwest that McLean's total majority was only 14.[5] The man who more than any other is entitled to the credit for the achievement of statehood by Illinois in 1818 was obliged to content himself for the time being with a minor state office.

In the election of state and county officers there was no general issue and there is no evidence that the political factions played

[4] *Intelligencer*, August 5, September 2, 1818.

[5] *Intelligencer*, September 23, October 7, 1818; *Illinois Emigrant*, October 17, 1818; *Niles' Register*, 15:192. The *Intelligencer* of October 14 gives McLean's majority as 6. Compare Washburne, *Edwards Papers*, 155.

any considerable part. The principal factor was doubtless the personal popularity of the respective candidates. An editorial in the *Intelligencer* of September 16 emphasized the importance of the election as

one which combines greater interest than any heretofore, or which may shortly follow. . . . Seven different grades of civil officers are to be elected—In this election, we are all vitally interested. The convention has left much for the legislature to do, and independent of the selections they have to make, of other officers, to fill highly responsible stations, their task will be no easy one. It will be such a one as will require the first talents in the state to perform; as it may be supposed, that they will not only go into the work of general legislation, but make a complete revision of our territorial laws. Who that possesses the smallest spark of public spirit can withhold his suffrage when so much is at stake?

As has been seen, Shadrach Bond had a clear field for the important post of governor. Only in Madison County, so far as is known from the incomplete returns available, were any ballots cast against him. There 19 voters indicated their preference for Henry Reavis, of whom nothing is known except that his name appears in the census schedule for Madison County. It would seem as though their only object must have been to show opposition to Bond. It may be significant also that in St. Clair County the ballots cast for governor numbered 117 less than the total vote for sheriff.[6]

For the office of lieutenant governor there were three candidates, Pierre Menard, William L. Reynolds, and Edward N. Cullom. Menard was a French-Canadian who had settled in Kaskaskia about 1791. Like Bond he had been popular with the voters. He had represented Randolph County in the legislature of Indiana Territory, and in every session of the Illinois territorial legislature he had presided over the council. It was natural that he should be chosen to fill a similar position under the state government, and, as has been seen, a section had been inserted in the schedule of the constitution for the sole purpose of making that possible. Reynolds was a physician from Ken-

[6] Churchill, "Annotations," no. 7; *History of St. Clair County*, 72.

tucky who located in Kaskaskia in 1809. In December, 1817, he gave up his practice on account of ill health, but the next July he announced his return to Kaskaskia and the resumption of his profession. He had never held any political office in the territory. Cullom was one of the foremost men of Crawford County. Coming from Kentucky, he had settled at Palestine in 1814 and had served in the territorial legislature and in the convention. Neither of these men had the slightest chance against Menard. Cullom carried his own county, Reynolds carried White and Pope, but both together received less than half the total vote. This result indicates what might have happened in the contest for representative to Congress had Bond remained in the race.

The number of candidates for seats in the legislature, judging from the counties for which returns are available, was generally about twice the number of positions to be filled.[7] Conspicuous among these candidates were at least 13 members of the convention, 12 of whom were elected, 5 to the senate and 7 to the house. The thirteenth was Dr. Fisher of Randolph, who was defeated for the senatorship by McFerron, over whom he had been victorious in the convention election. Thomas Cox, an unsuccessful candidate for the convention in Union County, was elected to the senate, while the three representatives of the county in the convention were returned to the lower house. Similarly, in Madison County, George Cadwell, who had received only a light vote in the convention election, secured the senatorship. Green B. Field, elected to the house of representatives in Pope County, had also been an unsuccessful candidate for a seat in the convention.

The most surprising thing about the personnel of the first state legislature is the fact that only two of its members had served in the legislature of Illinois Territory, Willis Hargrave of White

[7] For Menard, Reynolds, and Cullom, see Mason, *Early Chicago and Illinois*, 142-161; Reynolds, *Pioneer History*, 291, 368; *Intelligencer*, January 1, July 15, 1818; Perrin, *History of Crawford and Clark Counties*, 32. For announcements of candidates and election returns, see *Intelligencer*, July 15, August 12, August 19, August 26, September 9, September 23, October 7, 1818; Churchill, "Annotations," no. 7; *History of St. Clair County*, 72.

and Risdon Moore of St. Clair. Among the unsuccessful candidates who had been members of the territorial legislature was John Grammar of Union County. Two of the men elected, John Messinger of St. Clair and George Cadwell of Madison, had been members of the Indiana legislature before the division. Another candidate who had served in the Indiana legislature was William Biggs of St. Clair County, who ran for the senate; he was defeated, however, by William Kinney, a Baptist minister, who had never held office in Illinois before.[8] The election of Kinney and of another clergyman, Scott Riggs of Crawford County, is an interesting commentary on the action of the convention in rejecting the proposed section of the constitution which would have made ministers ineligible to seats in the legislature. Kinney was the only member of the senate who had not previously held some office of more or less importance, but there were 11 such men in the house. On the whole it would seem that the first state legislature was made up largely of men with little or no experience which would tend to fit them for the important work to be done. Even Nathaniel Pope, who in spite of his announced determination to retire from public life had been a candidate for the house in Randolph County, was defeated by two men without political experience.[9] It may be that the people believed in rotation in office, and this explanation would also serve to account for the fact that only 8 of the 28 members of this house of representatives were re-elected during the next ten years.

The first general assembly of the state of Illinois convened at Kaskaskia on Monday, October 5, 1818. The governor and lieutenant governor were qualified the following day and the governor then delivered his message. Before outlining the work to be done by the legislature he pleaded for an abatement of party

[8] Kinney took a prominent part in politics thereafter and was a candidate for governor against John Reynolds in 1830.

[9] Two months later, Pope was appointed register of the land office at Edwardsville by the President, and in March, 1819, he was appointed United States judge for the district of Illinois, a position which he held until his death in 1850. *Intelligencer*, December 9, 1818; Moses, *Illinois*, 1:237.

spirit. "If the minds of any of us," he said, "have heretofore been infected with a spirit of division which had not its foundation in a difference of principle; if the conduct of any has been hitherto influenced by unmerited partially [*sic*] or unjust resentment, let it be remembered that the period has now arrived when the public good and public justice imperiously require the extinguishment of that spirit, and the pursuance of a course of conduct that will do justice and do good."

GOVERNOR BOND'S HOME IN KASKASKIA
(Drawing owned by Chicago Historical Society)

On the same day, "the governor nominated and the senate confirmed the appointment of Elias Kent Kane, Esq. to the office of secretary of state." [10] Although Kane was a leader of one of the political factions, his selection was probably due to a recognition of his qualifications for the office. In the convention Kane had demonstrated his ability to do the sort of work that would be required of him as secretary of state. He had been especially useful in proposing changes to bring the various sections of the constitution into harmony with each other and to improve the English of the document. Just such a man was needed by Governor Bond, who was, to quote an early writer, "to a considerable

[10] *Intelligencer,* October 7, 1818.

degree, destitute of the advantages of education but, possessing
a strong mind, and a popular address, was successful in the administration of the duties of his office. His State papers were
usually attributed to his Secretary of State." [11] Whatever may
have been Bond's motive in choosing Kane for secretary, there
can be little doubt about the result from a political point of view.
Kane was soon in a position to dominate the administration.
Although "Shadrach Bond was our first State Governor," wrote
a contemporary, "I believe it was conceded that Mr. Kane was
chief ruler at the opening of our history." Party feeling, instead
of subsiding, increased, and the governor found it impossible to
maintain a neutral position. "You believe Gov. Bond to be your
friend—" wrote Cook to Edwards the following February, "I do
not. The nest which float around him are all against you." [12]

The third day of the session was spent in electing the two
United States senators. The candidates were Ninian Edwards,
Jesse B. Thomas, Leonard White, Michael Jones of Kaskaskia,
Joseph M. Street, and Robert Morrison. The last named was a
Pennsylvanian who had lived in Kaskaskia since 1798 and who
had been active in politics before the separation from Indiana.
After 1809 he was clerk of the general or supreme court at Kaskaskia.[13] Edwards was elected on the first ballot, having received
the vote of 32 of the 40 members present. White came second
with 17 votes, Thomas third with 15. Jones had 10 while Street
and Morrison received only 3 votes each and were dropped. On
the second ballot White led with 16 votes, Thomas had 14, and
Jones 10. Then the contest narrowed down to White and Thomas
with the advantage with Thomas, for he could hope to win over
more of the Jones supporters than could White. On the third bal-

[11] Brown, "Early History of Illinois," in *Fergus Historical Series,* no.
14:88.

[12] Lippincott, "Early Days in Madison County," no. 13; Washburne,
Edwards Papers, 150.

[13] Reynolds, *Pioneer History,* 165; James, *Territorial Records,* 7, 35.
The following account of elections by the legislature is based on *Senate
Journal,* 1 General Assembly, 1 Session, 17, 18, 28; *House Journal,* 1 General Assembly, 2 Session, 48; *Intelligencer,* October 14, 1818; *Illinois Emigrant,* October 17, 1818.

lot White had 18 votes and Thomas 19. On the fourth ballot Thomas received 21 votes, barely the number necessary to elect. The difference in the attitude of the members of the legislature toward Edwards and toward the other candidates is especially significant, if contrasted with the vote of the same assembly in the following February, when Edwards, who had drawn the short term, was up for re-election. Then Edwards was selected over a single competitor, Michael Jones, by the narrow margin of 23 to 19—a striking commentary on the height to which the events of four months had raised party feeling. The change was ascribed by Cook, in the letter already quoted, to the influence wielded by Kane.

On October 8, the legislature again met in joint session, this time for the election of justices of the supreme court. The *Intelligencer* of the preceding day contained an open letter to the general assembly from "A friend to an able judiciary," in which the importance of "the selection of proper Judges" was emphasized. Unfortunately, however, the salaries fixed by the constitution were not such as to attract "the best talents of the state," which this writer thought "should be called into the service." According to Reynolds, "the *material* for the bench was not as good as it might be. Human nature is easier persuaded to mount upwards than to remain on the common level." The candidates for supreme judge were Joseph Phillips, secretary under the territorial government, Thomas Browne, a Shawneetown lawyer belonging to the Edwards party, and Henry S. Dodge, a Kaskaskia lawyer and real estate dealer. Phillips received 34 of the 41 votes cast. The assembly then proceeded to elect three associate judges. There were nine candidates. John Reynolds, at that time a young lawyer, gives this account of how he happened to become one of them:

At the time of the session of the first legislature I resided in Cahokia, and had not the least intention to visit the seat of Government at all. I cared very little who was elected to any office—one thing was certain, I courted nothing myself. My friends urged me to visit, with them, the General Assembly in session at Kaskaskia, and I did so. When we reached the legislature, there was great excitement and turmoil in relation to the election of officers by the General Assembly. I had not

been in Kaskaskia only a few days, when it was urged on me to know
if I would accept of a judgeship, if I was elected. This broke in on me
like a clap of thunder. I was in truth persuaded to become a candidate
for the office. I had a great many personal friends both in and out of
the legislature who urged me much to consent to offer.

The other candidates were Thomas C. Browne; William P.
Foster, a man "of winning, polished manners" who had been in
the state about two months; [14] Henry S. Dodge; William Wilson,
clerk and recorder of Jackson County; C. R. Matheny, the antislavery advocate of the last territorial legislature, and circuit
attorney of the first district; Joseph Kitchell, senator from Crawford County; John Warnock, whom Edwards had appointed in
June as judge of the western circuit in place of Cook; and J. W.
Whitney, of whom nothing is known except that he lived in St.
Clair County. Browne and Foster were elected on the first ballot, Reynolds on the third. The choice of Foster proved an unfortunate one. The following May, A. F. Hubbard wrote to Kane,
"I have just been in the upper Country of Fosters Circuit
[White, Edwards, and Crawford counties]. He did not hold any
Court. The people are much enranged [*sic*] at him indeed and
every man all most has made it his own case and have joined in
complaint. I saw Judge Foster in Vincennes he told me the water
was too high that he was too unwell to get to Palestine on time,
and that his Son was to unwell to stay from him till after Edwards Court[?]." This confirms what Ford wrote of him: "he
was no lawyer, never having either studied or practiced law;
but . . . withal a very gentlemanly swindler. . . . He was believed
to be a clever fellow, in the American sense of the phrase, and a
good-hearted soul. He was assigned to hold courts in the circuit
on the Wabash; but being fearful of exposing his utter incompe-
tency, he never went near any of them. In the course of one year
he resigned his high office, but took care first to pocket his salary,
and then removed out of the State." [15]

[14] Reynolds, *My Own Times*, 212; Ford, *History of Illinois*, 29. Ford
states that he had been in Illinois about two weeks, but he registered a
slave in Randolph County on August 14, 1818.

[15] Chicago Historical Society Manuscripts, 52:185; Ford, *History of Illinois*, 29.

On the following day, October 9, the general assembly completed the elections by choosing Daniel P. Cook, attorney general; E. C. Berry, auditor; John Thomas, treasurer; and Blackwell and Berry, public printers. With the exception of Cook, it was but the reappointment of territorial officers and in no case were there more than five votes cast against the successful candidate.

When, the elections over, the general assembly turned to lawmaking, there appeared to be some doubt as to its power to legislate before Congress had ratified the constitution. Was Illinois a state? The enabling act had conferred the power "to form a constitution and State government"; the people, through their representatives in the convention, had adopted a constitution; and by the election and installation of officers a state government had been formed. Congress, however, had not yet accepted the constitution and admitted the state to the Union. There is every indication that, when the legislature assembled, an extensive program of legislation was contemplated. The governor's message recommended a thorough revision of the territorial code and the enactment of laws relating to education, the salines, the courts, and the militia. The house appointed committees on military affairs and on schools, both of which were directed to report "by bill." On October 9, however, the same day the elections were completed, the senate adopted a resolution "that a committee of two be appointed by the senate to confer with such committee as may be appointed by the house of representatives, to enquire into the expediency of an adjournment of the general assembly until a time sufficient for information to be received of the ratification of the constitution by the congress of the United States; and if an adjournment is expedient, to enquire what particular important business is necessary for the general assembly to provide for before such an adjournment." In this resolution the house concurred after changing it to direct the committees to confer with the governor on the subject, an amendment which was accepted by the senate.

On the following day a report of "the committee appointed to confer with the governor on the expediency of an adjournment" was adopted by the house in the form of a resolution that the general assembly

will not, at this present session, proceed to the enaction of any laws of a public or private nature.—but it being in the opinion of this legislature, necessary that a special meeting thereof ought to be held as soon as possible after this state has been regularly admitted into the union.

Be it therefore, and it is further resolved, that the governor of the state be, and he is hereby requested, as soon as he shall ascertain that this state has been so admitted into the union, to issue his proclamation for calling a special meeting of the general assembly of the state, at a convenient time thereafter.

This resolution was at once sent in a message to the senate, which amended it by inserting after the word "nature" the words "except such as may be recommended by the joint committee appointed to confer with the governor." The house accepted the amendment. Later in the day, however, when the joint committee presented its second report, a majority in both houses was found to be opposed to any legislation whatever. The report in question recommended the enactment of a law "to organize the supreme court" but considered it "advisable to fix the first terms of the courts at a period so far distant as to give time for the ratification of the constitution to be made known." A law to continue in force the territorial laws and another "to authorize the secretary of this state to receive into his possession the books, papers and records appertaining to the office of the late secretary of the Illinois territory" were also considered necessary. The senate refused to concur in this report, by a vote of 6 to 8, while in the house it was laid on the table. On Monday, October 12, the house adopted by a vote of 16 to 10 a resolution for immediate adjournment until the first Monday in January, 1819. Two unsuccessful attempts were made the next day to take the report of the joint committee from the table, but the senate adopted the resolution for adjournment after amending it by striking out the date for reassembling. The house concurred in the amendment and on Tuesday, October 13, at 4 P.M., the first general assembly stood adjourned to await the call of the governor.

While there seems to have been little or no opposition to postponing the program of general legislation to a later session, there was clearly a difference of opinion among the members of the general assembly as to the advisability of enacting the special laws thought necessary by the joint committee. A large minority in both houses appears to have favored such legislation but the general assembly adjourned without enacting a single law. This whole proceeding is probably to be explained by the existence of a fear that Congress might not consider the constitution with its article on slavery in accord with the ordinance and the enabling act and might therefore refuse to admit the state to the Union; there seems to have been no serious doubts as to the legality of passing laws before Congress acted, if only its action should prove to be favorable.[16]

Although the general assembly placed no laws upon the statute books at this first session, it did transact some other business of importance besides the election of officers. Of special interest is the action concerning the seat of government. The opponents of the plan adopted by the convention had by no means given up hope. The proprietors of Carlyle declared in their advertisement which appeared in the *Intelligencer* during September that they felt "assured notwithstanding the late decision of the Convention, that so soon as the lower counties can reconcile it to themselves to part with the legislature from the town of Kaskaskia, the seat of government will be fixed at this place, they having been creditably informed that there is no place above, that has the advantage of navigation, and a site sufficiently eligible for a town; for in every instance where a bluff puts in, an extensive bottom is opposite." Just across the Kaskaskia from the site of Carlyle, William and Robert Morrison had laid out on paper the town of Donaldson, and in an advertisement dated October 3, 1818, they declared: "The site is high, dry and commanding, and from its central position to the population, and its manifest advantages, holds out as fair a promise of its becoming

[16] Churchill, "Annotations," no. 7. The foregoing account of the proceedings of the legislature is based on *Senate Journal*, 1 General Assembly, 1 Session, 23, 25, 29, 31, 35, 39, 40, 41; *House Journal*, 1 General Assembly, 1 Session, 7-10, 21, 23, 25-28, 32-36; *Intelligencer*, October 14, 21, 1818.

the future capital of the state, as any other that can be mentioned." [17]

The legislature, however, obeyed the instructions of the convention and drew up a petition asking Congress

to grant and give gratuitously to this state the said four sections. . . . The said General Assembly do further present; that all the Land near the Above four Sections of Land belong to the United States, And that by establishing a seat of Government on the Land so granted it would enhance the Value of the Adjoining Unsold Lands of the United States —that the United States would not be injured by such donation; but should the congress of the United States be of a contrary Opinion from the General Assembly of this state, in making the Above donation: the said General Assembly do petition the congress of the United States, to give to this state the preemption in the purchase at two dollars per Acre of the said four sections of Land.

From the phraseology of the petition, it would seem that it represented not merely a formal compliance with the directions of the convention but also the real wishes of the legislature.[18]

The petition was presented to the House of Representatives in Washington on December 7, 1818, and was referred to the Committee on Public Lands. Two days later a remonstrance counter to this petition was received and referred to the same committee. The document bore the signatures of 53 "inhabitants of the state of Illinois" and protested against the granting of the petition on the ground that "the location of the seat of government upon the Kaskaskia river, was not the act of a majority of the People." In the first place, it was maintained, "the members of the Convention were apportioned among the several counties, without any regard to the actual population of the same," with the result that the 6 members from Madison and St. Clair represented a larger population than 14 members from seven other counties. Second, the provisions for fixing the seat of government "passed the Convention by the votes of only *sixteen* members out of the *thirty-three* members elected—one member having deceased, and

[17] *Intelligencer*, September 9, October 14, 1818.

[18] *Intelligencer*, October 21, 1818; original petition in House Files, December 7, 1818.

another refusing to vote." Especial emphasis was laid upon the fact that should the petition be granted, the location of the capital could not be changed for 20 years, except by the "intricate, expensive, and inconvenient" process of amending the constitution. "By rejecting the said petition," it was asserted, "your honorable body will leave in the hands of the people of this state a power of which they never ought to be divested—that of locating their seat of government where it shall be most convenient to them, and of removing it, when the public interests shall require its removal." A majority of the signers of this remonstrance were residents or owners of lots in the town of Upper Alton, a fact which raises a suspicion that that place also was in the race for the capital.

When the general assembly came together for its second session in January, 1819, Congress had not acted on the petition for a land grant for the capital. On February 25 Senator Thomas introduced a bill for the grant, and just before the close of the session of Congress it passed both houses, receiving the approval of the President on March 3. News of this action was several weeks in reaching Illinois, however, and some of the members of the state senate were becoming impatient. On March 16 they passed, by the casting vote of the lieutenant governor, a resolution to receive proposals for gifts to the state of land and money in return for the location of the capital "on the Kaskaskia river, at some point at or above Carlyle." The house refused to consider the resolution before hearing of the action of Congress, and the receipt of information from Washington put an end to the fight. An act for the location of the grant and the removal of the capital thereto passed both houses and was approved by the governor on March 30, 1819.

Another petition to Congress drawn up by the general assembly at its first session urged certain extensions in the right of pre-emption. A resolution further instructed the Illinois senators to endeavor to procure the passage of laws establishing the office of surveyor of the public lands in the state and authorizing the sale of land in 80-acre lots. On the last day of the session reports were received from the territorial auditor and treasurer which show the financial status of the state of Illinois at the beginning of its career. In his message the governor announced that "the treasury will be found in a state of present embarrassment," and the house refused to consider a report "from the committee to procure stationary . . . till a committee of ways and means be appointed to enquire into the state of the finances." The treasurer's report showed that from December 2, 1817, to October 1, 1818, the receipts were $3,979.72, the expenditures $4,039.25, leaving a deficit of $59.53. The auditor reported that the income expected up to December from various sources amounted to $8,771.20, from which were to be paid outstanding warrants for $7,588. This would leave a possible $183.20 with which to meet the deficit and start the new government. That an important source of revenue would be available when the state was admitted, however, is indicated in a report presented to the house on October 10 from a joint committee appointed to confer with the lessees of the salines. From this it appears that the lessees of the Ohio saline were willing to pay the state $10,000 a year if allowed to sell salt at $1.50 a bushel, and $8,000 if the maximum price were fixed at $1.25. The committee favored the latter proposition but no action was taken on the report.[19]

Shortly after the convention adjourned, the constitution was printed at Kaskaskia, and on September 11, 1818, Greenup, the secretary, forwarded a copy to Henry Clay, speaker of the national House of Representatives. Congress met on November 16, more than a month after the adjournment of the first legislative session, and on the first day Speaker Clay laid the Illinois constitution before the House, where it was tabled. Three days later McLean appeared in the House and asked to be sworn in, but the

[19] *House Journal*, 1 General Assembly, 1 Session, 7, 14, 32-36; *Intelligencer*, October 14, 21, 1818. That one of the counties at least was also in an embarrassed financial condition is seen from a note which the census enumerator for Johnson County appended to his returns. After showing that the annual revenue from taxes on taverns, slaves, and horses would be $138.50, for which must be deducted $80 for sheriff's and clerk's fees, he continued: "Johnson County oweth at present $2000—which at an Average will take some more than thirty-six years to Discharge the old Debt— Poor Little Johnson But is not yet on the Parish—the territorial tax in Johnson County this year is near about 48 or 50 Dollars from the Lands Returned to me for tax as will be seen more correct when I Draw off my Book in alpabetacle [*sic*] order."

speaker, in doubt about "the propriety of administering the oath to him, in consequence of Congress not having concluded the act of admission," submitted the question to the House. Poindexter of Mississippi thought it necessary "to see, first, whether the requisitions of the act of last session were complied with; and, secondly, whether the form of government established was republican," while Pitkin of Connecticut insisted that the presence in the territory of the population required by the enabling act should first "be officially established . . . and the resolution of admission passed." Harrison of Ohio claimed that there was precedent for immediate admission, but "it was decided apparently by a large majority that the SPEAKER should not at this time administer the oath of office." This event probably hastened matters, however, for the constitution was at once referred to a select committee consisting of Anderson of Kentucky, Poindexter of Mississippi, and Hendricks of Indiana, all western men.

On the following day, November 20, the committee reported a resolution for the admission of Illinois "on an equal footing with the original States." The preamble declared the constitution and state government framed by the convention to be republican and "in conformity to the principles of the articles of compact" of the Ordinance of 1787. After the resolution had been read twice, the question of population was again raised, this time by Spencer of New York, who wished to know if any documentary evidence on the subject had been transmitted. Anderson replied for the committee that the preamble of the constitution stated "that the requisitions of the act of Congress had been complied with . . . the committee," he said, "had considered that evidence sufficient; and he had, in addition, himself seen, in the newspapers, evidence sufficient to satisfy him of the fact, that the population did amount to forty thousand souls, the number required." The resolution "was then ordered to be engrossed for a third reading." [20]

[20] *Annals of Congress,* 15 Congress, 2 Session, 1:296-298. The resolution is printed in the appendix to the *Annals of Congress,* 15 Congress, 2 Session, 2:2548. Senator Edwards had asked Governor Bond for a statement of the population as returned to the convention. Washburne, *Edwards Papers,* **146.**

The principal debate took place in the House on November 23, when the resolution came up for final action. As a prelude to the controversy over the admission of Missouri, which opened a few months later, this debate and the vote which followed have an importance even greater for national history than for the history of Illinois—an importance which has not, as a rule, been recognized by historians.

The discussion was opened by Tallmadge of New York, the same man who was to lead the fight against the admission of Missouri with a constitution permitting slavery. Although he was inclined to demand further evidence that Illinois had the requisite population, he preferred to rest his opposition upon another point. "The principle of slavery, if not adopted in the constitution, was at least not sufficiently prohibited." After citing the provision against slavery in the Ordinance of 1787, he declared that:

The sixth article of the constitution of the new State of Illinois, in each of its three sections . . . contravened this stipulation, either in the letter or the spirit. These sections he separately examined, as to their construction and bearing, and felt himself constrained to come to the conclusion that they embraced a complete recognition of existing slavery, if not provisions for its future introduction and toleration; particularly in the passage wherein they permit the hiring of slaves, the property of non-residents, for any number of years consecutively. If Congress would observe in good faith the terms of the convention, he said, they were bound, under this circumstance, to reject the constitution of Illinois, or at least this feature of it.

He had no desire, the speaker said, "to invade the rights of the slaveholding States, or to assail their prerogatives, he believed they were equally sensible with him of the evils of slavery, and did what they could to control and regulate them." After referring to the excellent provisions of the Indiana constitution relative to slavery, he declared: "Our interest and our honor . . . calls on us rigidly to insist on the observance of good faith under the article of the ordinance I have referred to, so far as that no involuntary service be permitted to be recognised in the constitution of any State to be formed out of that territory." [21]

[21] The debate is reported in the *Annals of Congress,* 15 Congress, 2 Session, 1:305-311. It is summarized in the *Intelligencer,* December 23, 1818.

In replying to Tallmadge, Poindexter (whether deliberately or
not it is impossible to say) misrepresented the facts. After expressing his concurrence in the "solicitude to expel from our
country, whenever practicable, anything like slavery," he declared

that the article on the subject of slaves was almost literally copied from
the constitution of Ohio into that of Illinois. The third section of the
article in question, in the latter, was the only variation, and the necessity of that additional provision would be obvious to any gentleman who
would examine and reflect upon the subject. By an antecedent law of
the Territorial government, all persons, slaves or under indenture, in the
Territory, were required to be registered, as the only way in which they
could be discriminated from fugitives, &c. The constitution directs that
their children also shall be registered, that they may be secure of enjoy-
ing their freedom, when by the constitution they become entitled. From
their color, (being *prima facie* slaves in other States,) was it not more
secure to the freedom of the people of color, that their births, parentage,
&c., should be recorded in the new State, than otherwise? So far from
constituting an objection to it, Mr. P. said, he considered this a valuable part of the constitution of Illinois.

The speaker also maintained, with more truth, that "it would be
found impracticable, after admitting the independence of a State,
to prevent it from framing or shaping its constitution as it
thought proper. As to a constitution like that of Indiana, prohibiting the introduction of an amendment to it, of whatever nature,
if the people were to form a convention to-morrow, that provision
would be of no force: the whole power would be with the people,
whom, in their sovereign capacity, no provision of that nature
can control. Nor would Congress prevent them."

Anderson, another member of the committee, not only agreed
with Poindexter, but maintained that there was nothing binding
about the so-called articles of compact in the ordinance, since
"the people of the Northwestern Territory" were not "represented at all, nor consulted on the occasion." In his opinion
"there was nothing unconstitutional, in any view, in Congress
accepting what the people of Illinois have done, if they thought
proper; since the consent of the two contracting parties (sup-
posing the ordinance to be a compact) would thus be given."
"Are we," asked Tallmadge in reply, "to be drawn into a discussion of slavery, its merits and demerits, on abstract prin-

ciples? He would not enter into such a discussion; but must persist in stating it as his opinion, that the interest, honor, and faith of the nation, required it scrupulously to guard against slavery's passing into a territory where they have power to prevent its entrance." Nor would he admit that a state could change its constitution at will. He believed that it would "cease, by the very act, to be a component part of the Union" should it "violate the condition on which it was admitted."

William Henry Harrison, "as a Representative of Ohio," protested against this doctrine. The "people of that State," he said, "were fully aware of their privileges, and would never come to this House, or to the State of New York, for permission so to alter their constitution as to admit the introduction of slavery, the object of the gentleman's abhorrence, as, said Mr. H., it is of mine. They had entered into no compact which had shorn the people of their sovereign authority . . . he sincerely wished that Illinois had either emancipated its slaves, or followed the example of Indiana," and left "the question relating to this description of property . . . for the decision of the courts of justice. . . . In regard to the supposed compact, however, and its efficacy, Mr. H. said, he had always considered it a dead letter."

The yeas and nays having been requested by Livermore of New Hampshire, who was opposed to the resolution, the vote was taken and the resolution carried 117 to 34. The followers of Tallmadge in this vote were few as compared to those who supported him in the Missouri contest three months later, due probably to the fact that the issue was not so clear. It is significant, however, that only one of the 34, Reed of Maryland, voted against the Tallmadge amendment to the enabling act for Missouri. With the exception of Reed, all of those who opposed the Illinois resolution were from the five New England states, New York, New Jersey, and Pennsylvania. They included a majority of the representatives from New England. Clearly the opposition to the admission of Illinois was due to the provisions relative to slavery in the constitution and clearly, also, the extension of slavery was already a sectional issue in the United States in November, 1818.

The resolution for the admission of Illinois was received in the Senate on November 25 and was referred to the Committee on Public Lands. The following day the committee "reported the same without amendment." It was considered in committee of the whole on November 28 and 30, but if there was any debate, it was not reported. On December 1 the resolution passed the Senate without a division, and on the third it received the approval of the President. Illinois was now a state in the Union. The next day "NINIAN EDWARDS and JESSE B. THOMAS, respectively appointed Senators by the Legislature of the State of Illinois . . . took their seats in the Senate." In the House, "MR. JOHN McLEAN . . . took his seat as the Representative of the State of Illinois." [22]

By December 16, news of the action taken in the House had been received in Illinois. That news allayed any fear there had been that the state might not be admitted. In announcing it, the editors of the *Intelligencer* commented: "As the senate will act speedily on this subject, we may expect early information of our complete emancipation from territorial government." That information arrived in time for the governor to issue on December 22 the following proclamation:

Whereas information has been received that by a resolution of the Senate and House of Representatives of the United States of America in congress Assembled the State of Illinois has been declared to be one of the United States of America and has been admitted into the Union on an equal footing with the original States in all respects whatever

Therefore I Shadrach Bond Governor of the said State, by virtue of the power vested in me by the constitution do appoint the third monday in the month of January next for a meeting of the General Assembly of said state and I do hereby require all the members of each branch thereof to convene on said day at Kaskaskia the seat of Government.

In testimony whereof I have hereunto set my hand and private seal (there being no State seal provided) this twenty second day of December in the year of our Lord one thousand eight hundred and eighteen and of the Independence of the United States of America the forty-third.

[22] *Annals of Congress,* 15 Congress, 2 Session, 1:23, 26, 31, 32, 38, 342. The proclamation was printed in the *Intelligencer,* December 23, 1818. It is here copied from the manuscript Executive Register, secretary of state's office.

The figures in the accompanying table [p. 319], except where otherwise indicated, are the result of a careful checking up of extant schedules. Most of the commissioners who attempted to foot up the totals made errors of addition. The census of Franklin County had not been taken when the secretary made his report in June. The enumerator for Madison County appended to his schedule the following statements: "I beg leave further to state from good information that there are at

Fort Crawford	680 Souls
Fort Armstrong	150 Souls
Fort Edwards	70 "
do. Clark	80 "

Makeing in the whole 5466 Souls within the boundury of Madison County."

These 980 reputed inhabitants are not included in the schedule total but are included in the secretary's report and presumably in the final report to the convention. The schedule for St. Clair County has been burned in part and the figures given represent only what remains intact. Italics are used to indicate incomplete totals due to missing or incomplete schedules. The total of the secretary's report is a correct addition of the figures and is ten less than his total of the same figures as given in *Intelligencer*, June 17, 1818. The report to the convention is printed in the Illinois State Historical Society, *Journal*, 6:359.

JEFFERSON-LEMEN COMPACT

Edward Coles, in 1865, wrote that slavery "formed a prominent topic in the political discussions of Illinois previous to its becoming a State" and "at a very early period in the settlement of Illinois, the question was warmly agitated by zealous advocates and opponents of slavery." Letter quoted by Lippincott in his "Early Days in Madison County," no. 28.

The claim has been made that James Lemen, a Virginian, having made a secret compact with Jefferson to work for the exclusion of slavery in Illinois, came out for that purpose in 1786 and founded the settlement of New Design. During the Indiana period he is said to have exerted himself to prevent the success of the advocates of the introduction of slavery. From 1796 on, Lemen "was active in the promotion of Baptist churches and a Baptist Association." In 1808 he was licensed as a preacher and in the following year led a movement which resulted in the disruption of the association on the slavery question and the organization of "Bethel Baptist Church" on a strict antislavery basis. A document purporting to be a copy of an account written by Reverend John Mason Peck in 1851 states that the members of this church "formed what they called 'The Illinois Anti-Slavery League,' and it was this body that conducted the anti-slavery contest. It always kept one of its members and several of its friends in the Territorial Legislature, and five years before the constitutional election in 1818 it had fifty resident agents—men of like sympathies—in the several settlements throughout the territory quietly at work, and the masterly manner in which they did their duty was shown by a poll which they made of the voters some few weeks before the election, which, on their side only varied a few votes from the official count after the election." MacNaul, *Jefferson-Lemen Compact*, 7-25, 36.

The authenticity of this document and of all the so-called "Lemen family notes," only transcripts of which appear to be in existence, is very doubtful; and no other evidence has been found of the existence of an "Illinois Anti-Slavery League" in the territorial period.

LEMEN AND COOK

The claim has been made in a document purporting to have been written by Reverend John Mason Peck in 1857 that the plan was first suggested by Reverend James Lemen, Sr., reputed to have been an influential champion of freedom during the territorial period. It is said that he "had a government surveyor make a map showing the great advantages and gave them to Nathaniel Pope." MacNaul, *Jefferson-Lemen Compact*, 37-38, 55. Until more authentic evidence is presented the credit for the amendment must remain with Pope. If the slavery question was a factor in the matter, it is quite possible that Pope's nephew, Daniel Pope Cook, may have had a hand in it. As early as February 4, 1818, in a communication over the signature "A republican" in the *Intelligencer* he took a strong antislavery position, not merely with reference to Illinois, but for the nation as a whole; and in the issue of April 1, he presented a strong argument against the expediency or legality of providing for the toleration of slavery in the new constitution. Cook may have conferred with Pope in Washington in February or March, 1818, for, on January 6, he announced his intention of leaving Kaskaskia in the course of 15 or 20 days for Richmond, Washington, Philadelphia, and possibly New York. He could not have reached Washington, however, before the date of Pope's letter announcing his intention to work for the northern extension.

ABSTRACT OF THE CENSUS OF 1818

COUNTIES	ORIGINAL CENSUS							SUPPLEMENTARY CENSUS						Combined Total in Schedules	Report to Convention
	Heads of Families	Free White Males of Age	All Other White Inhabitants	Free People of Color	Servants or Slaves	Total in Schedules	Report of the Secretary in June	Heads of Families	Free White Males of Age	All Other White Inhabitants	Free People of Color	Servants or Slaves	Total in Schedules		
Bond	212	264	1105	0	15	1384	1382							1384	1398
Crawford	397	422	1549	78	20	2069	2074	121	179	698	0	0	877	2946	2839
Edwards							1948	42	71	227	0	0	298	298	2243
Franklin	171	218	943	52	15	1228								1228	1281
Gallatin	541	742	2397	83	218	3440	3256	75	167	250	9	85	511	3951	3849
Jackson	202	250	986	0	49	1285	1295	38	75	28	0	4	107	1392	1619
Johnson	117	118	535	1	24	678	678							678	767
Madison	717	1012	3393	34	77	4516	5456							4516	6303
Monroe	227	317	1007	6	41	1371	1358							1371	1517
Pope	322	399	1481	0	64	1944	1975							1944	2069
Randolph							2939	16	23	20	0	2	45	45	2974
St. Clair	497	683	2422	29	97	3231	4519							3231	5039
Union	392	439	2020	0	33	2492	2484							2492	2709
Washington	249	281	1382	19	23	1705	1707	16	26	82	0	5	113	1818	1819
White	572	720	2751	11	57	3539	3539							3539	3832
Totals	4616	5865	21971	313	733	28882	34610	308	541	1305	9	96	1951	30833	40258

No attempt has been made to make this a complete bibliography of the subject. It is primarily a list of works referred to in the notes, and is included for the purpose of enabling the reader to identify those works and to determine the editions used.

MANUSCRIPTS

American Fur Company Letter Book, 1816-20. Manuscript at Mackinac. Photostatic copy in Illinois Historical Survey.

Auditor of Public Accounts, Springfield, Land Office Records.

Chicago Historical Society Manuscripts: vols. 49, 50, 51, Edwards papers; vols. 52, 53, E. K. Kane papers.

Deed Record, A, in Pope County.

Draper Manuscripts, 1816-20. Originals in library of State Historical Society of Wisconsin. Photostatic copies of documents used in Illinois Historical Survey.

Eddy Manuscripts, Shawneetown, Illinois. Transcripts in Illinois Historical Survey.

George Knight to Charles Knight, June 21, 1818. Transcript in Illinois Historical Survey.

House Files. Archives of the United States House of Representatives, Washington. Photostatic copies of documents used in Illinois Historical Survey.

Indian Office Papers. Archives of the United States Indian Office, Washington. Photostatic copies of documents used in Illinois Historical Survey.

Messinger Manuscripts. Transcripts in Illinois Historical Survey.

Secretary of State, Springfield, Census Schedules; Correspondence; Executive Files, 1790-1821; Executive Register, 1818-32; manuscript journal of the legislative council, 1817-18; Miscellaneous Assembly Papers.

United States State Department, Bureau of Indexes and Archives, Miscellaneous Letters; Bureau of Rolls and Library, Papers and Records. Photostatic copies of documents used in Illinois Historical Survey.

OTHER SOURCES

Alvord, Clarence W. (ed.), *Cahokia Records* (Illinois State Historical Library, *Collections*, vol. 2. Springfield, 1907).

Alvord, Clarence W., *Illinois: The Origins* (*Military Tract Papers*, no. 3. Pontiac, 1910).

Alvord, Clarence W. (ed.), *Laws of the Territory of Illinois, 1809-1811* (Illinois State Historical Library, *Bulletin 1*, no. 2. Springfield, 1906).

American State Papers, 38 volumes (Washington, 1832-61).

Andreas, A. T., *History of Chicago, from the Earliest Period to the Present Time*, 3 volumes (Chicago, 1884).

Annals of Congress, 42 volumes (Washington, 1834-56).

Babcock, Rufus (ed.), *Memoir of John Mason Peck, D.D.* (Philadelphia, 1864).

Bailey, John R., *Mackinac, Formerly Michilimackinac* (Lansing, 1895).

Bancroft, Hubert H., *History of the Northwest Coast*, 2 volumes (San Francisco, 1884).

Biographical Review of Johnson, Massac, Pope, and Hardin Counties, Illinois (Chicago, 1893).

Birkbeck, Morris, *Letters from Illinois* (Philadelphia, 1818).

Birkbeck, Morris, *Notes on a Journey in America, from the Coast of Virginia to the Territory of Illinois* (London, 1818).

Blair, Emma H. (ed.), *The Indian Tribes of the Upper Mississippi Valley and Region of the Great Lakes as Described by Nicholas Perrot, French Commandant in the Northwest; Bacqueville de la Potherie, French Royal Commissioner to Canada; Morrell Marston, American Army Officer; and Thomas Forsyth, United States Agent at Fort Armstrong*, 2 volumes (Cleveland, 1911-12).

Boggess, Arthur C., *The Settlement of Illinois, 1778-1830* (Chicago Historical Society, *Collections*, vol. 5. Chicago, 1908).

Brown, Samuel R., *The Western Gazetteer; or Emigrant's Directory, Containing a Geographical Description of the Western States and Territories* (Auburn, New York, 1817).

Brown, William H., "Early History of Illinois," in *Fergus Historical Series*, no. 14.

Brown, William H., "An Historical Sketch of the Early Movement in Illinois for the Legalization of Slavery," in *Fergus Historical Series*, no. 4 (Chicago, 1876).

Buck, Solon J., *Travel and Description 1765-1865; Together with a List of County Histories, Atlases, and Biographical Collections and a List of Territorial and State Laws* (Illinois State Historical Library, *Collections*, vol. 9. Springfield, 1914).

Chittenden, Hiram M., *The American Fur Trade of the Far West. A History of the Pioneer Trading Posts and Early Fur Companies of the Missouri Valley and the Rocky Mountains and of the Overland Commerce with Santa Fé*, 3 volumes (New York, 1902).

Churchill, George, "Annotations" on Rev. Thomas Lippincott's "Early Days in Madison County," published in the *Alton Telegraph* in 1865. Scrapbook in possession of W. T. Norton of Alton. Transcripts in Illinois Historical Survey.

Dana, Edmund, *Geographical Sketches of the Western Country; Designed for Emigrants and Settlers: Being the Result of Extensive Researches and Remarks* (Cincinnati, 1819).

Darby, William, *The Emigrant's Guide to the Western and South-western States and Territories: Comprising a Geographical and Statistical Description of the States of Louisiana, Mississippi, Tennessee, Kentucky, and Ohio;—the Territories of Alabama, Missouri, Illinois, and Michigan* (New York, 1818).

Dowrie, George W., *The Development of Banking in Illinois, 1817-1863* (University of Illinois, *Studies in the Social Sciences,* vol. 2, no. 4. Urbana, 1913).

Dunn, Jacob P., Jr., *Indiana, a Redemption from Slavery* (American Commonwealth series, Boston, 1905).

Edwards, Ninian W., *History of Illinois, from 1778 to 1833; and Life and Times of Ninian Edwards* (Springfield, 1870).

Edwardsville Spectator, 1819-26 (Edwardsville, Illinois). Files in Library of Congress. Photostatic copies in Illinois Historical Survey.

Erwin, Milo, *History of Williamson County, Illinois, from the Earliest Times, down to the Present, 1876* (Marion, Illinois, 1876).

Fearon, Henry B., *Sketches of America. A Narrative of a Journey of Five Thousand Miles Through the Eastern and Western States of America* (London, 1819).

Flower, George, *History of the English Settlement in Edwards County, Illinois. With Preface and Foot-notes by E. B. Washburne* (Chicago Historical Society, *Collections,* vol. 1. Chicago, 1882).

Ford, Thomas, *A History of Illinois, from Its Commencement as a State in 1818 to 1847* (Chicago, 1854).

Harris, Norman D., *History of Negro Slavery in Illinois and of the Slavery Agitation in That State* (Chicago, 1906).

Harris, William T., *Remarks Made During a Tour Through the United States of America in the Years, 1817, 1818, and 1819* (London, 1821).

History of Gallatin, Saline, Hamilton, Franklin, and Williamson Counties, Illinois (Chicago, 1887).

History of Madison County, Illinois (Edwardsville, Illinois, 1882).

History of Marion and Clinton Counties, Illinois (Philadelphia, 1881).

History of St. Clair County, Illinois (Philadelphia, 1881).

History of Wayne and Clay Counties, Illinois (Chicago, 1884).

Hodge, Frederick W. (ed.), *Handbook of American Indians North of Mexico,* 2 volumes (Bureau of American Ethnology, *Bulletin 30.* Washington, 1907-10).

Hubbard, Gurdon S., *The Autobiography of Gurdon Saltonstall Hubbard, Pa-pa-ma-ta-be "The Swift Walker"* (Chicago, 1911).

Hubbard, Gurdon S., *Incidents and Events in the Life of Gurdon Saltonstall Hubbard. Collected from Personal Narrations and Other Sources and Arranged by His Nephew, Henry E. Hamilton* (Chicago, 1888).

Hurlbut, Henry H., *Chicago Antiquities: Comprising Original Items and Relations, Letters, Extracts, and Notes, Pertaining to Early Chicago* (Chicago, 1881).

Illinois, *Bluebook,* 1905 (Springfield, 1906); 1913-14 (Danville, 1914).

Illinois, "Journal of the Convention, 1818." The only known copy, in the office of the secretary of state, Springfield, contains pp. 3 to 72 inclusive only, the title page and a few pages at the end having been torn out. It is reprinted, with an introduction by Richard V. Carpenter, in Illinois State Historical Society, *Journal,* 6:327-425.

Illinois, *Journal of the House of Representatives,* 1818 (Kaskaskia, 1818); 1819 (Kaskaskia, 1819).

Illinois, *Journal of the Senate,* 1818 (Kaskaskia, 1818); 1819 (Kaskaskia, 1819).

Illinois, *Laws,* 1819 (Kaskaskia, 1819); 1820-21 (Vandalia, 1821).

Illinois Emigrant, December, 1818–September, 1819 (Shawneetown, Illinois). [Continued as *Illinois Gazette,* 1819-30.] Files in Library of Congress and American Antiquarian Society, Worcester, Massachusetts. Photostatic copies in Illinois Historical Survey.

Illinois Gazette. See *Illinois Emigrant.*

Illinois Intelligencer. See *Western Intelligencer.*

Illinois State Historical Library, *Collections,* 11 volumes (Springfield, 1903-16).

Illinois State Historical Society, *Journal,* 8 volumes (Springfield, 1908-16).

Illinois State Historical Society, *Transactions,* 1900-1915, 16 volumes (Illinois State Historical Library, *Publications,* nos. 4, 6-17, 19-21. Springfield, 1900-1916).

Illinois Territory, *A Law Establishing a Supreme Court and Documents* (Kaskaskia, 1814).

Illinois Territory, *Laws,* 1812 (Russelville, Kentucky, 1813); *Pope's Digest,* 1813-14, 2 volumes (Kaskaskia, 1815); 1815-16 (Kaskaskia, 1816); 1816-17 (Kaskaskia, 1817); 1817-18 (Kaskaskia, 1818). The last three are available in page-for-page reprints (Springfield, 1898).

Illustrated Encyclopedia and Atlas Map of Madison County, Illinois (St. Louis, 1873).

Indiana Historical Society, *Publications,* 5 volumes (Indianapolis, 1897-1915).

Indiana Territory, *Laws,* 1805 (Vincennes, n.d.); 1807 (Vincennes, 1807).

Intelligencer. See *Western Intelligencer.*

James, Edmund J. (ed.), *The Territorial Records of Illinois* (Illinois State Historical Library, *Publications,* no. 3. Springfield, 1901).

Kapper, Charles J., *Indian Affairs, Laws, and Treaties*, 2 volumes (Washington, 1904).

Kinzie, Mrs. John H., *Wau-Bun, the Early Day in the Northwest* (Philadelphia, 1873).

Lansden, John M., *A History of the City of Cairo, Illinois* (Chicago, 1910).

Leaton, James, *History of Methodism in Illinois, from 1793 to 1832* (Cincinnati, 1883).

Lippincott, Thomas, "Conflict of the Century," published in the *Henry Weekly Courier*, 1860. Transcripts in Illinois Historical Survey.

Lippincott, Thomas, "Early Days in Madison County," published in the *Alton Telegraph*, [1864]-65. Transcripts in Illinois Historical Survey.

McIlwain, Charles H. (ed.), *An Abridgment of the Indian Affairs Contained in Four Folio Volumes Transacted in the Colony of New York from the Year 1678 to the Year 1756. By Peter Wraxall* (Cambridge, 1915).

MacNaul, Willard C., *Jefferson-Lemen Compact. The Relations of Thomas Jefferson and James Lemen in the Exclusion of Slavery from Illinois and the Northwest Territory with Related Documents, 1781-1818* (Chicago, 1915).

Mason, Edward G. (ed.), *Early Chicago and Illinois* (Chicago Historical Society, *Collections*, vol. 4. Chicago, 1890).

Mason, Richard L., *Narrative of Richard Lee Mason in the Pioneer West* (New York, [1915]).

Mathews, Lois K., *The Expansion of New England. The Spread of New England Settlement and Institutions to the Mississippi River, 1620-1865* (Boston, 1909).

Michelson, Truman, "Contributions to Algonquian Grammar," in *American Anthropologist*, 15:470-477.

Minnesota Historical Society, *Collections*, 15 volumes (St. Paul, 1850-1915).

Morse, Jedidiah, *A Report to the Secretary of War of the United States, on Indian Affairs, Comprising a Narrative of a Tour* (New Haven, 1822).

Moses, John, *Illinois Historical and Statistical, Comprising the Essential Facts of Its Planting and Growth as a Province, County, Territory, and State*, 2 volumes (Chicago, 1892).

Niles' Weekly Register, 75 volumes (Baltimore, 1811-49).

Ogg, Frederic A. (ed.), *Personal Narrative of Travels in Virginia, Maryland, Pennsylvania, Ohio, Indiana, Kentucky; and of a Residence in the Illinois Territory: 1817-1818. By Elias Pym Fordham* (Cleveland, 1906).

Patterson, Robert W., "Early Society in Southern Illinois," in *Fergus Historical Series*, no. 14.

Perrin, William H. (ed.), *History of Alexander, Union, and Pulaski Counties, Illinois* (Chicago, 1883).

Perrin, William H. (ed.), *History of Crawford and Clark Counties, Illinois* (Chicago, 1883).

Perrin, William H. (ed.), *History of Jefferson County, Illinois* (Chicago, 1883).

Pope's Digest. See Illinois Territory, *Laws.*

Preble, George H., *A Chronological History of the Origin and Development of Steam Navigation, 1543-1882* (Philadelphia, 1883).

Quaife, Milo M., *Chicago and the Old Northwest 1673-1835. A Study of the Evolution of the Northwestern Frontier, Together with a History of Fort Dearborn* (Chicago, 1913).

Reynolds, John, *My Own Times, Embracing also, the History of My Life* (Illinois, 1855).

Reynolds, John, *The Pioneer History of Illinois Containing the Discovery in 1673 and the History of the Country to the Year 1818, When the State Government Was Organized* (Chicago, 1887).

Royce, Charles C. (ed.), *Indian Land Cessions in the United States* (Bureau of American Ethnology, *Eighteenth Annual Report*, pt. 2. Washington, 1899).

Schoolcraft, Henry R., *Personal Memoirs of a Residence of Thirty Years with the Indian Tribes on the American Frontiers: With Brief Notices of Passing Events, Facts, and Opinions, A.D. 1812 to A.D. 1842* (Philadelphia, 1851).

Schoolcraft, Henry R., *Summary Narrative of an Exploratory Expedition to the Sources of the Mississippi River, in 1820: Resumed and Completed, by the Discovery of Its Origin in Itasca Lake, in 1832* (Philadelphia, 1855).

Schultz, Christian, *Travels on an Inland Voyage Through the States of New York, Pennsylvania, Virginia, Ohio, Kentucky and Tennessee, and Through the Territories of Indiana, Louisiana, Mississippi and New Orleans*, 2 volumes (New York, 1810).

Scott, Franklin W., *Newspapers and Periodicals of Illinois, 1814-1879* (Illinois State Historical Library, *Collections*, vol. 6. Springfield, 1910).

Seybert, Adam, *Statistical Annals Embracing Views of the Population, Commerce, Navigation . . . of the United States of America Founded on Official Documents 1789-1818* (Philadelphia, 1818).

Shoemaker, Floyd C., *Missouri's Struggle for Statehood, 1804-1821* (Jefferson City, 1916).

Smith, William H. (ed.), *St. Clair Papers. The Life and Public Services of Arthur St. Clair, Soldier of the Revolutionary War; President of the Continental Congress; and Governor of the North Western Territory with His Correspondence and Other Papers* (Cincinnati, 1882).

Snyder, John F., *Adam W. Snyder, and His Period in Illinois History, 1817-1824* (Virginia, Illinois, 1906).

Snyder, John F., "Forgotten Statesmen of Illinois. Conrad Will," in Illinois State Historical Society, *Transactions*, 1905, pp. 349-377.

Spectator. See *Edwardsville Spectator.*

Table of Post-Offices in the United States, with the Names of the Post-Masters, and Counties and States in Which They Are Situated, and the Distances from the City of Washington (Washington, 1817).

Thorpe, Francis N. (ed.), *The Federal and State Constitutions, Colonial Charters, and Other Organic Laws of the States, Territories, and Colonies Now or Heretofore Forming the United States of America,* 7 volumes (Washington, 1909).

Thwaites, Reuben G. (ed.), *Early Western Travels, 1748-1846, a Series of Annotated Reprints of Some of the Best and Rarest Contemporary Volumes of Travel, Descriptive of the Aborigines and Social and Economic Conditions in the Middle and Far West, During the Period of Early American Settlement,* 32 volumes (Cleveland, 1904-07).

Treat, Payson J., *The National Land System, 1785-1820* (New York, 1910).

United States Public Documents, *Executive Documents*, 16 Congress, 2 Session, no. 8; *House Documents*, 15 Congress, 2 Session, vol. 1, no. 1; vol. 2, no. 46; *House Documents*, 26 Congress, 1 Session, vol. 7, no. 262; *House Journal*, 15 Congress, 1 Session; 2 Session; *Senate Journal*, 15 Congress, 1 Session.

United States, *Reports of the Secretary of the Treasury,* 2 volumes (Washington, 1828-29).

United States, *Statutes at Large,* 38 volumes (Boston and Washington, 1850-1915).

Walker, Charles A. (ed.), *History of Macoupin County, Illinois,* 2 volumes (Chicago, 1911).

Washburne, Elihu B. (ed.), *The Edwards Papers; Being a Portion of the Collection of the Letters, Papers, and Manuscripts of Ninian Edwards* (Chicago Historical Society, *Collections*, vol. 3. Chicago, 1884).

Washburne, Elihu B., *Sketch of Edward Coles, Second Governor of Illinois, and of the Slavery Struggle of 1823-4* (Chicago, 1882).

Western Intelligencer, 1816-18 (Kaskaskia, Illinois). [Continued as *Illinois Intelligencer,* 1818-19.] Files in Mercantile Library, St. Louis. Photostatic copies in Illinois Historical Survey.

Wisconsin Historical Society, *Collections,* 23 volumes (Madison, 1855-1916).

Woollen, William W., *Biographical and Historical Sketches of Early Indiana* (Indianapolis, 1883).

88-91, 317, 319; Monroe County, 83-84, 319; R. Morrison's report on, 189; ordered, 61-62, 219-220; pioneers' names taken from, 98, 101; Pope County, 75, 319; Randolph County, 80-83, 319; St. Clair County, 84-87, 319; and statehood movement, 214, 272-273; Union County, 77-79, 319; Washington County, 87-88, 319; White County, 69-71, 319
Chambers, Benjamin: signed 1805 petition, 188
Chambers, Lieutenant Colonel —: commander at Fort Crawford, 30
Chandonnais, Jean Baptiste: trader at Chicago, 31
Cheek, J.: advertised school, 166
Chester: Randolph County seat, 82
Chicago: agents at, 16-17, 20, 31; British influence at, 24; Deschamps' brigade at, 37; factory at, 5, 21; and fur trade, 21, 22-23, 26, 31; importance as lake port, 225, 226; military establishment at, 13, 16; Potawatomi near, 6
Chicago River: Conant and Mack's establishment near, 31; Deschamps' brigade on branch of, 37
Chippewa Indians: annuity to, 17; ceded land, 42, 43; W. Clark to conclude treaty with, 13; location of, 6
Chouteau, Auguste: and Indian treaties, 13, 43
Cincinnati: first Northwest Territory legislature at, 184; Fordham at, 109n
"A citizen": re slavery, 248-249, 256, 297
Claiborne, Thomas: on committee considering statehood memorial, 221

Clark, Fort: population at, 241, 317; post at, 16
Clark, George Rogers, 45, 93; occupied French villages, 97, 180
Clark, William: and Indian treaty, 13
Clark County, Ill., 64; settlement in, 66
Clark County, Ind.: opposed indenture law, 187; representatives did not sign 1805 petition, 188
Clay, Henry: laid Illinois constitution before House, 311
Clay County: formation of, 65, 67; settlement in, 67-68
Clinton County: Carlyle in, 289; formation of, 86; settlement in, 86
Clothing: French, 94, 95; Indian, 8; pioneer, 136-137
Coles, Edward, 123; characterization of, 242-243; governor, 242; probably "Agis," 242-245; re slavery in political discussions, 317; visited Kaskaskia, 243, 262
Columbia, 167
Comegys, John G.: failure of Cairo scheme of, 79
"Common Sense": re common law, 255
Compton, Levi: vote on slavery article, 281
Conant, Shubael. *See* Conant and Mack
Conant and Mack: establishment on Chicago River branch, 31
Connecticut: Daggett of, 229; emigrants from, 99; Pitkin of, 312
Cook, Daniel: re Bond's friendship for Edwards, 303; candidate for Congress, 233, 294-298; estimate of French population, 93n; interested in land, 155; interested in statehood movement, 209-214, 220-221, 232, 238; re Kane's influence, 304; laid out Waterloo,

of, 300; census in, 241, 260, 264, 317, 319; conditions for raising stock in, 143; convention candidates opposed to slavery, 256; convention delegates of, 228, 260, 280, 281, 285; Cook's interest in land in, 155; delegation from wanted franchise extended, 285; description and population of, 88-91; Edwardsville county seat of, 90, 145; establishment of, 90; Gilham of, 203n; large land holdings in, 57; Lofton of, 217; one representative assigned to, 197; one senator apportioned to, 285; opposed slavery, 261; opposition to Bond in, 299; Prickett of, 280, 281; Stephenson of, 280, 281; subscriptions to Edwardsville bank from, 150. *See also* Calhoun County; Greene County; Jersey County, Macoupin County

Malden: British distributed presents at, 14, 17

Mangham, John K.: death of, 267

Manufactures: of Indians, 8-9; of Kaskaskia, 82; of pioneers, 134-137, 148; trade encouraged by eastern, 148-149

Marietta: Northwest Territory seat of government, 182

Marion County: formation of, 65, 67; settlement in, 68

Marston, Major Morrell: re Indians, 7-8, 24-25

Maryland: emigrants from, 99, 100; Reed of, 315; Sprigg in, 205

Mary's River, 154

Mason, James: advertised for laborers, 144-145

Mason, Richard Lee, 83, 85; re experiences on early road, 124-127; re towns near Alton, 91

Mason and Dixon's line: settlers from south of, 99

Massac, Fort: Kaskaskia road to, 119

Massac County: formation of, 75, 76

Massachusetts: emigrants from, 99; Whitman of, 221

Matheny, Charles: candidate for judge, 305; opposed concessions to judges, 205; opposed slavery, 261n; positions held, 204n, 305; stand on indenture law, 216-217

Meachan, —, 155

Meigs, —, 155

Meisenheimer precinct, 78

Menard, Pierre, 96-97; favored advance to second grade, 186; and lieutenant governorship, 286, 299, 300; political activity of, 203; positions held, 17, 19, 187, 303; refused to join any faction, 206; resigned from Indiana council, 191; signed 1805 and 1807 petitions, 188, 190; vote on indenture law, 217

Menominee Indians: W. Clark to conclude treaty with, 13

Messenger, John. *See* Messinger, John

Messick, Dr. —, 176

Messinger, John, 270; interested in speculation, 292; member of Edwards faction, 292; positions held, 191, 280, 301; re religious observances, 178; vote on slavery article, 280. *See also* Pope, Messenger and Stephenson

Methodists: influence of, 174, 175-178

Metropolis, 76

Miami River, 14

Michigamea Indians: disappearance of, 5

Michigan, Lake, 14, 34, 37, 42-43, 182, 222; American Fur Com-

Vincennes, 67, 148; Vincennes-Kaskaskia, 87
Roberts, Thomas: votes on slavery article, 281
Rock and Cave, 176, 177
Rock Island, 7; Fort Armstrong on, 14, 16, 24
Rock River: Crafts sent trading outfits to, 31; G. Hubbard visited, 38; Indians on, 6
Ronalds, —: re plans for English settlement, 115
Rutherford, —, 124, 125, 126
Russellville: fort at, 66
Russia: Coles sent to, 243

St. Charles (S. Charles): mail route to, 129
St. Clair, William: signed 1796 petition, 183
St. Clair County, Ill., 62n, 88, 121, 228, 236, 237, 270, 272, 309; Amos of, 217; Belleville superseded Cahokia as county seat, 85; Bradsby of, 204n, 205, 213; census in, 264, 317, 319; convention delegates of, 227, 260, 280; courts in, 197-198; demand for roads in, 119; description and population of, 84-87; Edwards advertised land in, 154, 155; issues in, 203; Kinney of, 301; large land holdings in, 56-57; Lemen of, 280; Matheny of, 204n, 205; Messinger of, 280, 301; R. Moore of, 301; W. Moore of, 239; one senator apportioned to, 285; opposed slavery, 261; subscriptions to Edwardsville bank from, 150; two representatives assigned to, 197; vote for governor in, 299. *See also* Clinton County; Monroe County; Washington County
St. Clair County, Ind.: Biggs of, 186; Bond of, 186; for division

of Indiana, 192; and 1800 petition, 192; and 1805 petition, 188; R. Morrison re population of, 189; voted against advance to second grade, 186
St. Clair County, Northwest Territory: Bond of, 182; establishment of, 182; and 1796 petition, 183
St. Genevieve: merchants from wanted Illinois trade, 146
St. Jean, —, 29
St. Louis, 21, 75, 85, 86, 118, 126, 145, 155, 288, 289; banks in, 149; Deschamps' brigade reached, 38; distance of Augusta from, 148; Easton from, 90; Farnham traded at, 29-30; furnished funds for Edwardsville bank, 149-150; Goshen road joined road from Vincennes to, 119; Kaskaskia road to, 82, 83; merchants from wanted Illinois trade, 146; post for receiving supplies, 22; postal service to, 129, 130; trading activity at, 29-30; treaty negotiated at, 42; Vincennes road to, 67, 68, 123
St. Peter's River. *See* Minnesota River
Saint Vincents. *See* Vincennes
Salem, 68
Sales, 91
Saline. *See* Salt works
Saline County: formation of, 72; settlement in, 72-73
Saline Creek, 64; salt works on, 71; settlement along, 76
Saline River, 77, 120; U.S. reservation along, 57
Salt works, 87, 289; benefits to, from banks, 151; closing of Will's, 79-80; cost of salt from, 311; in Gallatin County, 71-72; government controlled, 71, 153; importance of roads to, 121; in